International Trade Policy

Søren Kjeldsen-Kragh

International Trade Policy

Copenhagen Business School Press
HANDELSHØJSKOLENS FORLAG

© *Copenhagen Business School Press, 2001*
Cover designed by Kontrapunkt
Book designed by Jørn Ekstrøm
Set in Plantin and printed by AKA-PRINT, Denmark

ISBN 87-16-13484-2 ✓

Distribution

Scandinavia:
Munksgaard/DBK, Siljansgade 2-8, P.O. Box 1731,
DK-2300 Copenhagen S, Denmark
phone: +45 3269 7788, fax: +45 3269 7789

North America:
Copenhagen Business School Press
Books International Inc.
P.O. Box 605
Hendon, VA 20172-0605, USA
phone: +1 703 661 1500, fax: +1 703 661 1501

Rest of the World:
Marston Book Services, P.O. Box 269
Abingdon, Oxfordshire, OX14 4YN, UK
phone: +44 (0) 1235 465500, fax: +44 (0) 1235 465555
E-mail Direct Customers: direct.order@marston.co.uk
E-mail Booksellers. trade.order@marston.co.uk

Contents

Preface

The purpose of this book is to provide an overall presentation of how the instruments of trade policy work, and how co-operation in international trade policy has functioned and developed in the post-war period.

In chapters 1 to 4, the effects of trade policy and industrial policy measures will be analysed. The point of departure is an analysis based on the presumptions that the market mechanism works perfectly, that there is perfect competition, and that there are no externalities. Over the last 15-20 years, a number of models have been developed which illustrate what happens when these assumptions no longer apply.

If the market structure changes so that there is imperfect competition, the effects of trade policy measures will be completely different. The effect of a measure varies a great deal according to the market structure. Is there imperfection at home, abroad or both? How many enterprises are there in a given market, and how do they behave? If there are externalities, i.e. positive or negative consequences of an activity, which are not reflected in the market mechanism, it will be perfectly reasonable to intervene.

The introduction of market imperfection or externalities opens up the possibility of increasing the level of economic welfare through trade policy and industrial policy measures.

In chapters 5-7, post-war co-operation in trade policy will be analysed. Global co-operation has taken place through GATT, which has established a set of principles for trade policy between its member countries, and has conducted international trade and tariff negotiations with a view to liberalizing trade. The results of GATT co-operation will be analysed. In addition to global co-operation, regional trading organizations have been set up in the form of customs unions and free trade areas. The setting up of the EC and NAFTA, as well as plans for East Asian co-operation, have triggered talk of a regionalisation of international trade. Developing countries have particular economic problems, and special trading arrangements have been made.

The final chapters of the book raise the question of which trade policy to pursue. This is a central question, both for developing countries and industrial countries. Developing countries want economic development. The question is, which trade strategy to pursue to attain this goal: a strategy based on primary exports, import substitution or export of industrial products? The analysis leads to the conclusion that there is no general answer, as it depends on the conditions in the individual developing country. The last chapter discusses the question of when free trade is the best solution. Is there a scientific argument for using trade policy and industrial policy instruments? The answer is clearly in the affirmative, but from an economic policy point of view, any intervention should be made with caution and after careful consideration.

Søren Kjeldsen-Kragh
Copenhagen 2000

1. Trade policy
– Perfect competition

In the following four chapters, the effects of the instruments of trade policy will be analysed. This chapter analyses the effect of trade policy measures in the case of perfect competition. The models used are partial equilibrium models in which the conditions relating to a single product are considered. In chapter 2, trade policy measures in markets with imperfect competition will be analysed. This analysis will also be based on partial equilibrium models. In chapter 3, we will return to a perfect competition market structure, and trade policy measures will be analysed on the basis of a general equilibrium model with two products. In chapters 1 and 3, it is assumed that the market mechanism operates perfectly. In chapter 2, it is assumed that there are imperfections connected with the market structure. In chapter 4, the theory of distortion will be studied, with examples of imperfections in the form of externalities. Is it necessary to intervene in such cases, and if so, how is this best done?

1.1 What is trade policy?

Most instruments of economic policy affect a country's exports and imports, either directly or indirectly. Therefore, many economic-policy measures affect international trade, even if the measures are not considered to be instruments of trade policy.

For a measure to be characterized as trade policy measure, two conditions must be satisfied. First, the purpose of the measure must be to influence the country's international trade in goods and services. Second, the measure must directly affect foreign trade, discriminating between domestic and foreign markets.

Trade policy affects a country's imports and exports of goods and services. The following are typical instruments directly affecting imports and exports:

Import tariffs	Export tariffs
Quantitative import restrictions	Export subsidies
Voluntary export restraint agreements	Export restrictions
Import subsidies	

Trade policy instruments may either be selective or general. In economic policy, there is a distinction between selective and general instruments. Selective instruments are those that affect a specific market. In contrast to this, general economic measures have a widespread effect on a number of central macroeconomic variables.

Trade policy is often associated with selective intervention. If tariffs are only imposed on selected goods or on goods from a narrow sector, the intervention is selective. If, however, a general tariff of 20 per cent is imposed on all imported goods, and at the same time subsidies of 20 per cent are granted on all exported goods, the result will be equivalent to a 20 per cent devaluation. In this case, the trade policy measures have a general effect.

Let us examine the delimitation between trade policy on the one hand and fiscal policy, monetary policy, foreign exchange policy and industrial policy, respectively, on the other.

Fiscal policy and monetary policy are general economic measures which, aim primarily at influencing domestic employment and domestic inflation. In this way, these policies will also affect the balance of payments. Here there is a connection with trade policy, since fiscal and monetary policies and trade policy all affect the balance of payments. However, it is not the intention of fiscal and monetary policy to affect trade. Nor do fiscal and monetary policies discriminate against foreign countries.

Foreign exchange policy is concerned with setting a country's exchange rates and laying down the rules that apply in relation to foreign exchange transactions, for instance in the form of exchange restrictions. Exchange rate policy has a significant impact on a country's foreign trade. An exchange rate is said to be in equilibrium if in the long term, disregarding more or less incidental fluctuations in foreign exchange earnings and foreign exchange expenses, the exchange rate will balance the current account of the country's balance of payments. If the exchange rate is overvalued, it will impede exports and encourage imports and the country will experience a balance of payments deficit. On the other hand, an undervalued exchange rate will result in a surplus in the current account of the country's balance of payments.

Foreign exchange policy is normally considered a general instrument. This is correct in a world where currencies are freely convertible. If, on the other hand, exchange restrictions are introduced, which has previously been the case, against trade with certain countries or against certain goods, such restrictions will function as a selective instrument.

Foreign exchange restrictions can be administered to establish a system with multiple exchange rates. In a system with multiple exchange rates, the rate may vary according to the type of product that is exported or imported. For example the exchange rate for the import of products which are considered to be luxuries can be higher than the exchange rate for goods which are considered necessities. If a country wants to support the production of goods within a specific sector, it may encourage the export of this sector's products by exchanging foreign currency at a particularly favourable rate.

Multiple exchange rates have previously been employed by a number of developing countries. Such systems contravene multilateral non-discriminating trade systems which aim at utilizing a country's potential for producing the goods it is relatively best at producing. The international exchange rate co-operation set up in connection with the establishment of the International Monetary Fund (IMF) therefore bans the use of exchange controls and multiple exchange rates except for temporary use in exceptional circumstances when a country is in serious trouble.

Even though foreign exchange policy and trade policy both affect a country's foreign trade, there is a sharp distinction between the two forms of policy. Exchange rate policy directly affects payments between countries, whereas trade policy directly affects trade between countries. This is how the two types of economic-policy measures are distinguished. Even though the distinction between exchange rate policy and trade policy is quite clear, obviously the two types of policy can have similar consequences in a number of situations. Exchange rate policy affects payments and thus trade, just as trade policy affects trade and thus also payments between countries.

Finally, industrial policy and consumer policy should be considered. The aim of industrial policy is to encourage industrial development through various support measures. The measures may be general schemes available to all, or they may be selective schemes available only to selected industrial sectors. If there is a wish to impede specific industries, duties may be imposed or production restrictions implemented.

Consumer policy aims at influencing the consumption of various goods through consumption subsidies or purchase taxes. Furthermore, consumer policy can ensure the qualitative standard of products through various technical and health-related regulations which products have to conform to.

Obviously, industrial policy and consumer policy measures can indirectly affect trade between countries as they affect domestic production and consumption, respectively. Moreover, product standards determine which goods a country can export and which goods it is willing to import.

Industrial policies which affect trade indirectly:	Consumer policies which affect trade indirectly:
Duties or subsidies related to production. Duties or subsidies related to the factors of production. Quantitative production restrictions.	Duties or subsidies related to consumption. Technical and health-related regulations.

In their definition, the distinction between industrial policy and consumer policy on the one hand and trade policy on the other is clear. Trade policy affects trade directly. Industrial policy and consumer policy affect trade indirectly. In practice, however, it may often be difficult to distinguish between the two types of policy, as the purpose of trade policy is mostly to support a country's own production.

Therefore, when analysing the effects of trade policy measures, it is also natural to consider how various industrial policy measures work, for instance production subsidies or production duties.

Trade and industrial policy instruments affect a number of economic factors, such as production, consumption, terms of trade, competition, income, income distribution, employment, balance of payments and government finances. The different instruments affect these economic factors in different ways. This will be apparent in the sections below in which the effects of various instruments will be analysed.

1.2 The effects of import tariffs

The impact of trade policy measures depends on whether a measure is implemented by a small country or a large country. The difference is that if a small country pursues a particular trade policy, it cannot influence the world market price because it is small in an international context. If, on the other hand, the country is large, its trade policy can affect world market prices, due to its international weight.

Tariffs in a small country

Figure 1.1 shows the demand, DD, and supply, SS, of a given product. If the world market price is P_w, the country will produce OA and demand OB, which means that imports will be AB. Now the country imposes a specific tariff, T, on imports. A specific tariff means that the tariff is a fixed amount per imported product unit as opposed to an ad valorem tariff, which means that the tariff is a percentage that is added to the price of an imported unit. Conse-

Figure 1.1: Import tariffs in a small country

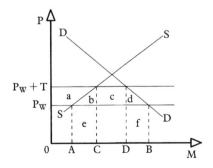

quently, the domestic price becomes $P_w + T$. The domestic demand is reduced to OD, and the supply is increased to OC. This means that imports are reduced to CD.

If welfare is measured by means of producer surplus and consumer surplus, we get the following result:

Producer surplus increase	a
Consumer surplus reduction	a + b + c+ d
Tariff revenue	c
Net loss	b + d

A redistribution takes place in favour of the producers, who make a gain of a. The consumers suffer a loss of a + b + c + d, but c is compensated for by the incoming tariff revenue which is assumed to be paid back to the consumers, for instance in the form of a tax relief.

If it is assumed that a loss of 1 euro suffered by the consumers can balance out a gain of 1 euro realized by the producers, the net loss will be b + d. The triangle b reflects a loss on the production side. The production costs of producing AC domestically are b + e, whereas the production costs abroad of producing this quantity are only e. The triangle d expresses a loss suffered by the consumers. By importing BD, the consumers derive a utility which equals d + f, but they only pay the amount f. There is a reduction in the consumption of the good, which yields a net loss of d.

Tariffs in a large country

If country A is a large country, and it imposes a tariff on a product, it is necessary to consider not only the conditions in country A, but also the conditions in the rest of the world, here referred to as country B. The conditions of supply and demand for A and B are set out in figure 1.2 in part figures a and c. Part figure b shows country A's import demand and country B's export supply.

In the initial situation, the world market price is P_{wo}. Country A now imposes a specific tariff, T, on the product. As a result, country A's reduced imports make the world market price fall to P_{w1}. The domestic price in country A becomes $P_{w1} + T$, and the price in country B becomes the world market price P_{w1}. The fact that coun-

Figure 1.2: Import tariffs in a large country

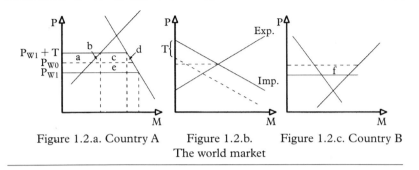

Figure 1.2.a. Country A   Figure 1.2.b.   Figure 1.2.c. Country B
The world market

try A imposes the specific tariff T on the imported product means that country A's import demand shifts downwards in part figure b with the tariff T. Consequently, country A's imports are reduced, but other things being equal, the import reduction is not as large as is the case when a small country imposes the same specific tariff. The reason for this is that the world market price is reduced when a large country imposes a tariff.

If the change in welfare is still measured on the basis of changes in consumer surplus and producer surplus, it may be concluded that country B loses welfare to the extent of the area f. In country A, the following situation arises:

Producer surplus increase	a
Consumer surplus reduction	a + b + c+ d
Tariff revenue	c + e
Net effect	e – b – d

If e > b + d, the country realizes a net gain. Area e is the gain made by country A due to its ability to import at a lower world market price than before. In other words, area e expresses the improvement in terms of trade achieved by country A because the tariff T puts pressure on the world market price.

By looking at a figure corresponding to figure 1.2a, it is possible to illustrate what happens to e – b – d, when starting with a modest tariff which is gradually increased. With a small tariff, b and d will be small, whereas e will be larger. Even though a small tariff only

Figure 1.3: Connection between tariff level and welfare

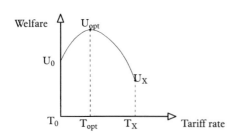

slightly improves the terms of trade, the improvement is noticeable because the volume of imports is relatively large. When the small tariff is increased, e – b – d will also increase. At a given tariff level, e – b – d will reach its maximum. If the tariff is increased beyond this level, e – b – d will decrease. When the tariff becomes prohibitive, i.e. when it eliminates all imports, e becomes 0. The tariff level at which the net benefit of e – b – d reaches its maximum is known as the optimal tariff.

The connection between welfare and the tariff level can be illustrated in a figure in which welfare is on the vertical axis and the tariff rate on the horizontal axis, cf. figure 1.3.

Under free trade, the tariff is 0, which gives welfare U_0. When the tariff rate is gradually increased from the initial level under free trade, the level of welfare will increase. The optimal tariff is found at the point where welfare reaches its maximum level. With the tariff rate T_x, the tariff is prohibitive, which means that U_x is the welfare under conditions of autarky. As $U_x < U_0$, the welfare level under autarky will be lower than under free trade.

For a large country which is able to affect the international price level through tariffs, free trade does not yield the highest level of welfare. This can only be reached by imposing the optimal tariff.

Looking at welfare in the two countries combined, measured in terms of consumer surplus and producer surplus, free trade will be the best solution. Even if one of the countries imposes the optimal tariff and therefore maximises e – b – d, the other country will experience a loss of f. As f is larger than e, then e – b – d – f will always be negative, which means that free trade is the optimum solution. If we take one country's total consumer and producer surplus and add it to the other country's total consumer and producer surplus, the total amount will never exceed that generated under free trade.

The effect of import subsidies

Import subsidies are the opposite of import tariffs and may be considered a negative tariff. Direct import subsidies are hardly ever used. Import subsidies stimulate imports and reduce the price obtainable by domestic manufacturers and payable by consumers.

If a small country introduces import subsidies, the world market price will remain unchanged. If a large country introduces import subsidies, the world market price will rise, the country's terms of trade will deteriorate, and the fall in the domestic price will be smaller than the amount of the import subsidies. This can be analysed in figures corresponding to figure 1.1 and figure 1.2 for a small and a large country, respectively.

1.3 Import restrictions and voluntary export restraint agreements

The effect of import restrictions

Instead of tariffs, import restrictions may be applied as a means of restraining imports. An import restriction sets a quantitative limit to the volume of imports. Figure 1.4 shows an illustration corresponding to figure 1.1.

Figure 1.4: The effect of import restrictions

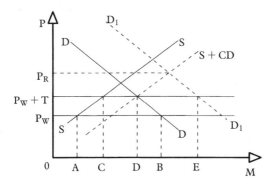

The amount AB is imported under free trade. If a small country imposes the tariff T on the imported good, imports are reduced to CD. If instead of the tariff T, an import restriction is imposed, which corresponds exactly to the imports CD with the tariff T, this will result in a total supply as indicated by the curve S+CD. This means that an import restriction which allows a maximum import of CD will have the same effect as the tariff T. An import restriction can thus be converted into a tariff equivalent which is exactly the tariff rate that enables the same level of imports as under the import restriction.

On the face of it, it seems that a tariff and an import restriction have the same effect. However, there are two crucial differences.

The first difference has to do with adjustments when there are changes to the conditions of supply and demand. It is assumed that the demand curve shifts from DD to D_1D_1. If a country imposes the tariff T, the volume of imports will increase from CD to CE, and the price will remain the same, namely $P_w + T$. If instead of this a country has an import restriction which only allows import of the quantity CD, the volume of imports cannot be increased. However, the increased demand means that the price will rise from $P_w + T$ to P_R. If the domestic supply SS rises, a tariff would cause the volume of imports to fall, whereas an import restriction would imply that the domestic price would fall. With tariffs, adjustments are made through the volume of imports. With import restrictions, adjustments are made through price.

The other difference has to do with who benefits from the import restriction. In the case of tariffs, the state gets a tariff revenue which benefits the taxpayer. It is assumed that the tariff revenue is either paid back to the taxpayer or is used to lower other taxes correspondingly. In the case of import restrictions there is no tariff revenue. The difference between the domestic price and the world market price benefits those who obtain the import licences. If domestic importers obtain the import licences, they will reap the benefit. If foreign exporters obtain the import licenses, they reap the benefit. The government may obtain benefit by selling the import licences to the highest bidding importers. By doing this, it will also be possible to avoid a distortion of competition between those who obtain a cost-free right to import and those who do not obtain such a right.

The effect of voluntary export restraint agreements

Instead of imposing import restrictions, an importing country may turn to exporting countries and ask them »voluntarily« to restrain their exports.

The effects of a voluntary export restraint agreement are illustrated by figure 1.4. CD is now no longer an import quota, but an export quota which limits the import to the country. The market effects of voluntary export restraint are identical to the effects of import restrictions. Voluntary export restraint increases the domestic price above the level of the world market price in exactly the same way as an import restriction.

However, there is a difference between the ways in which the effects of the two types of intervention are distributed. In the case of voluntary export restraint, the exporting country centralizes sales by granting export licences. In the case of import restrictions, it is normally the importing country that issues import licences. Under voluntary export restraint agreements, the difference between the domestic market price and the world market price goes to the exporting country. When import licences are granted to the country's importers, foreign exporters are only able to sell at world market prices.

This may explain why exporting countries accept voluntary export restraint agreements. The exporting country obtains an improvement to its terms of trade, while its volume of exports is reduced. If the alternative to voluntary export restraint is that the importing country introduces trade barriers, then voluntary export restraint will be preferred by the exporting country.

The exporting country can seek to get round the quantitative limit by using the freed capacity to produce other types of products which are not included in the export restraint agreement, and which can therefore be exported. For instance, Japan entered into a voluntary export restraint agreement concerning the export of »standard cars« to the USA. As a result, Japan used the freed capacity for producing more luxurious cars which were not included in the export restraint agreement, and which were then exported to USA. Subsequently the US has also sought to make an export restraint agreement for this type of car. This example illustrates the well-known fact that once restraints have been introduced within a certain area, they tend to spread to other areas because of the derived effects.

Voluntary export restraint agreements gained much ground during the last 20 years before the new WTO-agreement. The reason for this was that the immediate alternative, namely the imposition of import restrictions, was not allowed under GATT. We will return to this in section 5.6.

1.4 Product standards

In order for a product to be exported from one country to another, the product must live up to requirements set by the importing country. There are technical and health-related regulations that must be observed in order to protect consumers. Electrical equipment must be of a standard that enables consumers to use it without risk of accidents. Food must be of such quality, both in terms of hygienic standards and in composition, that it does not cause illness.

Such requirements are quite legitimate. Since traditional trade policy instruments such as tariffs and import restrictions are being more or less phased out, questions of product standards have become more important. Producers in the individual countries have attempted to adopt product standards which they find easy to maintain, but which foreign producers may find more difficult to adhere to. The public authorities in such countries may also have an interest in favouring the interests of domestic manufacturers.

Consumer interests should be acknowledged, but if product standards are dictated principally by the interests of national industrial policy, they have the same effect as trade barriers. In practice, it may be difficult to distinguish between consumer interests and protectionism.

In recent years, consideration for the environment has played a role in connection with international trade. Environmental problems are typically connected with production processes. Should it be possible for an individual country to impose standards for the environmental impact of production processes, not only for the products produced by the country itself but also for the products it imports? This is not currently permitted under WTO rules. Should such an environmental code be adopted as a condition for free import? One argument for this could be the desire to reduce cross-border pollution. Another argument could be the wish to avoid a situation where an individual country does not dare to adopt stricter environmental regulations than other countries out of fear that its competitiveness may be weakened. The solution might be a harmonization of the countries' environmental regulations.

The issue of social clauses in the WTO rules has also been debated. Should individual exporting countries meet certain minimal standards for labour market conditions before goods can be freely exported to other countries? This concerns the working environment, minimum wages, a ban on child labour, acceptance of trade unions etc.

Product requirements in the form of technical and health-related standards can make it more difficult for developing countries to compete. If environmental and social standards are introduced in relation to the production processes, this will also affect developing countries. Therefore, such measures should be approached with caution.

Regulations of a technical, health-related and social nature will have the same effect as a ban on imports. The standards set by an importing country determine which goods other countries can export to it. If the standards are met, there is free access to the importing country's market. If the standards are not met, there is no access to the market.

Common international standards will impede the abuse of regulations by a country in order to promote its own industrial interests. Reaching agreement on such common standards is not easy because countries have different priorities.

1.5 The effects of export subsidies and export tariffs

Export subsidies

If a country wants to increase its exports, it may grant export subsidies. Imagine two large exporting countries A and B, and an importing country C. One exporting country, A, wants to increase its exports and thereby its domestic production. Country A seeks to achieve this by granting export subsidies.

Figure 1.5: The effect of export subsidies

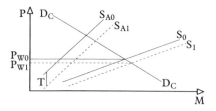

In figure 1.5, S_{AO} is country A's export supply curve at time 0. Country B also has an export supply curve which rises from left to right. A horizontal addition is now made of the two countries' export supplies, which is the sum of the two countries' exports at a given price. We thus get the total export supply, which is the curve S_0. Country C's import demand is $D_C D_C$. The world market price in the initial situation is P_{W0}.

Country A now introduces an export subsidy T, which remains constant per exported unit. This means that country A's new export supply curve moves downwards with T. If S_{A1} is combined with B's export supply, we get the new total export supply curve S_1. The result will be a fall in the world market price to P_{W1}.

Country A's volume of exports is increased, but its terms of trade deteriorate because exporters have to sell at a lower world market price. The importing country C will profit from the export subsidies because the importing country can import at a lower price. The major loser will be country B, which will experience both a reduced volume of exports and deteriorated terms of trade.

Export tariffs

If, instead of this, country A imposes a tariff on exports, this will of course have the opposite effect of an export subsidy, as shown in figure 1.5. In this case, the curve S_{A1} moves upwards with the size of the tariff. Country A's volume of exports will be reduced, but on the other hand, the country's terms of trade will be improved. Country B will be the major winner, because it can both increase its volume of exports, and get a higher world market price for its exported goods.

Instead of imposing an export tariff, a country may set a quantitative limit on the volume of exports. This requires export sales to be monopolized. In this case, the volume of exports will fall, and the world market price will rise. Other exporters will benefit from country A's quantitative limit on the volume of exports.

A small exporting country will not be able to cause the world market price to rise, either through export tariffs, or through quantitative limits on exports. If several small exporting countries act together in an export cartel, i.e. they make an agreement that each country shall reduce volumes, the world market price can be increased. The more exporting countries that join such a cartel, the higher the increase in the world market price. OPEC is an example of such an export cartel, whose very purpose has been to increase the world market price of oil. If several oil-exporting countries are not part of the export cartel, OPEC's chances of causing a rise in the world market price will decrease.

Today, many developing countries impose export tariffs on agricultural products which are exported. This lowers the domestic price level to the detriment of producers and to the benefit of consumers. Low consumer prices may be a goal, but low producer prices can hardly be a goal. If export tariffs were abolished, producers would get higher prices, and the higher consumer prices which would also be an outcome could be avoided by granting consumption subsidies. The problem with consumption subsidies is that they are a burden on government budgets, which are already overstretched in most developing countries.

On the other hand an export tariff produces a revenue for government finances, which is a principal goal of export tariffs. Administratively, export and import tariffs are an easy way of generating government revenues, as opposed to normal commodity taxes and income taxes. Tariffs are collected at the border, which is administratively easy. General purchase taxes and income taxes require a large administrative apparatus, with widespread opportunities for evasion if there is a predominantly subsistence economy.

Individual developing countries are so small that, acting alone, they are not able to improve their terms of trade through export tariffs. If all countries made use of export tariffs, there would be the possibility of an increase in the world market price.

1.6 Subsidies for and duties on production and consumption

Subsidies or duties related to production will affect output. The same applies to consumption if consumption taxes are levied, or if consumption subsidies are granted.

Since exports and imports constitute the difference between production and consumption of a given product, such subsidies and duties will indirectly affect the trade volume and the types of products traded.

The subsidies and duties dealt with in the following are excise subsidies and excise duties, i.e. subsidies granted on specific products or duties imposed on specific products, and not general subsidies or general duties granted or imposed on all products.

The effects of production subsidies

If a country wishes to support a domestic industry which is exposed to foreign competition through imports, an import tariff may be imposed or a similar direct intervention in the form of a restriction may be implemented as described above. An alternative option is to grant a production subsidy. Here we are dealing with a small country whose conditions do not affect the world market price, which is determined by external factors only.

Figure 1.6 shows the demand D and the supply S_0 for a country. The world market price is P_w, and the country produces OA, consumes OB and imports AB.

To support domestic production, production subsidies T are granted at a fixed amount per produced unit. This means that the country's supply curve is lowered with T to the curve S_1. Produc-

Figure 1.6: The effect of production subsidies

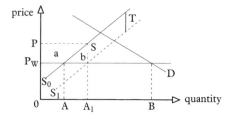

tion is increased to OA_1, consumption remains unchanged, and imports are reduced to A_1B. The consumer price is still P_w, but the producer price including the subsidy is P.

What are the consequences of the production subsidies on welfare? The consumer surplus is not affected by production subsidies. The producer surplus is increased by area a, which is paid by the state, and involves a tax payment of a + b. In terms of welfare, the total net loss will therefore be area b, which reflects the additional costs connected with producing the volume AA_1 rather than importing the same quantity.

A comparison between a tariff, cf. figure 1.1, and production subsidies shows that the effects are identical on the production side. The effects on the consumption side, however, are different. Production subsidies do not affect the consumer price and thus do not affect consumption. A tariff causes an increase in the consumer price and consequently a reduction in consumption. Imports are reduced more when a tariff is imposed than when production subsidies are granted. The loss in terms of welfare when imposing a tariff is the areas b + d (cf. figure 1.1). The welfare loss connected with granting production subsidies is only b. Production subsidies and tariffs result in the same distortion on the production side. However, as opposed to tariffs, production subsidies do not entail any distortions on the consumption side.

In this analysis it has been assumed that the collection of the taxes a + b to finance the production subsidies does not cause distortions in other parts of the economy. Increased income taxes to finance subsidies may for instance be assumed to affect the labour supply negatively.

If, rather than a small country, as assumed in figure 1.6, it is a large importing country that introduces production subsidies, the world market price may be affected. Production subsidies reduce imports and thus tend to lower the world market price.

This analysis concerns production subsidies. Similarly, the analysis may illustrate the effect of a production tax, which will have the exactly opposite effect.

The effects of input subsidies

The domestic production sector may receive support in the form of subsidies related to the volume of production. Another method of support is to grant subsidies on inputs e.g. in the form of wage sub-sidies, subsidies for capital or subsidies for other inputs such as energy or fertilizers.

Such input subsidies will cause a reduction in the production costs. The supply curve in figure 1.6 will move downwards. How much the curve moves downward depends on how much the mar-ket prices fall for those inputs receiving subsidies. The share of the total costs which is related to the subsidized input factors is also important. Finally, the possibilities of substitution between the use of non-subsidized input factors and subsidized input factors will influence the cost reduction.

Cost reduction will be maximised if the market prices of the subsi-dized input factors fall by an amount equal to the subsidies. The mar-ket conditions will determine whether subsidies granted on the use of input factors prompt the factor suppliers to raise their prices. Also, in the case of perfect competition in the market for the input factors, the increased demand may force up the prices of input factors.

Cost reduction will be greatest if the subsidized input factors make up a large proportion of the total costs. Finally, costs will be reduced further if there is a possibility of substituting non-subsi-dized input factors with subsidized inputs.

Input subsidies therefore tend to work in the same way as pro-duction subsidies when it comes to increasing the domestic pro-duction and reducing the import of finished goods. However, if the subsidized input factors are imported, imports of these goods will of course rise.

There is a crucial difference between production subsidies and input subsidies. Production subsidies only distort conditions for the production of finished goods. Input subsidies also distort con-ditions for the production of finished goods, but as well as this, the combination of the different input factors is distorted.

The effects of duties on input factors are in direct contrast to the effects of subsidies.

The effects of consumption subsidies

If the government grants consumption subsidies on a good, the consumption of this good will rise. The conditions in a small coun-try, which is not able to affect the world market price, are shown in figure 1.7.

Figure 1.7: The effect of consumption subsidies

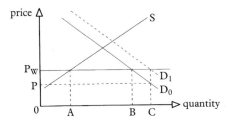

S is the domestic supply curve and D_o is the demand curve. At the price level P_W, the quantity AB is imported. When consumption subsidies are granted as a fixed amount per purchased unit, the demand curve will rise vertically with this amount to D_1. The new consumption will be OC, where consumers can buy at a lower price P, which includes the consumption subsidy. The producer's price is still P_w, which equals the import price. The volume of production in the country remains the same. The increased consumption is covered by increased imports.

Food is a necessity which for social reasons should preferably be inexpensive. Therefore, there are many examples of food subsidies, for instance from the US, from Central and Eastern European countries and from many developing countries. Usually, food subsidies are granted on individual food products and to particular low-paid groups. The reason for this is simply that general food subsidies which either cover all products or the entire population represent a considerable burden on government finances. In figure 1.7, the expenditure for consumption subsidies is $OC \cdot (P_w - P)$.

The purpose of granting food subsidies is to obtain a situation in which, for social reasons, consumer prices are low, and, for production reasons, selling prices for farmers are high.

Obviously, consumption duties again have the opposite effect to consumption subsidies.

1.7 Measuring the level of protection

There are significant problems connected with measuring a country's level of protection. Various policy instruments are available, each of which has a different impact on the economic variables mentioned at the end of section 1.1 above.

Nevertheless, it is important to have an idea of the extent of protection in different countries within different industrial sectors. This plays a role in connection with international tariff and trade negotiations in GATT/WTO. The principle of reciprocity prevails, which means that if a country eases its protection it can expect similar relaxation from other countries. In such negotiations it is necessary to have an idea of the levels of protection in the individual countries.

The extent of the tariff protection alone can be difficult to measure. The customs tariff contains a large variety of different rates for different goods. Different tariff rates may be averaged, but there is a question as to which weighting to use. Imports cannot be used as a basis for weighting because the average tariff rate thus found will underestimate the extent of protection. This is due to the fact that a higher tariff rate gives more protection in the form of lower imports. The higher the tariff rate, the lower the imported volume, and the lower the weighting of the high tariff rate in the calculation of the average tariff rate. A prohibitive tariff eliminates imports, and this tariff will not even be included in the calculation of the average tariff rate. When calculating the average rate it is better to use the value of consumption of the different products as the basis for weighting. In this case, the average tariff rate will be an indication of how much higher the internal price level is due to protection. Even this method of measuring has flaws, as world market prices may be affected to differing extents by the tariffs imposed by different countries. If a big country and a small country have the same average tariff protection rate, the protection in the bigger country will be more distorting than the same protection in the small country. The protection in the big country will distort the world market prices, which will not be the case for the small country.

It should be added that the tariff protection level does not express anything about the resulting distortion or the loss of welfare which equal the two triangles b and d in figure 1.1. These losses depend on the elasticity of the supply and demand curves for the different products. The smaller the elasticities, the smaller the reduction in demand, and the smaller the increase in domestic production. Small elasticities mean small welfare losses.

In order to measure *the effect of import restrictions*, it is natural to calculate the corresponding tariff equivalent, cf. section 1.3. This can be calculated if the conditions of supply and demand are known, which is rarely the case in practice. To this should be added the problem that the tariff equivalent changes when the conditions of supply and demand change. The effect of import restrictions on domestic demand and production also depends on how the import restrictions may affect domestic competitive conditions. Import restrictions may lead to the establishment of a domestic monopoly or oligopoly, which is not the case when tariff protection is applied. Finding a common measure for tariff protection is problematic. Other problems arise when measuring the protection given by import restrictions or voluntary export restraint. Since it is problematic to find an agreed measurement of protection as regards each individual instrument of trade policy, it is obviously even more problematic to find a common measurement of the protection given by all instruments in combination.

In measuring the protection given by each individual instrument, there is an additional problem to be kept in mind. Let us take a look at the tariff protection for a single product as an example. The nominal tariff protection, which is the size of the tariff in relation to the world market price, disregards the fact that some of the raw materials and semi-manufactured products used in the production may also be subject to a protective tariff. It should also be noted that the primary production factors, labour and capital, can of course also receive subsidies or be subject to duties. The fact that tariffs are imposed on raw materials and semi-manufactured products is in itself a negative protection of the finished good, compared with a situation where no tariffs are imposed on inputs. The reason is that where tariffs are imposed on raw materials and semi-manufactured products, the domestic production costs will be higher.

Therefore, the nominal protection of the finished good says nothing about the actual protection enjoyed by the manufacturing process. An example with figures illustrates the conditions. Two countries, A and B, both produce the same finished good using the same production technique. The value of inputs in each country is 50, and the increase in value is also 50. Country A has an import tariff on inputs of 10 per cent and a finished good tariff of 20 per cent. In country B, there are no tariffs, either on inputs or on fin-

Table 1.1: Calculation of effective tariff protection

The price of producing the product in country A:		The price of importing the product from country B:	
Inputs	50	Inputs	50
Tariff 10 per cent	5	Tariff 0 per cent	0
	55		50
Value added	50	Value added	50
Production costs	105	Production costs	100
		Tariff on exports to country A 20 per cent	20
		Import price in country A	120

ished goods. It is now possible to calculate the so-called effective tariff protection in country A. This is illustrated in table 1.1.

It appears from the table that country A can allow a factor return which is 15 units higher in the tariff protection situation compared with country B. The activity in country A being protected by the tariff is the value added of 50, which means that the effective tariff protection is 15/50 = 30 per cent. The effective tariff protection is larger than the nominal tariff protection, because inputs are subject to a lower nominal tariff than finished goods. Such a system is known as tariff escalation. Most industrial countries have a tariff structure where raw materials are not subject to tariffs. Moderate tariffs are imposed on semi-manufactured goods, and higher tariffs are imposed on finished goods. This means that the processing of raw materials and semi-manufactured goods enjoys larger real protection than is shown by the nominal tariff on the finished good.

If an input-output model is available for a country, it is possible to calculate the effective tariff protection for a given product j. The effective tariff protection for product j will be:

$$e_j = \frac{t_j - \sum_{i=1}^{n} a_{ij} t_i}{1 - \sum_{i=1}^{n} a_{ij}}$$

where t_j is the percentage tariff rate on the finished good j, and where t_i is the percentage tariff rate on input i. In total, there are n inputs, and a_{ij} is the »technical coefficient« indicating how large a share of the product price, excluding tariffs, is spent on the purchase of inputs, excluding tariffs. If the production conditions are identical at home and abroad, so that the »technical coefficients« in the two areas are the same, the factor income in the two countries will be:

$$1 - \sum_{i=1}^{n} a_{ij}$$

provided that none of them make use of tariffs. If one of the countries imposes the tariff rates t_i and t_j, this country will get a different total factor return than the country which does not make use of tariffs, namely:

$$1 + t_j - \sum_{i=1}^{n} a_{ij} t_i$$

To simplify, it is now assumed that all semi-manufactured goods are subject to the same percentage tariff rate t_i. There are now three possibilities, namely:

$t_j = t_i$
$t_j > t_i$
$t_j < t_i$

If the tariff rate on the finished good equals the tariff rates on the inputs used, the effective tariff protection e_j will equal the nominal tariff protection t_j. It is assumed that all inputs used are protected by $t_i = t_j$. Whether the inputs in question are actually imported or produced domestically is irrelevant, as long as it is assumed that the domestic price of inputs equals the world market price plus tariffs.

If there are no tariffs on inputs, or if the level of these tariff rates is below the level of the rate on finished goods, i.e. $t_j > t_i$, the effective tariff protection e_j will be larger than the nominal tariff protection. If, on the other hand, the tariff rate on semi-manufactured goods is higher than the tariff rate on finished goods, the effective tariff rate e_j will be below the nominal tariff rate.

The objections to the input-output model can also be raised against the calculation of the effective tariff protection. The input-output model is based on fixed technical production coefficients which do not allow for substitution of inputs when there are changes to the input prices as a result of different tariffs being imposed on different inputs.

1.8 Summary

As an introduction, a delimitation is made of those measures which may be characterized as trade policy measures. In practice, all economic policies affect economic relations between countries. Some measures such as tariffs, import restrictions, export subsidies etc. may be characterized as »pure« trade policy measures. Other measures such as production taxes/subsidies, consumption taxes/subsidies and input taxes/subsidies, which are industrial and consumer policy measures, have such significant consequences on trade that their impact on international trade should also be analysed.

Next, the effects of the different trade policy measures are analysed on the basis of a partial equilibrium model. The analysis examines how the measures affect the conditions for a single product, assuming that the measures will have no implications for other products. The analyses describe the effects of applying trade policy instruments. Using the concepts of producer and consumer surplus, it is shown how applying instruments of trade policy in a perfectly competitive market, without the presence of externalities, gives rise to so-called distortion losses, illustrated for instance in figure 1.1 by the triangles b and d.

However, the analyses can also be used normatively to illustrate which trade policy a country should pursue. The conclusion was that there is a crucial difference between a small country pursuing trade policy and a large country pursuing a trade policy. If a small country wants to avoid the distortion losses connected with a trade policy measure, it should abstain from pursuing that trade policy. By virtue of its size, however, a big country is able to affect the international terms of trade. Therefore, it is possible for a big country to achieve a better position through trade policy measures than could have been achieved under free trade. The theory of the optimal tariff shows exactly which tariff a large country should impose in order to reach the highest attainable welfare.

Different goods will normally be protected by varying extents. Finding a system of measurement for the effects of several different types of trade policy intervention in relation to a single product is not easy. The problems of measurement become even greater when trying to find a total measure for all products combined. The nominal tariff protection does not show the real protection because there are often different levels of protection for finished goods, semi-manufactured goods and raw materials. This is taken into account when calculating the so-called effective tariff protection.

Literature

There is a very comprehensive literature concerning international trade policy. It is not the intention to give references to this extensive literature. Below there are references to publications which survey international trade policy issues, and which also include detailed references to the literature. Such survey publications are:

Bhagwati, J.N. (ed), *International Trade: Selected Readings,* Cambridge, MIT press, 1987.
Caves, R.E. and H.G. Johnson (eds), *Readings in International Economics,* Homewood, 1968.
Greenaway, D., (ed), *Current Issues in International Trade,* Macmillan, 1996.
Greenaway, David and Alan Winters (eds), *Surveys in International Trade,* Blackwell, 1997.
Jones, Ronald and Peter Kenen (eds), *Handbook of International Economics,* Volume 1 and 2, Elsevier Science Publishing Company, 1984.

At the end of each chapter of this book the most important publications relating to the content of the chapter will be referred to. For chapter 1 important references are:

Baldwin, R.E., »Non-tariff Distortions of International Trade« in Baldwin, R.E. and J. D. Richardson (eds), *International Trade and Finance,* Boston, 1974.
Corden, W.M., »The Structure of a Tariff System and the Effective Protection Rate«, *Journal of Political Economy,* 74, 1966.
Corden, W.M., *The Theory of Protection,* Oxford, 1971.
Corden, W.M., *Trade Policy and Economic Welfare,* Oxford 1974.
Greenaway, D., *International Trade Policy: From Tariffs to the New Protectionism,* London, 1983.
Hamilton, C. and G.V. Reed, »Economic Aspects of Voluntary Export Restraints« in Greenways, D. (ed), *Current Issues in International Trade,* London, 1996.
Krauss, M.B., *The New Protectionism, the Welfare State and International Trade,* Oxford, 1979.
Malmgren, H., *International Order for Public Subsidies,* London, 1977.

2. Trade policy
– Imperfect competition

One of the benefits of free trade is the intensification of competition when domestic manufacturers compete with foreign manufacturers. This way of thinking dates back to Adam Smith, who believed the size of the market to be absolutely decisive for economic development. The idea that the market structure changes under free trade and that one of the advantages of free trade is indeed intensified competition is one that has existed in the shadow of factor proportion theory, which ascribes to foreign trade the comparative advantages related to different factor endowment. Factor proportion theory assumes that there is perfect competition within individual countries, even without international trade.

During the last 15 to 20 years, international trade theory has focussed on analyzing the effects of trade policy measures in situations of imperfect competition. Imperfect competition comes in many shapes, and the literature is consequently quite comprehensive with conclusions very much depending on the assumptions fed into the model. The conclusions also depend on whether imperfection is an exclusively domestic or foreign phenomenon, or whether there is imperfection domestically as well as abroad.

In the following, a number of central models will be discussed. In sections 2.1 and 2.2, there are imperfect domestic markets with perfect competition abroad. In section 2.3, there is perfect domestic competition and imperfect competition abroad. In section 2.4, markets operate imperfectly both domestically and abroad. In sections 2.5 and 2.6, the models are evaluated. Most models which analyse trade policy measures under conditions of imperfect competition are partial equilibrium models. It is important to note that careless application of these partial models can easily lead to wrong conclusions. If a country bases its trade policy on such models, it must not forget that trade policies can easily lead to retaliatory measures from foreign countries which should thus be built into the model. Section 2.7 of this chapter discusses a general equilib-

rium model for two countries, both with monopolistic competition
in one sector.

2.1 Domestic monopoly

The effects of tariffs

In the following there is one domestic manufacturer of a given good,
in this illustration called a monopolist, even though the manufacturer in question does not have power over the market. The sole
manufacturer's power over the domestic market is dependent on
whether there is a trade policy intervention. A tariff would improve
the monopolist's market power. The monopolist's power accelerates
as the tariff increases. The power of the monopolist also depends on
the trade policy instrument applied. Other things being equal, an
import quota will result in greater market power than would be the
case with a tariff, as will become clear in the next sub-section.

The situation of the monopolist is illustrated in figure 2.1. D is
the domestic demand, and MC is the monopolist's marginal cost
curve. There is perfect competition in the world market, and the
world market price is P_W, which is constant.

X_W is the quantity produced by the monopolist under free trade.
If the monopolist's price is fixed at a higher level, it will immediately be competed out of the market by foreign manufacturers.

A tariff is now imposed. The tariff t increases the domestic price
to $P_W(1+t)$. It is now assumed that the tariff t is gradually aug-

Figure 2.1: Monopolist in a country imposing a tariff

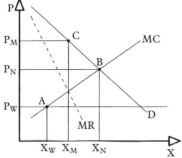

mented. There are three possibilities for the size of the tariff, which will influence the production of the monopolist.

The domestic price:	The monopolist's production.
$P_W < P_W (1+t) < P_N$	AB
$P_N < P_W (1+t) < P_M$	BC
$P_M < P_W (1+t)$	C

If the domestic price is between the world market price P_W and P_N, which is the price in perfect competition in a closed economy, the production of the monopolist will follow the MC curve along the line AB. The tariff has the same impact as it would have under perfect competition.

If, as a consequence of the tariff, the domestic price rises above P_N, but remains below the monopoly price P_M, production will be determined by the line BC on the demand curve. The monopolist will now become the sole supplier of the good on the domestic market, but the monopolist alone cannot fix the price, which is determined by $P_W + t$.

Only in the case where $P_W (1+t)$ is equal to or larger than P_M can the monopolist fix its optimum price, which is the monopoly price P_M. If $P_W (1+t)$ is higher than P_M, the monopolist is protected against potential competition from foreign manufacturers. However, this does not apply if $P_W (1+t)$ is lower than P_M.

The effect of an import quota

In this illustration, instead of a tariff, an import quota is now introduced, which imposes a quantitative restriction on imports. Figure 2.2 shows the same demand curve and the same marginal cost curve as in figure 2.1. The size of the import quota is $X_H X_I$, which is lower than the imports $X_F X_I$ realized under free trade.

This means that the monopolist can deduce its own demand for the good, which equals the aggregate demand of the country less the import quota. This curve is shown by D_M. MR_M is the marginal revenue curve which corresponds to D_M. This means that the monopolist's optimum price becomes P_M, and the optimal production X_M. The retail price for the imported volumes will also be P_M.

While the market power of the monopoly enterprise depends on the size of the tariff, the monopolist will immediately gain market

Figure 2.2: Monopolist in a country which introduces an import quota

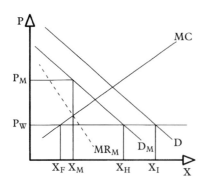

power, in the sense that the monopoly price is immediately obtainable, when the import quota takes effect. It is evident that the monopoly price increases as the import quota decreases.

In figure 2.2, the import quota restricts imports compared to the level of imports under free trade. This is known as a binding import quota. If the import quota is larger than the actual imports under free trade, it is not binding. In a figure corresponding to figure 2.2, it can easily be shown that even where there is a non-binding import quota, it is possible for the domestic enterprise to obtain the monopoly price in the same way as shown in figure 2.2. Even a non-binding import quota can thus give the monopolist power over the price mechanism.

An import tariff may result in exports

In figure 2.1, an import tariff was imposed. This means that under given conditions, the monopolist can obtain the optimum monopoly price on the domestic market. The monopolist cannot export, however. If P_M is the domestic price in figure 2.1, export is only possible if the monopolist receives export subsidies. If export subsidies of $P_M - P_W$ are granted, the monopolist will produce a quantity corresponding to the point where the $P_M C$ line crosses the MC curve. The additional manufactured output which is not sold on the domestic market can be exported, but this is only possible because of export subsidies.

Even without export subsidies it is possible that an import tariff

Figure 2.3: Monopolist exports as a consequence of the tariff

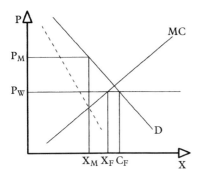

will trigger exports. In figure 2.3, the demand curve and the marginal cost curve are the same as in figure 2.1, but the world market price P_W is higher.

Under free trade, the country imports the volume $C_F X_F$. If the country's tariff policy makes it possible for the manufacturer to obtain the domestic price P_M, the manufacturer will, in addition to producing X_M for the domestic market, benefit from exporting the volume $X_M X_F$.

Monopoly with diminishing unit costs

In the above it is assumed that the monopolist has a production plant of a given size with given fixed costs and marginal costs which increase with output. It is now assumed that the monopolist can produce in plants of varying size. There are economies of scale

Figure 2.4: Falling costs

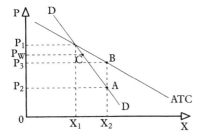

which entail that the average total costs (ATC) fall when there is a total adjustment of the enterprise. Figure 2.4 illustrates that the monopolist faces diminishing unit costs with increasing output. The country's demand is shown in the demand curve DD.

In order for a sole manufacturer to be able to survive in the market, its price must be higher than its average unit costs, which means that the price must be equal to or higher than P_1. The world market price P_W is lower than P_1. Therefore, the enterprise will not be competitive.

If the country introduces a tariff of $P_1 - P_W$, the enterprise will become competitive. The disadvantage of this is that the retail price rises. The level of welfare will fall because the consumer surplus will fall while the manufacturer will only have its expenditure covered.

However, in the scenario with falling unit costs there is an alternative. Production subsidies may be granted. If the enterprise commits itself to produce the quantity OX_2, the state will release subsidies corresponding to P_3BAP_2. These subsidies will merely allow the enterprise to survive.

Through subsidies an enterprise is maintained that otherwise would not have existed. Welfare will rise if the increase in the consumer surplus exceeds the public expenditure on subsidies. The consumer surplus increases by $P_W CAP_2$, and the public expenditure on subsidies will be P_3BAP_2. By introducing production subsidies it is possible to increase welfare.

In this analysis it is assumed that the domestic monopolist cannot export the good to other countries, for instance because other countries have imposed a tariff on imports. If it is possible to export, it will not be necessary to grant production subsidies. The enterprise can utilize the existing economies of scale by exporting at the price P_W.

2.2 Domestic oligopoly

The monopoly situation discussed above is not very typical. On the contrary, the market structure is often characterized by there being either a large or a small number of firms in the market.

It is assumed that the country has k firms, each manufacturing the same product. If k is small, there is an oligopoly with a few large firms in the market. If k is large, a market structure of perfect competition is approached.

The price established in such a market depends partly on the market structure, i.e. the number of manufacturers, and partly on the behaviour of the individual manufacturers.

The influence of behaviour on the price mechanism

Firms may behave either conjecturally or autonomously. Conjectural behaviour means that the firm in question takes into consideration how other firms will react to what the firm itself does. If a firm considers lowering its price, it will be acting conjecturally if it takes into consideration that other firms may respond by lowering their prices. If a firm acts autonomously, it will assume that what it does will not affect the actions of other firms. If firms act autonomously, an individual firm may choose to adjust its output assuming that the others will maintain their production level. This means that the market will determine the price. This is called Cournot competition. Firms may also choose to change their prices assuming that the competitors will maintain their prices, which means that the market determines the quantities sold. This is called Bertrand competition.

There is a connection between market structure and behaviour. The smaller the number of firms in the market, the more likely it is that they act conjecturally. It is assumed that one's own actions will influence the actions of competitors.

Figure 2.5: Co-ordinated behaviour

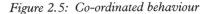

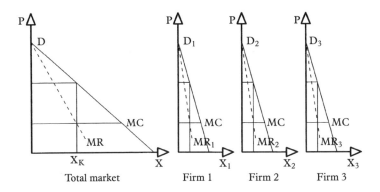

Figure 2.6: The price with co-ordinated and autonomous behaviour

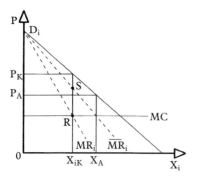

There are k manufacturers in the domestic market. These firms face an aggregate demand in the market, which is described by D in figure 2.5. For the sake of this example k is assumed to be three. It is assumed that there are three domestic manufacturers each with the same costs. Further, it is assumed that the firms co-ordinate their production, as they collectively calculate the optimum price and output for the entire market. Each of them then manufactures a third of the aggregate optimal production. Each firm considers one third of the aggregate demand as its demand curve. Each firm manufactures a quantity for which the marginal revenue equals the marginal cost of the enterprise. This is the case of a cartel agreeing on finding the optimal output for the entire market and then distributing this output equally between the enterprises.

Let this be the starting point for one of the enterprises whose conditions are displayed in figure 2.6.

The curve D_i is the demand curve for firm i. If each of the k firms believes that it has $1/k$ of the total market, because all the firms are simultaneously changing the quantities produced in a similar way, then D_i is the demand curve for each of the k firms.

In the case of linear demand functions we have a total demand curve for the whole market equal to:

$$P = A - B \sum_{j=1}^{k} X_j$$

and a demand curve for firm i equal to:

$$P = A - kBX_i \qquad (2.1)$$

In this case of conjectural behaviour the marginal revenue curve MR for firm i and for the other producers will be:

$$MR = A - 2kBX_i$$

In this case each of the firms will produce X_{iK}, and the market price will be P_K, see figure 2.6.

If firm i behaves autonomously the firm i will have a perceived marginal revenue curve $\overline{MR}$.

The turnover for firm i is equal to:

$$P \cdot X_i = \left[A - B \sum_{j=1}^{k} X_j \right] \cdot X_i$$

where firm i believes X_j for $j \neq i$ to be a fixed quantity. When we differentiate the turnover function in relation to X_i we get the following:

$$\frac{d(P \cdot X_i)}{dX_i} = A - B \left[\sum_{j \neq i}^{k} X_j + 2X_i \right]$$

When initially X_j for all j different from $j = i$ is equal to X_i we will get the following perceived marginal revenue curve:

$$\overline{MR} = A - B \cdot (k+1)X_i \qquad (2.2)$$

In the case of conjectural behaviour the MR has a slope numerically equal to $2kB$, and in the case of autonomous behaviour a slope equal to $B(k+1)$. For $k>1$ the first term is always bigger than the second term, which means that the perceived marginal revenue is always flatter than the MR.

If all the firms behave antonomously the $\overline{MR}$ curve will be the relevant one for each of the firms, and they will each produce the quantity X_A, and the market price will be P_A, see figure 2.6.

Equation (2.1) is the firm's demand curve and equation (2.2) the perceived marginal revenue curve. When k increases, the perceived marginal revenue curve approaches the firm's demand curve. In this case we are approaching a perfect competition equilibrium, where the market price is determined by the intersection of the total demand curve and the marginal costs curve.

Relations to the outside world

The foregoing discussion of the price mechanism under an oligopoly is related to a closed economy without trade. Let us examine some examples which also include foreign countries.

In the first case it is assumed that the same good is produced abroad at a world market price which equals MC in figure 2.6. In this situation, the domestic manufacturers cannot obtain any market power. If they sell at a price above MC, they will be competed out of the market. They can only obtain a higher price if the country introduces an import tariff t. The price they can then get will equal MC + t. This oligopoly case is completely parallel to the monopoly case in section 2.1.

The introduction of a tariff reduces domestic consumption and increases the market price. There is a fall in consumer surplus which exceeds the rise in producer surplus.

In the second case, we look at an exporting country. It is assumed that the k manufacturers do not sell the good domestically, but only on the export markets. D_i is the foreign countries' import demand for each of the k manufacturers' production.

In this situation, it is an advantage for the country if the enterprises co-ordinate their actions, i.e. each asks the price P_K and sells the quantity X_{iK}. In a situation of autonomous behaviour, the export price will be lower, i.e. P_A.

If the firms are not able to form an export cartel, the country can improve its welfare by implementing an export tariff of RS. Without an export tariff, the enterprises will act autonomously, which means that each of the k manufacturers will get a producer surplus of $(P_A - MC) \cdot (OX_A)$. If an export tariff is introduced, there will be a producer surplus of $(P_K - MC) \cdot (OX_{iK})$. When the last area of figure 2.6 is larger than the first one, an export tariff will improve the country's welfare.

In the third and final case, the k enterprises sell their products on the domestic as well as on the export markets. Figure 2.6 still shows the conditions on the export markets, which means that in the case of exports it will be an advantage to introduce an export tariff if the enterprises themselves cannot agree on establishing an export cartel.

However, in this case an export tariff may also lead to higher domestic prices, which will be to the detriment of consumers if the producers act conjecturally rather than autonomously in the domestic market. This loss can become so large that the introduction of an export tariff is not suitable.

Generally, it can be said that in relation to export markets, the country may be interested in a »strong« oligopoly, which can be obtained through an export tariff, but in relation to the domestic market the country will be interested in a »weak« oligopoly.

2.3 Imperfect competition abroad

It is now assumed that domestically there is perfect competition, but a foreign enterprise or enterprises enjoy a certain market power. By applying an import tariff or import subsidies, the importing country may obtain a share of the profit which the foreign enterprises may generate because of the market situation. This is referred to as »rent snatching«, which means that the domestic market »snatches« part of the gain.

Monopoly abroad

Only in rare cases will there be just one foreign manufacturer. This scenario is discussed nevertheless, because the main conclusions here also apply to oligopolies. We are dealing with a homogeneous product. Domestically, there is a straight import demand D, as shown in figure 2.7.

Under free trade, with perfectly competitive markets abroad, the

Figure 2.7: Monopoly abroad

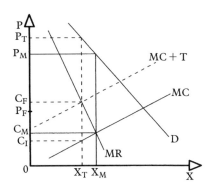

price will be P_F. Where there is a monopoly abroad, the price of the good will be P_M where the marginal revenue MR crosses the marginal cost curve. The monopolist will achieve a supernormal profit of $(P_M - C_M) \cdot X_M$.

For the importing country, this situation is clearly worse than the free trade situation. If the importing country could introduce a price regulation which only allowed imports at a maximum price of P_F, the domestic market would attain the same situation as under free trade.

If such a price regulation is not possible, the second best solution would be to impose an import tariff. An import tariff of T increases the marginal costs of the monopolist. After the imposition of a domestic tariff, the optimum price on the market will be P_T, and the output sold X_T. The price P_T is determined by the intersection of MR and the monopolist's new marginal cost curve, which is MC + T.

The monopolist's supernormal profit is now $(P_T - C_F) \cdot X_T$, and the tariff revenue of the country is $(C_F - C_I) \cdot X_T$. The monopolist's supernormal profit falls compared to the non-tariff situation. This is because the slope of MR is steeper than the slope of D. In other words, the domestic price increase causes a smaller rise in consumer expenditure than the tariff revenue now realized.

In this case, the importing country's situation will be improved by the tariff. This is often called »rent snatching«. The supernormal profit which the monopolist obtains, known as the monopoly rent, is reduced when the importing country imposes a tariff. The tariff means that the importing country gets part of the monopoly rent.

However, this is not the case if the slope of MR is less steep than the slope of D. Figure 2.8 shows an isoelastic import demand curve in which the price elasticity numerically is above 1. It can be shown that in this case, the slope of the marginal revenue curve MR for any X will be less steep than the slope of D for the same X.

It is assumed that the foreign manufacturer's marginal costs MC are horizontal. In the monopoly situation, the price will be P_M, and the imported quantity of goods X_M. If the importing country imposes a tariff, the retail price will be P_T, and the imported volume X_T. In this case, the price of the manufactured goods will increase by more than the tariff rate. This means that the monopolist's supernormal profit increases. The fall in the domestic consumer surplus will be larger than the tariff revenue.

Figure 2.8: Foreign monopolist in the case of isoelastic import demand

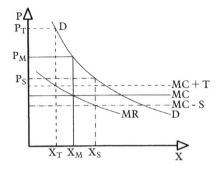

If instead the country grants an import subsidy of S, domestic welfare will increase. The domestic price will fall to P_S. This means that the price drop will exceed the subsidy. In that case, the consumer surplus will increase more than the subsidy expenditure.

The central element in this model is that through tariffs and subsidies, the foreign manufacturer can be deprived of part of its monopoly gain.

As shown above, the character of the import demand exercises decisive influence on whether the country's situation can be improved through tariffs or subsidies. To illustrate this further, the case of a kinked import demand can be analysed. The kink may, for instance, occur because there is a basis for a domestic production of the good in question. D_Q and S_Q in figure 2.9.a are domestic

Figure 2.9: The kinked demand curve

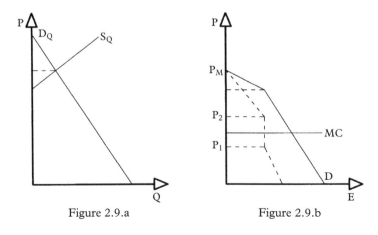

Figure 2.9.a   Figure 2.9.b

demand and domestic supply. In figure 2.9.b, the domestic import demand is inferred on the basis of figure 2.9.a. The import demand is kinked at the highest price, where there is no longer a basis for a domestic production.

The marginal cost curve of the foreign manufacturer is MC. If MC crosses the marginal revenue curve between the prices P_1P_2, where the marginal revenue curve is vertical, the optimum price will be P_M.

In this situation, the importing country may get part of the foreign manufacturer's monopoly gain by imposing a tariff which equals the difference between P_2 and MC.

Oligopoly abroad

The existence of a foreign oligopoly is a more realistic case. The individual oligopolist enterprise which acts autonomously will see a more shallow marginal revenue curve than where the enterprises act in co-ordination. It appears from the analysis in connection with figure 2.6 that autonomous behaviour will result in a lower price than can be obtained by a cartel capitalizing on its monopoly.

An analysis of the oligopoly case leads to the same conclusion as with a monopoly case. If the marginal revenue curve has a steeper slope than the import demand, it may be an advantage for the importing country to impose an import tariff, so it may »snatch« part of the oligopolists' profit, cf. figure 2.7 which now illustrates the conditions for each of the oligopolists. The total profit of the oligopolists is largest when the oligopolists act as a cartel. This situation provides the most profit to »snatch« by imposing an import tariff. If the enterprises act autonomously, the price will decrease with the number of enterprises in the oligopoly. If there are k enterprises, the price obtained in the oligopoly market will tend towards the price obtained in a perfectly competitive market, when k increases towards infinity. Therefore, the smaller the number of enterprises in the oligopoly, the higher will be the optimal import tariff.

In figure 2.7, the import price before the tariff is OP_M. After the imposition of the tariff T, the import price, exclusive of the tariff, will equal $OP_T - C_IC_F$. The country's terms of trade will be improved after the tariff has been imposed. Where there is imperfect competition, even a small country may obtain a gain in terms of trade by imposing a tariff. As shown in section 1.2, only large countries can obtain a gain in terms of trade by imposing tariffs if the markets are perfectly competitive.

In practice, there are examples which show that there can be reductions in price connected with imports to a small country. Denmark imports cars which are subject to substantial registration taxes. In principle, this is a domestic tax, but since Denmark does not produce cars itself, the tax functions as a tariff. As a consequence of the high Danish registration tax, car manufacturers sell cars to Denmark at lower import prices than those which apply in other countries which do not have correspondingly high registration taxes.

If in the oligopoly case there is a marginal revenue curve with a more shallow slope than the import demand, it would be optimal to grant subsidies provided that the marginal costs are constant (see figure 2.8), or increase with the production volume.

2.4 Imperfect competition at home and abroad

So far it has been assumed that there are imperfect markets either domestically or abroad. It cannot be ruled out that there are differences in market structures in different countries. The smaller a country is, the stronger is the possibility that there are only one or a few manufacturers. Often, however, if there is an oligopoly in one country, the same will apply in other countries. In the following it is assumed that there are imperfect markets at home as well as abroad.

The definition of strategic trade policy

When market imperfection exists at home and abroad, there is scope for an initiative called a strategic trade policy. Strategic initiatives may be regarded as actions which are not in themselves desirable, but which make others change their behaviour in a way which suits the interests of the originator of the strategic measure.

Private enterprises implement strategic measures to influence competitors' behaviour. A monopolist may abstain from obtaining the monopoly price in the short term because the enterprise risks that a high price will open a window for other enterprises to enter the market. The monopolist will thus maintain a lower price than the optimal price in the short term.

An enterprise may decide to invest in larger capacity than can be utilized in the near future. The existence of spare capacity sends a signal to potential competitors that production can be extended quickly if new manufacturers penetrate the market. In the short term, the monopoly price can be obtained. If this price attracts potential new competitors, it can quickly be reduced and production can be extended so that competitors abstain from entering the market. With excess capacity it is possible to obtain the monopoly price while avoiding attracting new competitors to the market.

When a country pursues a strategic trade policy, the objective is to influence the competitive relationship between domestic and foreign manufacturers in a way that enables a larger production potential for domestic manufacturers to the detriment of foreign competitors. In the following, examples will be given of strategic export and import policies.

Strategic export policy

The aim here is to analyze the strategic aspects of trade policy. It is therefore assumed that countries A and B both manufacture a good, but there is no domestic consumption of the good. The two countries only export to a third country. Such assumptions are not realistic, but they help to isolate the strategic aspects of trade policy.

For the sake of simplification, it is further assumed that each country has one manufacturer and that both manufacturers produce the same homogeneous product. This is a duopoly in which each manufacturer fixes the output produced on the basis of the output supplied by the other manufacturer. Each manufacturer determines its quantity in order to maximize its profits. Each of the two firms acts autonomously, as each of them assumes that the competitor will not change its supply in reaction to a change in its own supply. It is possible to deduce the reaction curves as shown in figure 2.10. The R_A curve shows the optimal quantity for the manufacturer in country A, when the manufacturer in country B produces the quantity indicated on the X_B axis, and when the domestic marginal costs are MC_A. Correspondingly, R_B shows the optimal

Figure 2.10: Reaction curves and profit functions in duopoly

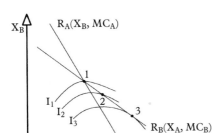

output for the enterprise in country B when X_A is given and when the foreign marginal costs are MC_B. The Cournot equilibrium is found at point 1.

The I curves are isoprofit curves for the enterprise in country A. An isoprofit curve is based on the demand curve and the cost function for the enterprise in country A. An isoprofit curve shows the combinations of X_B and X_A which give the enterprise in country A a constant profit. They will all have their highest points where the isoprofit curves I_1, I_2 and I_3 cross the R_A curve. The further down the isoprofit curve, the larger the revenue of the enterprise in country A, because the foreign competitor produces less.

When the two manufacturers act autonomously with regard to output, 1 will be the only point of equilibrium. This applies when the manufacturer in country B acts autonomously even though the manufacturer in country A could increase its profits by going from point 1 to point 2 and further to point 3 at which the manufacturer in country A gets the maximum profit obtainable.

This situation arises if the firm in country A departs from its autonomous behaviour and instead acts as »volume leader«, i.e. the manufacturer which declares its production volume to which the manufacturer in country B adapts. Point 3 is called a Stackelberg equilibrium. Being the volume leader, the firm in country A adjusts its production to the volume on the reaction curve R_B, which maximizes the profit of the firm in country A.

If a domestic firm assumes volume leadership, and the foreign firm acts autonomously, point 3 will become the point of equilibrium. This situation leaves the country A better off and country B worse off.

Figure 2.11: The effect of production subsidies

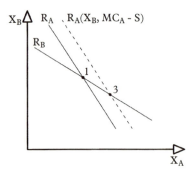

If a domestic firm does not act as volume leader, domestic subsidies may be used to shift the reaction curve of the domestic manufacturer to the right. This is shown in figure 2.11. Subsidies of S are granted, reducing the marginal costs. There is a level for subsidies which implies that the domestic reaction curve becomes the broken line crossing R_B at point 3, which is the Stackelberg equilibrium, cf. figure 2.10, point 3.

This maximizes the earnings of the firm in country A, but at the same time requires public expenditure on subsidies. A lower subsidy level than S can be found which maximizes the sum of the earnings of the firm and the public expenditure on subsidies. This example proves that a higher level of welfare can be obtained through export subsidies.

However, such a conclusion must be treated with some reservation, as the result is based on the assumptions chosen. If the two firms do not adjust through changes in volume but through changes in price, it can be shown that a country should always impose an export tariff on the good in order to obtain a gain.

In general, it can be questioned whether it is relevant to assume either Cournot behaviour or Bertrand behaviour. Could it not be reasonable to assume that over time, one firm discovers how the other reacts and incorporates this experience into its own decision-making process? This is referred to as a conjectural behaviour.

Furthermore, it can be shown that even in the Cournot adjustment example above, the outcome of subsidies is unclear if there is a domestic oligopoly. It was illustrated in section 2.2 that a domestic oligopoly will put added pressure on the export price when the oligopoly firms act autonomously. This implies that a tariff should always be imposed on the exported good in order to make the enterprises reduce their output, thus provoking a price increase. On the other hand, it means that the domestic oligopoly loses sales to the foreign competitors on the domestic market. This fact seems to suggest that subsidies should be granted to the domestic oligopoly.

It is not possible to generalize about the net results. The only conclusion is that when one moves from a domestic monopoly to an oligopoly, the argument for granting export subsidies is severely weakened.

In the above it was assumed that there is a fixed number of manufacturers in the country considering applying a strategic trade policy. Now, it is assumed that enterprises enter and leave the market freely, until the moment when there is no supernormal profit. In the initial situation, there is no supernormal profit. If the country grants export subsidies, the existing enterprises will obtain a supernormal profit which will attract new enterprises until the supernormal profit is eliminated. The final outcome is that enterprises both before and after the introduction of export subsidies only get the »normal« profit which is necessary for their survival. In other words, export subsidies do not lead to a supernormal profit in this case. On the contrary, society incurs a net loss which equals the value of the export subsidies.

Whether it is reasonable to grant export subsidies or to impose an export tariff very much depends on the model chosen and the assumptions behind this model.

Apart from this, models such as those used here are problematic to apply. The models are partial, as they only consider the conditions of one sector. In a general equilibrium model, the advantages of a trade policy measure are smaller, and the effects may even become adverse, as the expansion of one sector leads to the contraction of another. Moreover, the above models do not consider the risk that the other country may implement retaliatory measures. These objections will be discussed below.

Strategic import policy

Again we consider two countries, A and B, with imperfectly competitive markets, as each of the countries has one manufacturer. In

Figure 2.12: The impact of a tariff in duopoly

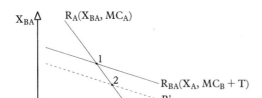

country A, the firm produces X_A which is only destined for the domestic market. In country B, the enterprise manufactures for the country itself and exports to country A. The export from country B to A is called X_{BA}.

Figure 2.12 shows the reaction curves of the two manufacturers with respect to the market in country A. Point 1 is the Cournot equilibrium in the initial situation.

When country A imposes a tariff on imports from country B, the reaction curve for the enterprise in country B will shift from R_{BA} to R'_{BA}. The aggregate supply in country A will fall. The market price will consequently rise. The enterprise in country A increases its earnings, because both the quantity produced and the price increase. The enterprise in country B experiences a decline in its profits. At the same time, country A gets a tariff revenue.

Another example of a strategic import policy is in a situation with significant economies of scale in production. There is only scope for the production of the good in question in one of the countries. This means that one of the countries manufactures the good, which is then sold on its domestic market and exported to the other country.

If country A enjoys a comparative advantage in production, this production will be located in country A. If country B imposes a tariff on imports, production of the good can be established in country B, which renders the survival of the enterprise in country A impossible. Exports to country B are a condition for the existence of the enterprise in country A.

This is an example of how country B, which is less favourable for the production of a given product, can »snatch« the production from country A by imposing a tariff on the good.

Measures to avoid monopoly

The previous examples in this section have mostly included two producers, one in each country. The individual country may support its own manufacturer through strategic trade policy.

Let us now assume that there is only one manufacturer in the market, and let us examine a concrete example, viz. the aviation industry. In the US, Boeing has specialized in constructing very large aircraft. Boeing enjoys a very strong position, which approximates to a monopoly situation on the world market. The expenses connected with establishing aircraft production plants are very significant, and there are large research and development costs related to the development of new types of aircraft.

Europe has to import aircraft from the USA, and since USA has a monopoly in this respect, Boeing can obtain a monopoly gain which is paid for by Europe. For this reason, a number of European governments join forces to establish an Airbus company to produce aircraft corresponding to the types produced by Boeing.

The market conditions for an Airbus company are as set out in figure 2.4. The unit costs decline significantly with increased production, but the sales are relatively limited. If Boeing delivers aircraft at a price of P_W, the basis for a European aviation industry is eliminated. However, if the European governments intervene and grant subsidies, there is a basis for establishing Airbus. The inherent advantage is that Boeing's monopoly is broken, and that European purchasers get access to cheaper aircraft than previously.

Breaking up such a monopoly can in itself be a benefit, seen from a European viewpoint. Even though Boeing may deliver aircraft produced at a lower cost by virtue of its large production, deliveries from Airbus can be cheaper, even taking into account the public subsidies, because the monopoly price previously paid to Boeing is avoided.

The establishment of Airbus reduces Boeing's sales, and causes their unit costs to rise. Even if Boeing can survive this competition, they might feel occasioned to apply for increased public support in the USA. This could be a clear signal to Airbus not to establish exports of aircraft to third countries to which Boeing has delivered so far.

Production subsidies can thus be used not only to break a monopoly, but also to »threaten« a competitor into not exhibiting too »aggressive« behaviour in markets where the country already has a dominant position.

2.5 Problems with partial models

The models applied above have been partial models. In order for such models to be satisfactory, a couple of assumptions must be fulfilled.

First of all, the production costs in the analysis must reflect the socio-economic costs. This assumption is only valid if there is perfect competition in all the other sectors, both in the markets for the goods themselves and in the factor markets. It is realistic to assume that there is also imperfection in other parts of the system. If production is increased in the sector analysed, resources will be drawn from other sectors in which, because of imperfection, the costs do not reflect the socio-economic costs, unless optimal economic intervention is effected in these sectors.

Secondly, a partial model does not take into account the capacity limitations of a society. Any extension of the production of an important sector will necessarily affect goods and factor prices in other sectors of the economy.

The conditions in one export sector affect the conditions in another export sector, just as the conditions in the rest of the economy may be influenced. In order to illustrate this interaction, it is assumed that there are two export sectors with oligopoly. The rest of the economy is assumed to be perfectly competitive.

For each of the two oligopoly sectors it is assumed that the »true« marginal revenue curve MR and the actually »perceived« marginal revenue curve $\overline{MR}$ are known. It is assumed that each of the two export sectors uses specially skilled labour which is not used in the rest of society, and for which the supply is fixed. It is assumed that one labour unit is used in the production of one product unit in each of the two sectors.

This simple model is illustrated in figure 2.13. The length of the horizontal axis equals the quantity of labour L. It can be applied in either sector a or sector b, in which the output volumes X_a and X_b are measured on the basis of O_a and O_b, respectively. Each of the two sectors will manufacture a volume for which it applies that MR = MC, with MC being the marginal costs. The marginal costs are

Figure 2.13: Imperfect market conditions in two sectors

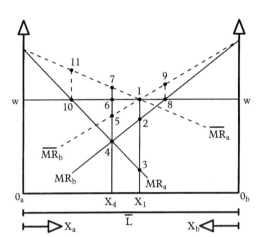

MC = w + t − s, where w is the wages, t is an export tariff, and s is export subsidies. Moreover, it applies that L = X_a + X_b.

Point 1 shows the equilibrium reached when the two oligopolist sectors attempt to maximize their income, and w becomes the wages. This equilibrium differs from the best scenario from a socio-economic point of view. Figure 2.13 illustrates the problems connected with applying a partial model.

Firstly, the use of partial analysis may lead to a »wrong« allocation of production. If one only looks at sector b in figure 2.13, one will reach the conclusion, that point 8 is the optimal production level. At this production level the »true« marginal revenues equal the marginal costs. To induce a move from point 1 to point 8 it is necessary to impose a production tax equal to the vertical distance 8-9. From a socio-economic point of view the situation at point 8 is worse than the situation at point 1. The optimal solution is in fact point 4, which involves an increase in the production of commodity b.

If one only looks at sector a, figure 2.13 shows that one should impose a tax on commodity a equal to 10-11, so that the production point would move from 1 to 10. If one applies a partial model to each of the two commodities, the result would be that each of the two sectors should pay a production tax. The result would be that the labour force corresponding to the distance 8-10 would be unemployed.

Secondly, the analysis shows that one can only reach the optimal point 4 by looking at both sectors simultaneously, and one can only reach the optimal situation by intervening in both sectors. The production of commodity b should be increased by giving subsidies corresponding to 5-6. On the other hand the production of commodity a should be reduced by imposing production taxes corresponding to 6-7.

Thirdly, a partial application of the model will give a wrong impression of the economic gains associated with the move from point 1 to point 4. If we only look at the production increase in sector b we will obtain a gain equal to $2X_1X_44$. But this production increase can only be realized by a reduction of the production in sector a. In sector b the reduction in income will amount to $3X_1X_44$, so that the net gain in income will be equal to the area 234.

Fourthly, the analysis shows that knowledge of the data needs to be quite comprehensive in order to facilitate the choice of the »right« level of duties and subsidies.

If the right values are not found immediately, there will either be an excess demand or a lack of demand for the labour in question.

2.6 Retaliatory measures

The starting point is the duopoly scenario illustrated in figure 2.11. There are two firms which are located in countries A and B, respectively. They both sell the good in question to a third country market. It is assumed that each of the firms adjusts its export volumes in order to maximize its profit. Each firm assumes the supply of the other to be fixed.

The reaction curves of the two enterprises are shown in figure 2.14, in which point 1 is the point of equilibrium.

If each firm acts autonomously, neither of the firms in situation 1 can improve its situation by changing its supply.

Figure 2.14 shows that country A can use export subsidies to change the reaction curve of the enterprise located in the country. The reaction curve shifts from $R_A{}^0$ to $R_A{}^1$, and the new intersection will be point 3, with the firm in country A receiving a larger profit and the firm in country B a smaller one compared to point 1.

If country B now retaliates by also granting export subsidies, the firm in country B gets a new reaction curve $R_B{}^1$. The new equilibrium point will be point 4 when the two countries have decided on

Figure 2.14: Both countries pursue a trade policy

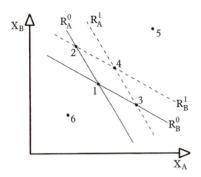

the level of export subsidies corresponding to R_A^1 and R_B^1. At point 4, the firm in country A obtains a lower profit than at point 3, while the enterprise in country B obtains a higher profit than at point 3. Profit functions can be inferred as illustrated in figure 2.10. It can be shown that at point 4, the profit of the two firms, less the export subsidies paid by the state, will be lower than at point 1 for each of the enterprises. From a socio-economic point of view, both countries will thus incur losses when moving from point 1 to point 4.

If country A introduces export subsidies, country A may obtain a socio-economic advantage, but only at the expense of country B. Therefore, if country B initiates countermeasures, country B will be able to reduce its loss, but in total, after each country has introduced export subsidies, they will both be worse off than if they both abstained from subsidizing exports.

The question therefore is, why the countries grant export subsidies leaving both of them worse off.

The reason is that the two countries do not co-ordinate their actions, which can be illustrated by an example corresponding to the case of the »Prisoner's Dilemma« game. Each country makes assumptions about the behaviour of the other country without any communication between them. Regardless of the action of country B, country A will benefit from introducing export subsidies, and the same applies to country B. It appears from table 2.1 that if country B were not to introduce export subsidies, it would still be an advantage for country A to do so. If country B does grant export subsidies, it will still be an advantage for country A to do so. The situation is the same for country B. The countries will thus end up

Table 2.1: The countries' gain from alternative behaviour[1]

Country A \ Country B	No export subsidies	Export subsidies
No export subsidies	Country A: 10 Country B: 10	Country A: 0 Country B: 15
Export subsidies	Country A: 15 Country B: 0	Country A: 4 Country B: 4

[1] The gains of the countries are measured as the profit of the enterprise less the expense for export subsidies.

in a situation in which they both subsidize exports even though they would both benefit if neither of them gave export subsidies.

As a consequence of this, which is inherent in the Prisoner's Dilemma, the two countries can initiate mutual increases of export subsidies in order to obtain a larger gain than would have been realized if the export subsidies had not been increased. The result would be a situation in equilibrium, for instance at point 5, at which neither of the countries would benefit from increasing export subsidies. However, for each of the countries, point 5 is less favourable than point 1, which would be the outcome if the countries co-ordinated their behaviour and agreed to abstain from the use of export subsidies.

Point 1 is not the best solution in the actual example in figure 2.14. The two countries could benefit from agreeing to impose an export tariff so that a price and an export volume to third country markets are obtained which correspond to what the countries would get if the two firms exploited their monopoly through an export cartel. The export tariff implies that the reaction curves of the two countries shift to the left. An intersection at point 6, for instance, would lead to a reduction of the two countries' exports, maximizing the aggregate gain of the countries.

2.7 Monopolistic competition with differentiated products domestically and abroad

In the following, a model is analysed which shows that it is an advantage to introduce an import tariff in order to obtain increased production of »advanced« products. The model was developed by

Venables (1987), and is different from the partial models discussed so far in this chapter, as it is a general equilibrium model taking into consideration the existence of capacity limitations in a country's economy.

Production in a country takes place within two industries or two sectors. One sector manufactures a differentiated product D, which consists of n variants. The other sector produces a homogeneous product Q with constant returns to scale.

There are two factors of production. One production factor is unskilled labour, called L, and it is used in the production of each of the two product lines. The other factor of production is skilled labour, called K, which is only used in the sector which manufactures n variants of the differentiated product.

In the production of the homogeneous product, a fixed quantity of L per unit produced is used, as indicated by k_{LQ}. The differentiated sector also uses a given quantity of unskilled labour per unit produced, namely k_{LD}. In the differentiated sector, each variant is manufactured in enterprises each using Z units of skilled labour. The expenses for skilled labour represent fixed costs.

For all firms, the price will be fixed at the point where the marginal revenue equals the marginal cost. In the sector producing the homogeneous product Q there is perfect competition which means that:

$$P_Q = w_L \, k_{LQ}$$

where w_L is the wages for the unskilled labour.

In the sector manufacturing differentiated products, each firm, which each produces one variant, faces the same demand curves:

$$X = f(P)$$

which is assumed to be isoelastic with the elasticity e. According to the price theory, the optimum price $P^\star$ equals:

$$P^* = MC\left(\frac{e}{e-1}\right)$$

with MC being the marginal costs. For each manufacturer of the differentiated product, the optimum price P_D equals:

$$P_D = \frac{w_L \cdot k_{LD} \cdot e}{e-1}$$

In order to be in equilibrium, the price of each of the differentiated product must equal the average costs. Each enterprise requires Z units of skilled labour.

The number of enterprises must thus be:

$$n = \frac{K}{Z}$$

with K being the total quantity of available skilled labour.

The model assumes that the wages for skilled labour are adjusted so that the earnings of the enterprises less the cost of unskilled labour are used to pay the skilled labour.

This means that:

$$w_K \cdot Z = P_D \cdot X - w_L k_{LD} X$$

with w_K being the wages of the skilled labour and X the volume produced.

It is now assumed that there are two countries, A and B, in the model shown above. The demand structure is identical in the two countries. Each of the two countries will now also demand the other country's differentiated products, which are distinct from the country's own product variants. The demand function for all product variants is the same, not only in the individual country, but also between the countries. However, it is assumed that the conditions for the production in each of the two sectors are different in the two countries, A and B. This can be deduced from the different technical production coefficients in each sector for the two countries.

In countries A and B the price of the homogeneous product before trade is:

$$P_Q^A = w_L^A \cdot k_{LQ}^A$$
$$P_Q^B = w_L^B \cdot k_{LQ}^B$$

where the upper exponent refers to the country. This means that after trade, when $P_Q{}^A$ equals $P_Q{}^B$, the following will apply:

$$\frac{w_L^A}{w_L^B} = \frac{k_{LQ}^B}{k_{LQ}^A}$$

which means that the wages of unskilled labour are determined by labour productivity.

As regards the differentiated product, the price of the individual product variant before trade equals:

$$P_D^A = \frac{w_L^A \cdot k_{LD}^A \cdot e^A}{e^A - 1}$$

$$P_D^B = \frac{w_L^B \cdot k_{LD}^B \cdot e^B}{e^B - 1}$$

If the two countries' demand elasticities for the differentiated products are the same, we get:

$$\frac{P_D^A}{P_D^B} = \frac{w_L^A \cdot k_{LD}^A}{w_L^B \cdot k_{LD}^B} = \frac{k_{LD}^A \cdot k_{LQ}^B}{k_{LD}^B \cdot k_{LQ}^A}$$

The trade in the homogeneous product, which obtains the same price in the two countries, means that the price relations between the differentiated products in the two countries are also fixed.

This factor is important when discussing the effects of a tariff. It is assumed that country A imposes a tariff on the import of the differentiated product from country B. Such a tariff makes the domestic price of the differentiated products equal the foreign price, which is constant, plus the tariff. The structure of the model does not allow for a change in the terms of trade.

There are three effects of the tariff. First, the domestic price of the imported differentiated products rises. Secondly, the country obtains a tariff revenue. Thirdly, there will be a substitution involving a move away from the imported differentiated products towards the domestic differentiated products.

The net effect on welfare is apparent, as the two first effects largely balance each other out. The net effect will thus equal the third effect, which is an increase of the domestic production of the differentiated products. The output of the differentiated product D increases, and the price remains unchanged. This means that the domestic manufacturers of the differentiated products obtain larger gross margins, which are transferred into higher wages for skilled labour. At the same time, country A will decrease its production of the homogeneous product. Country A's national income increases at the expense of country B.

The model can also be used to illustrate the effect of a retaliatory measure by country B in the form of a tariff on differentiated products imported from country A.

If country B introduces a similar tariff on country A's products, country A's gain from an import tariff will be neutralized by a corresponding loss from reduced exports to country B. The retail price level for the differentiated imported goods increases in each of the two countries. Consumption therefore shifts towards the homogeneous product. The reduced demand for differentiated goods in both countries leads to a fall in the demand for skilled labour, and consequently also in the wages of this group.

In other words, a tariff may prove beneficial to the individual country if the other country does not take countermeasures, but if the other country retaliates, both countries will incur losses by imposing tariffs.

2.8 Summary

Chapter 1 analysed the effects of trade policy measures in situations with perfectly competitive markets and no externalities. This chapter has carried out corresponding analyses of cases with imperfect competition. As was the case in chapter 1, the analyses are descriptive, which means that they show what actually happens when countries engage in trade policy intervention. However, as in chapter 1, the analyses may be used normatively to examine whether it is reasonable for a country to intervene.

In an attempt to keep the different factors distinct, it is practical to divide the analyses into three groupings. The first situation shows domestic imperfections, but perfectly competitive markets abroad. In the second situation, there is perfect domestic competition and imperfect competition abroad. In the third case, the markets operate imperfectly, domestically as well as abroad.

If there is perfect competition abroad, a domestic sole producer of a homogeneous product can only sell at the world market price, if there is free trade. The sole producer's domestic market power increases with the level of tariff protection (figure 2.1). An import quota in the place of a tariff allows the sole producer always to sell at the monopoly price (figure 2.2). The protection of a good in an importing country can make the country not only self-sufficient, but also make it possible for the country to export the good (figure 2.3). If the sole producer has falling unit costs, the producer may only be able to compete if it receives support. Production subsidies can improve welfare (figure 2.4).

There is a domestic oligopoly in which each manufacturer produces the same good, which is differentiated from the good produced abroad under perfect competition. If the domestic market imports from abroad, an import tariff will increase the retail price (figure 2.6). If, on the contrary, the oligopoly exports, an export tariff will improve the country's terms of trade while reducing the volumes exported (figure 2.6).

The country may obtain improved terms of trade through an export tariff, but if the oligopoly also sells the good domestically, the outcome could be that the domestic price increases as well. If this is the case, it will in itself reduce the level of welfare. In that case, an export tariff is a two-edged sword.

We assume now that there is perfect competition at home, but imperfect competition abroad. This situation allows the domestic market to use trade policy to »snatch« part of a gain which would otherwise go to the enterprises abroad. In the case of monopoly or oligopoly, a tariff can shift part of the profits from foreign firms to domestic firms. This will be the case if the slope of the marginal revenue curve is steeper than the slope of the import demand curve (figure 2.7). If the slope of the marginal revenue curve is less steep than the slope of the import demand curve, import subsidies will cause profits to be transferred from foreign to domestic firms by means of reduced import prices (figure 2.8).

If the markets operate imperfectly, domestically as well as abroad, it is possible for the country to pursue a type of policy known as a strategic trade policy. The simplest way of illustrating this is in a model with one manufacturer in each country. In such a case, an exporting country can obtain an improvement by granting export subsidies (figure 2.11). If the country imports the good, it may be an advantage to impose a tariff (figure 2.12).

It can thus be shown that under imperfect competition there may be situations in which a country can improve its position by employing trade policy measures. However, it is inadvisable to apply the results of these analyses uncritically. Two points must be observed. Firstly, the models are mostly partial equilibrium models for a single market. If there are several markets with imperfection, the indications provided by the single product models may lead to a wrong allocation of resources. Secondly, it is vital to bear in mind that if one country engages in trade policy, other countries may feel prompted to initiate retaliatory measures. As a result, all countries may end up worse off than would have been the case under free trade.

The last section of the chapter shows a 2 country/2 sector model in which there is monopolistic competition in one of the sectors. The model illustrates that in a case such as this, one country may obtain a larger production within the »advanced« sector by imposing an import tariff. Again, the premise for this conclusion is that the other country does not implement countermeasures.

Literature

Brander, J. A. and B. J. Spencer, »Tariffs and the Extraction of Foreign Monopoly Rents under Potential Entry«, *Canadian Journal of Economics*, 14, 1981.

Brander, J. A. and B. J. Spencer, »Export Subsidies and Market Share Rivalry«, *Journal of International Economics*, 18, 1985.

Eaton, J. and G. M. Grossman, »Optimal Trade and Industrial Policy under Oligopoly«, *Quarterly Journal of Economics*, 101, 1986.

Haberler, G., »Strategic Trade Policy and the New International Economics: A Critical Analysis« in Jones, R.W. and A.O. Krueger (eds), *The Political Economy of International Trade*, London, 1990.

Helpman, E., »Imperfect Competition and International Trade: Evidence from Fourteen Industrial Countries«, *Journal of the Japanese and International Economics*, 1, 1987.

Helpman, E. and P. Krugman, *Trade Policy and Marketing Structure*, Mass. 1989.

Kierzkowski, H. (ed), *Monopolistic Competition and International Trade*, Oxford, 1984.

Krueger, A.O., »The Political Economy of the Rent-seeking Society«, *American Economic Review*, 64, 1974.

Krugman, P. (ed), *Strategic Trade Policy and the New International Economics*, Cambridge, Mass., 1986.

Spencer, B.J. and J. A. Brander, »International R & D Rivalry and Industrial Strategy«, *Review of Economic Studies*, 50, 1983.

Venables, A.J., »Trade and Trade Policy with Differentiated Products: A Chamberlinian-Ricardian Model«, *Economic Journal*, 97, 1987.

Vousden, N., *The Economics of Trade Protection*, Cambridge, 1990.

3. Trade policy
– General intervention

In chapter 1, the effects of trade policy measures were analysed. It was assumed that the markets were perfectly competitive. Trade policy measures were selective in the sense that only one out of many kinds of goods was subject to intervention. Therefore, we applied a partial model, in which we could rightly disregard the relations between the goods on the supply side and the demand side. If we take one out of n goods, changes for this one good mean very little to the remaining n – 1 goods.

In this chapter, trade policy instruments will also be analysed under the presumption of perfectly competitive markets. In contrast to chapter 1, the model applied will be a general equilibrium model in which changes for one good have an impact on the others.

We are dealing with an economy with two sectors, i.e. production of two different goods. All factors of production are fully utilized, which means that the increase in one sector necessarily implies a reduction in the other. On the demand side, incomes are spent on the purchase of the two products. If the consumption of one product increases, this will have an impact on the consumption of the other.

In this chapter, trade policy measures are implemented which are aimed at one sector. The measures are no longer selective. They must be considered as general measures even if they are only directed towards one sector, because they will have a general impact on the entire economy.

First, the effects of tariffs, duties and subsidies in a small country will be analysed. Then we will turn to the effects of tariffs in a large country, including the consequences of another large country imposing retaliatory measures. This leads to a discussion of the advantages gained when countries co-ordinate their trade policy.

3.1 The effects of tariffs in a small country

The conditions under free trade

The country whose conditions are being analysed is so small that it is not able to affect the international terms of trade, which must therefore be considered to be determined by external factors (exogenously determined).

Two types of goods, a and b, are produced and consumed. TT is the country's transformation curve illustrating which combinations of the two types of goods the country can produce when all factors of production are fully utilized.

The international terms of trade $P_a/P_b = P_w$ are exogenously determined. The slope of the straight line P_w indicates these terms of trade. The country will produce at point A_1 and consume at point B_1 which means that the country is on indifference curve I_1. The country exports product a and imports product b.

The situation under free trade results in a Walras equilibrium. A Walras equilibrium means that the DRT (Domestic Rate of Transformation), the DRS (Domestic Rate of Substitution) and the FRT (Foreign Rate of Transformation) are the same. The domestic marginal rate of transformation is indicated by the slope of the tangent at A_1 (the production point), and the domestic marginal rate of substitution in consumption is indicated by the slope of the tangent at B_1 (the consumption point). The foreign marginal rate of transformation indicates the marginal increase in the volume of imported goods that can be obtained by a marginal increase in

Figure 3.1: Free trade and tariffs in a small country

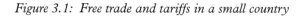

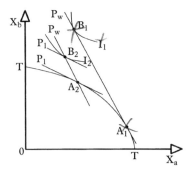

exports. In the case of a small country which is not able to affect its terms of trade, the foreign marginal rate of transformation will equal the relative prices in international trade, which equals the slope of P_w.

The effects of import tariffs

The country now imposes an ad valorem tariff t on the imported product b. This means that t is a given percentage. The world market prices of the two goods remain unchanged. Consequently, the domestic price relation is $P_1 = P_a/P_b(1+t)$. This is the price relation that domestic producers and consumers are faced with.

P_1, shown in figure 3.1, has a slope which corresponds exactly to these new domestic price relations. There is a new equilibrium at the point where P_1 is tangential to the transformation curve and an indifference curve, respectively, (curve I_2 in the figure), while the straight line connecting the two points of tangency has the slope P_w, which represents the international terms of trade.

In the new equilibrium, the country produces at point A_2 and consumes at point B_2. This means that the tariff imposed on product b causes a change in the production composition as well as in the consumption composition of the two products. The import of product b decreases, and so does the export of product a. In terms of welfare, the tariff leaves the country worse off, as after imposing the tariff, the country is located on the lower indifference curve I_2.

Obviously, the import tariff is a measure which benefits the import-competing sector in terms of production. The partial model in chapter 1 comes to the same conclusion. What the partial model does not take into account is that the support received by one sector will harm the other. This is clearly illustrated by the general model, which shows precisely how the production possibilities in the other sector are reduced.

When an import tariff is imposed, DRT still equals DRS, and both rates equal the relative domestic prices. However, FRT deviates from this, as FRT equals the relative international prices.

The effects of export tariffs

Instead of imposing an import tariff on the import-competing sector, an export tariff q could be imposed on the export good. This implies that the internal price relations will be $P_a(1 - q)/P_b$. As a result, the new equilibrium with an export tariff will be exactly the same as with an import tariff provided that:

$$\frac{P_a(1-q)}{P_b} = \frac{P_a}{P_b(1+t)}$$

which again means that:

$$q = \frac{t}{1+t}$$

An export tariff of this size will lead to exactly the same point of equilibrium as an import tariff of t. The export tariff will harm the export-competing sector and benefit the import-competing sector.

This analysis can also illustrate the effect of imposing an import tariff on industrial products (product b) and an export tariff on agricultural products (product a) simultaneously. This situation has been seen in many developing countries. It means that the domestic relative prices will be:

$$\frac{P_a(1-q)}{P_b(1+t)} \qquad\qquad (3.1)$$

which implies strong discrimination against the agricultural sector. Revenue in the agricultural sector will fall, and industrial products must be purchased at higher prices.

If a country introduces an import tariff and export subsidies simultaneously, the two measures will neutralize each other in our two-sector model. Export subsidies may be considered a negative tariff. If q in (3.1) is equal to $- t$, this will result in the same domestic relative prices as under free trade, where neither import tariffs nor export subsidies exist.

3.2 A three-sector model

However, the above results, showing firstly that an import tariff in the import sector has the same effect as a corresponding export tariff in the export sector, and secondly that an import tariff in the import sector will be neutralized by corresponding export subsidies in the export sector, only apply in a two-sector model.

The results are no longer valid in a three-sector model where, apart from the import-competing and the export-competing sectors, there is a home market sector, a service sector, which is not in competition with foreign countries.

This may be illustrated quite easily by looking at the producer prices in the export sector P_X, the home market sector P_H, and the import-competing sector P_M in different scenarios, as shown below:

The initial situation:	P_X	P_H	P_M
The export tariff scenario:	$P_X (1-q)$	P_H	P_M
The import tariff scenario:	P_X	P_H	$P_M (1+t)$
The import tariff and export subsidies scenario:	$P_X (1+q)$	P_M	$P_M (1+t)$

Compared to the initial situation, an export tariff has the effect that the producer price in the export sector decreases relative to the producer prices in the other two sectors. If the initial situation is then compared with the scenario in which a tariff is imposed on the imported good, the producer price in the import sector will increase compared to the producer prices in the other two sectors.

The result in the first scenario with an export tariff is that the export sector will release factors of production to the home market sector and the import sector, because the factor return is higher in these sectors. In the scenario with an import tariff, the import sector will attract factors of production from the other two sectors. The pattern of the relocation of resources resulting from the two measures is illustrated in diagram 3.1.

In the import tariff scenario, the import-competing sector will grow because resources will be relocated from the export sector as well as from the home market sector. In the export tariff scenario,

Diagram 3.1: Relocation of resources resulting from an import tariff and an export tariff

both the import-competing sector and the home market sector will grow. The home market sector will be reduced by import tariffs, but increased by export tariffs.

In the situation where a tariff t is imposed in the import sector, and export subsidies q, which equal t, are granted in the export sector, the relative prices between the two sectors with foreign competition will remain unchanged. The important thing is, however, that the price relation between the sectors with foreign competition and the home market sector shifts to the benefit of the former. Support for sectors with foreign competition will therefore have the effect that each of the sectors will receive resources from the home market sector.

A combination of import tariffs and export subsidies works in the same way as a devaluation. The effect of a devaluation is precisely to change domestic producer prices in the sectors competing with foreign countries, compared to the producer prices in the home market sector. In the case of a devaluation, the export and import sectors obtain relatively higher prices compared to the home market sector. A revaluation may thus be compared with the situation in which import subsidies are combined with an export tariff.

3.3 The effects of duties and subsidies in a small country

The country whose conditions are now analysed is still a small country, which means that the international prices are exogenously determined. There are two perfectly competitive sectors.

If the country introduces production duties/production subsidies or consumption taxes/consumption subsidies in one of the sectors, this will affect international trade.

A closed economy

In the initial situation, we are dealing with a closed economy in which consumption and production are the same. Figure 3.2 shows the transformation curve.

If the country does not intervene, the result will be equilibrium at the point where the indifference curve I_1 is tangential to the

Figure 3.2: The effects of duties and subsidies in a closed economy

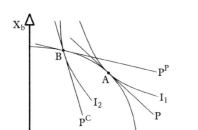

transformation curve. The relative prices are indicated by the slope of tangent P.

If duties are imposed on the production of a good a, the retail price of good a, $P_a{}^C$, will exceed the producers' selling price $P_a{}^P$. This means that the relative retail prices will equal the numeric value of the slope of P^C, and the relative selling prices for the producers will equal the numeric value of the slope of P^P. The new equilibrium point will be B, where the level of welfare is lower. The difference between the slopes of P^C and P^P equals the percentage size of the duty.

If, instead of imposing a production duty on good a, the country grants production subsidies for good b, the result will be the same. If a production duty on good a is replaced by a consumption tax on the same item, the result will also be the same. Similarly, consumption subsidies for good b will have the same effect as production subsidies for the same sector. These findings are apparent in table 3.1.

Thus, it may be concluded that in a two-sector model, it makes no difference whether production duties are imposed on product a, or whether subsidies are granted to the production of product b. Taxation of one sector implies indirect support to the other. This result also applies when international trade is opened up.

The other conclusion is that in a closed economy, it makes no difference whether duties are imposed on the production or the consumption of a given product. In fact, this is not surprising since production and consumption are the same in a closed economy. This equivalence between production duties/production subsidies

Table 3.1: The effect of duties and subsidies on prices

	Sector a	Sector b	Relative prices
Prices in the initial situation	P_a	P_b	$\dfrac{P_a}{P_b}$
Production duty q on product a	$P_a^C = P_a^P(1+q)$	P_b	$\dfrac{P_a^C}{P_b} = \dfrac{P_a^P(1+q)}{P_b}$
Production subsidies s for product b	P_a	$P_b^C = P_b^P(1-s)$	$\dfrac{P_a}{P_b^C} = \dfrac{P_a}{P_b^P(1-s)}$
Expenditure tax r on product a	$P_a^C = P_a^P(1+r)$	P_b	$\dfrac{P_a^C}{P_b} = \dfrac{P_a^P(1+r)}{P_b}$
Consumption subsidies Z for product b	P_a	$P_b^C = P_b^P(1-z)$	$\dfrac{P_a}{P_b^C} = \dfrac{P_a}{P_b^P(1-z)}$

and consumption taxes/consumption subsidies does not apply in an open economy. In an open economy, the following applies:

$$\text{Production} = \text{Consumption} \quad \begin{array}{l} + \text{ Exports (for exported goods)} \\ - \text{ Imports (for imported goods).} \end{array}$$

If we are dealing with exported goods, a production duty will affect consumption and export, whereas a consumption tax will only affect domestic consumption. In the case of imported goods, a production duty will not affect imports, whereas a consumption tax will.

The effect of production subsidies in a small country

If the country wants to increase its production in the import-competing sector, an import tariff may be imposed, as described in section 3.1 in this chapter. Figure 3.1 is repeated in figure 3.3. Under free trade, the country will be at point A_1 in terms of production, and at point B_1 in terms of consumption. If the country wants a production of product b corresponding to A_2, it may impose a tar-

Figure 3.3: Production subsidies

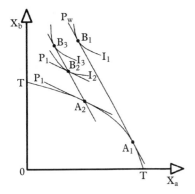

iff. The production point will be A_2, and the consumption point will be B_2, located on indifference curve I_2. This shows that the level of welfare has decreased.

Instead of imposing a tariff t on product b, a production subsidy could be granted. If production subsidies equal to t are granted for product b, the domestic selling price will be the same in both cases. Therefore, when granting subsidies, the production point A_2 will also be the same.

The tariff also affects the relative retail prices, which is not the case with production subsidies. If production subsidies are granted, the relative retail prices will equal the relative world market prices. In the subsidy scenario, the consumption point will thus be B_3, whereas in the tariff scenario, it will be B_2. B_3 is on indifference curve I_3, which gives a higher level of welfare than indifference curve I_2, which was the level of welfare in the tariff scenario. It has thus been proved that production subsidies lead to a higher level of welfare than a tariff. In other words, if there is a wish to protect sector b, subsidies should be preferred to tariffs.

Instead of granting production subsidies to sector b, production duties could be imposed on sector a. The effect will be the same in a two-sector model.

The effect of consumption subsidies in a small country

It is not possible to affect the production pattern in a small country, whose international terms of trade are exogenously determined, through consumption subsidies. This is illustrated in figure 3.4. The world market relations, which are indicated by the slope of P_w, are tangent to the transformation curve in A_1. Without subsidies, the consumption point will be B_1 on indifference curve I_1. Consumption subsidies are now granted for product b. This means that the retail price P_b^C will fall. Therefore, the relation between the retail prices in country $C_1 = P_a/P_b^C$ will be larger than the relative world market prices P_w.

The new point of tangency between C_1 and an indifference curve which at the same time is on the line P_w will be B_2. The indifference curve I_2 is below I_1. Therefore, the level of welfare will decrease.

Figure 3.4: Consumption subsidies

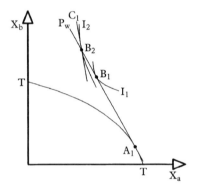

3.4 The effects of tariffs in a large country

The possibility of influencing the terms of trade

Economically, the crucial difference between a small country and a large country is the possibility which a large country has of influencing the international terms of trade.

A large country can do this even in perfectly competitive markets. A large country buys a considerable quantity of the products traded internationally. By imposing an import tariff, the country can cause a fall in the world market price. Alternatively, a large country which exports a great deal of the volumes traded on the world market can limit its own export by imposing an export tariff, and thus cause a rise in the world market price of its export goods.

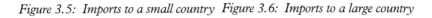

Figure 3.5: Imports to a small country   Figure 3.6: Imports to a large country

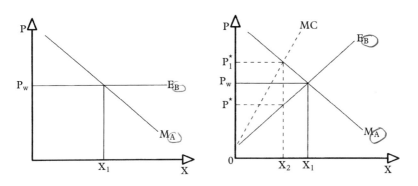

To illustrate this, the following example is based on a situation in which a country imports a good. Figures 3.5 and 3.6 show the conditions for a small country and a large country, respectively. Country A is the importing country, and the curves M_A in the two figures represent country A's import demand. Country B is the rest of the world, and E_B indicates the foreign export supply curve. The crucial difference between a small importing country and a large importing country is that the small country faces a horizontal export supply curve, whereas a large country faces an export supply curve which rises from the left towards the right.

Each of the two countries may impose an import tariff t on the import price. In the initial situation under free trade, the world market price is P_w, and the two countries import quantity X_1. If the tariff t is imposed on the world market price, the domestic price will rise, and the volume of imports will fall. The difference between the two countries is that in the case of a small country, the world market price P_w will remain unchanged after the imposition of the tariff. In the case of large country, however, the import price will fall when a tariff is imposed. This is because E_B, which reflects the export supply, is a curve which rises from the left towards the right.

For the small country, the marginal cost of imports is constant, whereas for the large country, the marginal cost of imports is the broken line MC. The reason for this is that if the large country wants to increase its imports by one unit, it has not only to pay a higher world market price for this unit, but also for all the other import units purchased as well.

Country A's marginal cost MC when importing an additional unit may be expressed as:

$$MC = P + X \cdot \frac{dP}{dX} = P\left(1 + \frac{1}{e_s}\right) \qquad (3.2)$$

where P is the world market price of the additional unit, and where $X \cdot dP/dX$ is the increased cost of imports as a result of the other goods imported becoming more expensive. e_s is the export supply elasticity, i.e. the elasticity in the foreign export supply E_B. The expression (3.2) shows that MC is located above E_B, because e_s is positive.

Country A will reach its optimal level of welfare at the point where the domestic price P equals the marginal cost MC. The price P expresses the marginal utility of the imports, and MC expresses the marginal costs in this connection.

The optimal consumer price is therefore $P_1^\star$. This situation can be reached by country A if the country imposes a tariff on the imported good which equals $P_1^\star - P^\star$. The large country makes a gain since, through a reduction of imports, compared to the free trade situation, the country will have the advantage that the import price will fall from P_w to $P^\star$. At the same time, country A receives a tariff revenue of the tariff $E^\star = P_1^\star - P^\star$ multiplied by the volume of imports OX_2.

The optimal tariff $t^\star$ can be calculated by means of expression (3.2). The optimal situation implies that $P_1^\star = MC$ which implies that:

$$P_1^\star = P^\star(1 + t^\star) = P^\star\left(1 + \frac{1}{e_s^\star}\right)$$

where the asterisk refers to the optimal situation. From this it can be deduced that:

$$t^\star = \frac{1}{e_s^\star} \qquad (3.3)$$

from which it follows that the optimal tariff depends on the elasticity of the foreign export supply curve. The more horizontal the E_B

curve, the larger the e_S. When $e_S \rightarrow \infty$, the E_B curve will be horizontal, which is the situation faced by the small country, cf. figure 3.5. In this case, the optimal tariff, cf. expression (3.3), will be zero.

Instead of imposing an optimal import tariff, a large country may choose to impose an optimal export tariff. In section 3.1, it was shown that in a general equilibrium model, an export tariff has the same effect as an import tariff. This means that a large country can place itself in an optimal position by imposing either an import tariff or an export tariff. Moreover, it can be proved that in a general equilibrium model with two sectors, the optimal export tariff will equal the optimal import tariff.

The size of the tariff and welfare

In section 1.2 above, where tariffs in a large country were analyzed by means of a partial model, it was shown that a small tariff increases the level of welfare, whereas a large tariff reduces the level of welfare. The same applies in a general equilibrium model.

If the large country imposes a small tariff which improves the country's terms of trade, the country will make a gain in terms of welfare. This is shown in figure 3.7.

Under free trade, the country produces at point A_1 and consumes at point B_1. The country will be on indifference curve I_1. If a small tariff is imposed, the production point will shift to A_2 and the consumption point to B_2. The improved international terms of trade more than cancel out the negative effect from reduced trade

Figure 3.7: The effect of a small tariff

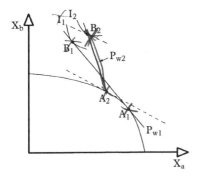

Figure 3.8: The effect of a large tariff

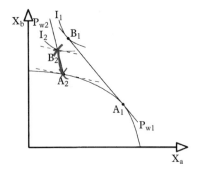

arising as a result of the import tariff. Therefore, the country's level
of welfare increases, illustrated by the fact that B_2 is on indifference
curve I_2, which is further out in the plane than the original indifference curve I_1.

If the import tariff is higher, the production point will move further to the left, and the improvement in the terms of trade will be
larger. This is shown in figure 3.8.

The new production point will be A_2, and the new consumption
point will be B_2. B_2 is on indifference curve I_2, which is located
below indifference curve I_1, which is the situation under free trade.
In this case, the import tariff will reduce the level of welfare.

The higher tariff in figure 3.8 reduces international trade more
than in figure 3.7. Even though the terms of trade improve with an
increase of the tariff, this improvement in the terms of trade will
only be beneficial for a reduced import volume. The loss resulting
from reduced foreign trade more than cancels out the gain from the
improved terms of trade.

When a small tariff causes improved welfare and a large tariff
causes reduced welfare, there must be a tariff rate at which a maximum welfare effect is achieved. As mentioned previously, this tariff
rate is referred to as the optimal tariff.

The optimal tariff illustrated by offer curves

The effects of a tariff may be illustrated by means of offer curves,
which illustrate how much of the exported good a country is willing to »offer« to obtain a given quantity of the imported good. Fig-

Figure 3.9: Offer curves for country A

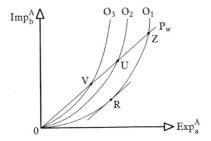

ure 3.9 shows an offer curve for country A. On the vertical axis we find

$$Exp_a^A = X_a^A - C_a^A$$

where Exp_a^A is the export of product a from country A, which equals the difference between production and consumption of product a in country A. On the vertical axis we find $Imp_b^A = C_b^A - X_b^A$, where Imp_b^A is the import of product b to country A, which equals the consumption less the production of this product in country A. An offer curve shows a country's demand for the imported good when a given quantity of the exported good is supplied. The figure shows the offer curve OO_1, which rises from the left towards the right.

The slope of a tangent to the offer curve, for instance the slope of the tangent at R, expresses how much a country marginally wants to import when it marginally increases its export supply. For country A, the slope of the tangent equals $dImp_b/dExp_a$. The marginal relation between imports and exports increases. This shows that the larger the country's export of product a, the larger the marginal increase in the imports required when there is a marginal increase in the export.

At point Z, the relative world market prices $P_w = P_a/P_b$ are indicated. At point Z it applies that:

$$\frac{Imp_b}{Exp_a} = \frac{C_b - X_b}{X_a - C_a} = \frac{P_a}{P_b} \qquad (3.4)$$

which means that the balance of payments is in balance.

The offer curve OO_1 illustrates conditions under free trade. It is now assumed that country A imposes a tariff on product b, which is the imported good. It can then be shown that if a tariff is imposed on the imported good, the offer curve moves upwards. If international prices are not affected by the tariff, so that the slope of P_w still indicates the international terms of trade, the domestic price of the imported good b will rise relative to the price of product a as a result of the tariff. In expression (3.4) this means that C_b will fall and X_b will rise. At the same time, $X_a - C_a$ will also fall because the production of product a decreases due to a relative fall in the domestic price of product a, and the consumption of product a increases for the same reason. At unchanged international prices, exports and imports will decrease by the same percentages. In figure 3.9, it is assumed that U indicates the new volumes of imports and exports after the imposition of a tariff. For all points on the OO_1 curve, it is possible to make a corresponding inference of the impact of a given tariff. With a given tariff, a new offer curve can be drawn, which is OO_2. If the tariff imposed is higher than the tariff corresponding to the offer curve OO_2, the offer curve will move further to the left, because the higher tariff causes a further reduction of the volumes of imports and exports. It has now been shown that an increasing tariff will cause a leftward move of the country's offer curve.

Figure 3.10 shows two offer curves for two large countries. OO_1 is the offer curve for country A, and ON is the offer curve for country B under free trade. The point of equilibrium is at point Z, and the international prices are indicated by the slope of P_{w1}.

The slope of FRT_1, which is the slope of the tangent to country B's offer curve in the equilibrium situation Z, indicates the additional quantity of the imported good b that can be obtained by

Figure 3.10: The optimal tariff

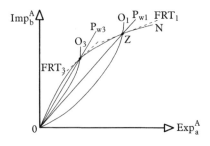

country A when there is a marginal change in the export of product a. The slope of FRT_1 is:

$$\frac{dImp_b^A}{dExp_a^A}$$

which expresses the marginal rate of transformation in international trade faced by country A.

For country A, under free trade, where there is equilibrium at point Z, it is the case that:

$$DRT = DRS = P_w$$

If country A is a small country which cannot influence the international terms of trade by imposing a tariff, country B's offer curve ON is a straight line, which means that:

$$\frac{dImp_b^A}{dExp_a^A} = P_w$$

Therefore, the domestic marginal rates of transformation and substitution equal the international rate of transformation, which again equals the relative world market price.

If, on the other hand, country A is a large country which is able to affect the international terms of trade through a tariff, then:

$$FRT < P_w$$

which means that the foreign marginal rate of transformation does not correspond to the domestic marginal rates.

Country A is thus in a position where it can cause a reduction in the world market price of the imported good by imposing a tariff. If country A imposes a tariff resulting in the offer curve OO_3, we will get P_{w3} (where $P_w = P_a/P_b$), which is larger than P_{w1}, because the relative import price has been reduced.

The international marginal rate of transformation at point V is increased relative to point N. If it applies to point V that:

$$DRT = DRS = FRT \qquad (3.5)$$

the result will be a situation in which country A cannot improve its level of welfare through a reallocation of its resources. By moving from the free trade situation at Z to the tariff situation at V, due both to the reduction in the international trade resulting from the import tariff and to the reallocation of resources, country A achieves an improvement in its terms of trade so that its level of welfare is increased. The tariff which realises the validity of expression (3.5) is the optimal tariff, which gives country A the highest possible level of welfare.

3.5 Tariffs and retaliatory measures

The above section, which dealt with two large countries, A and B, showed that country A can increase its level of welfare through tariffs. The optimal tariff is the rate at which country A maximizes its level of welfare. This is shown in figure 3.10.

If country A and country B have different factor endowments, cf. factor proportion theory, each country has comparative advantages which are best exploited under free trade. By imposing a tariff which is gradually increased, the full advantages of product specialization will not be exploited. The higher the tariff, the greater the loss incurred by not exploiting the advantages of specialization in country A. However, country A will obtain improved terms of trade. In the case of modest tariff rates, the improved terms of trade will carry more weight than the loss incurred by a lesser degree of specialization. With the optimal tariff, the marginal gain from improved terms of trade equals the marginal loss from the lesser degree of specialization.

In the analysis in the above section, it is assumed that country B would not react. Country B maintains free trade. As a consequence of country A's tariff policy, country B suffers a loss. Country B experiences a loss in terms of specialization, just like country A, as country B cannot fully exploit its comparative advantages. In addition, country B will experience deteriorated terms of trade corresponding to country A's improved terms of trade.

It is not realistic to believe that country B will not respond by similarly imposing an import tariff on country A's exports. Therefore, there will be a situation in which each country's tariff protection gradually escalates.

It is assumed that the two countries act autonomously. First, country A imposes an optimal tariff based on the assumption that country B will not respond to it, but will maintain its free trade policy. Next, country B acts autonomously. Country B assumes that in the future, country A will maintain the tariff rate corresponding to the optimal tariff when country B imposes a tariff on country A's products. On the basis of the offer curve OO_3 in figure 3.10, i.e. country A's offer curve with the optimal tariff, country B now imposes a tariff which is optimal for country B. When country B has imposed an optimal tariff, country A's tariff will no longer be optimal in relation to the offer curve OO_3. Country A will therefore increase its tariff to a higher level which has now become optimal.

Each country acts autonomously. This means that each country does not expect that its own actions will influence the actions of the other country.

Where does this mutual tariff escalation, resulting from autonomous behaviour, end? It can be shown (Johnson 1953-54), that the end result may be an equilibrium such as the one described in figure 3.11.

If the two countries do not impose tariffs on the respective imported goods, the result will be the free trade situation Z.

After mutual tariff escalation, prompted by the desire to achieve better terms of trade by imposing the optimal tariff, the countries reach point U, the co-ordinates of which show how much the two products are traded. The new terms of trade will be the slope of the line OU.

U is a point of equilibrium, provided that the following applies to the two countries:

Country A: $DRT_A = DRS_A = FRT_A$

Country B: $DRT_B = DRS_B = FRT_B$

Figure 3.11: Mutual escalation of tariff protection

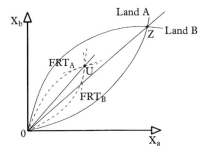

FRT$_A$ and FRT$_B$ are the slopes of the two tangents to the new offer curves at point U. The price relation between product a and product b is different in the two countries. The price relation P_a/P_b in each country equals the foreign marginal rate of transformation faced by the individual country.

The equilibrium situation at U is a Nash equilibrium. A Nash equilibrium is defined as the situation in which neither of the two countries can improve its own situation by changing its tariff policy, when the other country has decided on a given tariff.

With the Nash equilibrium at point U, one country may be better off than under the free trade situation Z. The other country will always be worse off. Most often, both countries will be worse off than under free trade. As a result of the tariff protection in both countries, they cannot fully exploit their comparative advantages. As a consequence of mutual tariff escalation, the terms of trade will change. All in all, one country's terms of trade gain will neutralize the other country's terms of trade loss, while both countries will suffer a loss by not exploiting their comparative advantages.

Therefore, both countries ought to have an interest in free trade. However, since both countries act autonomously, they may end up at point U. The individual country assumes that its imposition and gradual increase of a tariff will not prompt the other country to take countermeasures.

If both parties act conjecturally, i.e. they both take into account the possible response from the other party, it could be assumed that both parties would abstain from using the tariff instrument. The countries would thus maintain the optimal situation Z, in which there is free trade.

In practice, both countries will often have a tariff initially. If the tariff is optimal for both areas, the countries are at point U. The problem in this situation is that it may be difficult to move from U to Z, unless the countries agree that they will both abolish the tariff.

If one country reduces its tariff, without having agreed on a co-ordinated, joint scaling-down, the other country will be able, through its tariff policy, to place the first country in a worse position, after the first country has reduced its tariff in an attempt to reach point Z.

If tariffs have already been imposed, one country has no guarantee that it will benefit from scaling down its tariff if it takes such an initiative unilaterally, i.e. on its own without making an agreement with the other party.

Even if initially there is free trade or a low degree of protection, there is no guarantee that protection will not be increased, even though this will harm both parties. This will be the case if the countries act autonomously, as exemplified by the mutual escalation of agricultural support in the EC/EU and in the US in the years from 1970 to 1990.

3.6 Co-ordination of trade policy

In the above section, it was shown that in the case of two large countries, a mutual escalation of tariff rates may take place. Country A acts autonomously, which means that it benefits from imposing the optimal tariff on imported goods. In response, country B will impose a tariff on its imported good. The end result will be that the countries will suffer an overall loss, because they will not be able to exploit their comparative advantages. This will be elaborated in the present section.

Country A imports product b, and t_b is the tariff imposed by country A. Product a is country B's imported good, and t_a is the tariff imposed by country B. There are two decision makers who both have a tariff instrument at their disposal. Both countries' welfare is a function of both tariff rates (t_b, t_a), which in turn means that each country's welfare depends on the actions of the other country.

Let us assume that each country has a welfare function corresponding to the utility function of the individual household. This means that:

$$W_A = W_A (t_b, t_a)$$

$$W_B = W_B (t_a, t_b)$$

where W is the welfare function which depends on t_a and t_b. Figures 3.12 and 3.13 indicate the conditions in the two countries A and B.

If country B does not impose a tariff on product a, i.e. $t_{a1} = 0$, country A will impose the tariff t_{b1}, which is the optimal tariff. This results in a level of welfare corresponding to curve W_{A1}. If country B imposes a tariff equal to t_{a2}, it would be best for country A to

Figure 3.12 Welfare function and reaction curve for country A

Figure 3.13 Welfare function and reaction curve for country B

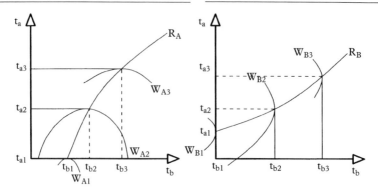

impose a tariff t_{b2}, where the horizontal line t_{a2} is tangent to the lowest W_A. The lower the position of W, the higher the level of welfare in country A. It appears that the welfare function W_A corresponds to the isoprofit curves in figure 2.10 in the previous chapter. In this way, it is possible to deduce country A's reaction curve R_A, which shows country A's optimal tariff when country B has fixed its tariff rate.

Figure 3.13 shows the reaction curve for country B deduced in the same way. When country A has fixed its import tariff rate for product b, the W_B curves show the optimal tariff for country B. Figure 3.14 shows the two reaction curves from figures 3.12 and 3.13. The reaction curves illustrate the behaviour of the individual country when it acts autonomously on tariff policy. The two countries

Figure 3.14: Reaction curves for country A and B

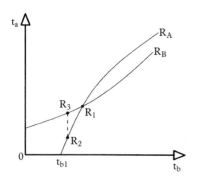

do not discuss which tariff policy to pursue, even though each country is dependent on the actions of the other party.

If country A is the first to impose the optimal tariff t_{b1}, country B will impose a tariff as indicated by R_B. This again causes an increase in country A's tariff. Finally, equilibrium will be reached at R_1, where some trade will still take place. This is called a Nash equilibrium.

If both parties' behaviour is still autonomous, i.e. non-cooperative, a unilateral tariff reduction to R_2 on country A's part will simply result in country B fixing its tariff at R_3, and the end result will be R_1.

An alternative to this non-cooperation is for the two countries to start discussing a mutual scaling-down of the tariffs, since the aggregate welfare of both countries will thus be increased. The individual country will not achieve the expected gain by reducing its tariff unless it enters into an agreement with the other country on an appropriate tariff policy.

This example shows how important it is that countries confer before each implements a protection policy. It shows the importance of the international trade policy co-operation in GATT/WTO, which will be discussed in further detail in chapter 5.

Once protection has been introduced, it is reasonable to ask why countries do not start a process towards liberalization. This has been done in the post-war period, but it is a lengthy process. There are several reasons for this.

Firstly, the world does not consist of two countries, but of many groups of countries with different interests. This in itself makes it a difficult process.

Secondly, it is best to find a compromise with which everybody is satisfied. Some countries are »free riders«, i.e. they are not willing to grant the concessions that others expect of them. In an international context, such countries are often of minor importance. Other countries are »foot draggers«, i.e. large and important countries which will not accept a compromise until other important countries have granted additional concessions.

Thirdly, countries' economies are adjusted to the level of protection currently in force. Liberalization always requires readjustments which imply costs in the short term, and which are only beneficial in the long term. If a country is already suffering from a recession, adjustment will be even more difficult.

Finally, the idea that every country is led by a government and parliament which seek to maximize the welfare functions for its society is very naive. In the discussion above, we have applied welfare functions. As a hypothesis this is useful, but a concrete formulation of a welfare function for society gives rise to a number of theoretical and practical problems.

In any society, there are various pressure groups with different priorities. Some will suffer from liberalization, whereas others will benefit. There will be a redistribution of income which may theoretically be compensated for if the country as a whole ends up better off. If the groups that suffer from liberalization have no confidence that they will receive the compensation they find appropriate, they will resist it. Often, those who would suffer from liberalization will have more power and greater understanding than those who would benefit from the changes.

3.7 *Summary*

This chapter analyses the trade policy instruments available when there is perfect competition and no externalities. The chapter is based on the same assumptions that applied in chapter 1. As opposed to chapter 1, in which the method of analysis was a partial model, this chapter applies a general equilibrium model. Therefore, in this chapter, trade policy measures can be considered general measures, whereas the measures described in chapter 1 were of a more selective nature.

If a two-sector model is applied, the analysis generally shows that support for one sector implies taxation of the other. This is also reflected in the fact that if one sector receives support in the form of an import tariff, while the other sector receives support in the form of export subsidies, the two measures will neutralize each other. These conclusions are based on a two-sector model. In the case of a three-sector model with an export sector, an import-competing sector and a home market sector, the above conclusions no longer hold.

The effect of an import tariff depends on whether it is a large or a small country that imposes the tariff. In the case of a small country, the optimal tariff equals zero, whereas for a large country it equals the reciprocal of the foreign elasticity of export supply in relation to the world market price. The optimal tariff can also be illustrated by offer curves. The offer curve method shows that under free trade, DRT = DRS ≠ FRT. The optimal tariff is precisely the tariff that eliminates the sign of inequality. By using the offer curve method it is also possible to analyse the effects of retaliatory measures.

When two countries act autonomously, they may end up in a situation in which both are worse off. For the two countries in combination, a situation with mutual tariff escalation is always worse than a free trade situation. As a result of this, it is desirable that countries co-ordinate their trade policy.

Literature

Corden, W.M., *Trade Policy and Economic Welfare*, Oxford, 1974.

Harberger, A.C., »Reflections on Uniform Taxation« in Jones, R.W. and A.O. Krueger (eds), *The Political Economy of International Trade*, London, 1990.

Johnson, H.G., »Optimal Tariffs and Retaliation«, *Review of Economic Studies*, 21, 1953-54.

Lerner, A., »The Symmetry Between Import and Export Taxes«, *Economica*, 11, 1936.

Markusen, J.R., »The Distribution of Gains from Bilateral Tariff Reduction«, *Journal of International Economics*, 11, 1981.

4. Trade policy and the theory of distortions

Chapter 3 discussed a general equilibrium model. If a country's economy functions in accordance with the premises built into the model, this will result in a Walras equilibrium in which DRT = DRS, i.e. the domestic marginal rate of transformation in production equals the domestic marginal rate of substitution in consumption. This balance again equals the relative prices P_a/P_b of finished goods. It can be shown that a Walras equilibrium is also a Pareto optimum, which implies that it is not possible to improve anyone's welfare without lowering the welfare of others.

The model is based on a number of assumptions. First of all it is assumed that there is perfect competition in the goods markets. Secondly, it is assumed that there are no externalities, either in production or in consumption. Thirdly, it is assumed that there is perfect competition in the factor markets. Finally, it is assumed that each of the countries is so small that none of them can, in isolation, influence the international terms of trade through trade policy intervention.

4.1 The theory of distortions

The theory of distortions applies precisely to those cases in which the above assumptions do not apply. These distortions may be linked to production, consumption, production factors or trade. Each of these four types of distortion has its own characteristics. Table 4.1 provides examples of the four types and their individual characteristics.

The examples provided in table 4.1 all represent market imperfection, and their specific content will be discussed in the following. The term »endogenous« distortions is often used instead of market imperfection, because such distortions are inherent in the economy. In contrast to market imperfection or endogenous distortions there may be exogenous distortions in the form of policy intervention. Let us now imagine that we have an economic system which operates as illustrated in the introduction to this chapter, i.e. without market imperfections. Earlier, policy intervention has been made in a way that leads to distortions of the same kind and with the same characteristics as the four distortions listed in table 4.1.

If a country has introduced production duties or subsidies, distortion type I will occur. If, instead, consumption taxes or consumption subsidies are implemented, the result will be distortion type II. A high wage rate, above the equilibrium level, caused by strong trade unions, represents a distortion of type III. If the country has imposed a tariff on a product, it is a distortion of type IV.

Exogenous distortions, stemming from policy intervention, can be divided into two types. One type consists of policy measures which are historically determined, as they represent a heritage which may not be so rationally motivated today as before. The other type consists of policy measures which aim at achieving a number of non-economic goals. Several countries grant support to their own weapons industry for security considerations. Some countries support agricultural producers out of a desire to maintain a certain degree of self-sufficiency, because import deliveries may fail in a war. Here, non-economic factors are taken into consideration.

A distinction can thus be made between three types of intervention. The first type is due to »failure« in the economic system, and the measures aim at repairing the market imperfections at hand.

The second type of intervention is policy measures that create distortions, and which are only motivated by a desire for protection. The third type of intervention is policy measures that create distortions, and are motivated by the desire to attain various non-economic goals.

In the following, we will begin by analysing situations in which there are market imperfections. Here, the question is whether free trade improves the situation. If this is not the case, it can be asked which type of measure should be implemented. The next situation is the case of historically-determined policy intervention which distorts and is less rationally motivated. This case will not be discussed, because the solution is very simple: such measures should be abolished in order to avoid distortions. The last situation is the

Table 4.1: Different types of distortion

Type of distortion	Distortions in connection with:	Examples:	Characteristics:
I	Production	Externality, Monopolized (oligopolized) production	DRT ≠ DRS = FRT
II	Consumption	Externality	DRS ≠ DRT = FRT
III	The factor market:		The country is not on the »right« transformation curve
	The labour market	Frozen wages, Externalities	
	The capital market	Interest rate deviates from the society's time preference	
IV	Trade	The country is large	DRT = DRS ≠ FRT

one in which a number of non-economic goals exist. The question of which measures best secure these goals will be discussed at the end of this chapter.

4.2 Distortions in production

As illustrated in table 4.1, there may be imperfection in the market structure, for instance in the form of an oligopoly in the import-competing sector. In this situation, free trade would be preferred over a tariff, as a tariff would help strengthen the oligopoly. If there is free trade, and if the world market price is determined by foreign countries with perfect competition, the domestic oligopoly enterprises must accept this price.

Distortions may also be derived from externalities which can be either positive or negative. If there are externalities, the social costs of production will not equal the private costs.

The following model is a two-sector model in which product a represents industrial products and product b represents agricultural products. It is assumed that there is a negative externality in agricultural production in the form of environmental pollution. For the sake of simplicity, it is assumed that there are no externalities in the industrial production.

Figure 4.1 displays the socio-economic transformation curve TT. This is a transformation curve which shows the production possibilities that are available when the pollution has been cleaned up. In the initial situation, the country is at point T_1. For this point it applies that:

$$\left(\frac{dX_b}{dX_a}\right)^S < \left(\frac{dX_b}{dX_a}\right)^P = \frac{P_a}{P_b}$$

where the first term is the socio-economic rate of transformation in production, taking into consideration that pollution caused by agriculture entails socio-economic environmental costs.

The slope of line 1 indicates the social rate of transformation. The second term is the private rate of transformation when the environmental costs are not taken into consideration. The relative prices equal the private rate of transformation. This is indicated by the slope of line 2. T_1 is a situation of autarky, as the indifference curve I_2 penetrates point T_1 with a slope corresponding to the relative prices.

Trade is now opened up. In relative terms, world market prices

Figure 4.1: Externalities in production

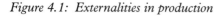

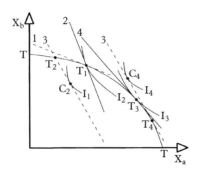

correspond to the slope of line 3. The fact that the slope of line 3 is shallower than the slope of line 2 implies that the world market price of agricultural products is relatively higher than in autarky. The country will therefore specialize further in agricultural products. After trade, the production point will be T_2 and the consumption point C_2, which is tangential to indifference curve I_1.

In figure 4.1, free trade has caused the level of welfare to fall compared to autarky. If the curves were different, a situation could be reached in which welfare rose after the introduction of free trade. The pivotal factor is that free trade may result in a lower level of welfare. Therefore, if the country introduces a prohibitive tariff so that the autarky point T_1 is reached, the welfare may be improved as compared to the situation under free trade.

The question is whether the country could have intervened in other and better ways than by using the tariff instrument. The answer is in the affirmative.

If country A had imposed a production duty on agricultural products, the production point T_1 would move to the right. When the production duty is so high that the relative prices of finished goods equal the slope of tangent 4, a new autarky situation T_3 is reached at which the »true« marginal rate of transformation equals the marginal rate of substitution in consumption, which again equals the relative prices of finished goods. The level of welfare is higher at T_3 than at T_2.

If the country moves to point T_3 and if international trade is opened up, the production point will be T_4 and the consumption point C_4. The slope of tangent 3 indicates world market prices. When trade is opened up, the level of welfare will increase. The country moves from indifference curve 3 to curve 4.

Hence, it can be concluded that in situations with externalities in production, free trade can produce a worse outcome than if a tariff is imposed. A tariff can increase welfare in this situation, but tariffs are not the best solution. If the country uses a production duty to adjust for the externality, the situation will be improved in autarky. If trade is opened up after the adjustment, a further improvement may be achieved.

Adjusting for the externality by using a production duty produces a better result than a tariff. In this example, a production duty is an optimal type of intervention, because it eliminates the negative externality causing the market imperfection.

4.3 Distortions in consumption

The possibility of externalities in consumption is well-known. Some products such as tobacco and alcohol are injurious to health. It is assumed that consumers underestimate health-related problems when choosing such products, and that they do not consider public expense, in the form of hospital care etc., which is related to the consumption of harmful consumer goods. Should a tariff be imposed here, or would other instruments be better?

Product a is a product with a negative influence on health, whose influence does not form part of consumer preferences.

In the initial situation, the country is at T_1. The broken line I_1 is the »true«, i.e. the socio-economic, indifference curve. The indifference curve on the basis of which consumers act is tangential to T_1, and the marginal rate of substitution in consumption equals the slope of tangent 1. This curve is not shown in the figure. It is the case that:

$$\left(\frac{dC_b}{dC_a}\right)^S < \left(\frac{dC_b}{dC_a}\right)^P = \frac{P_a}{P_b}$$

where the first term is the true rate of substitution, the second term is the rate of substitution experienced by consumers, and the last term is the relative price. This means that the social marginal utility of product a in relation to the marginal utility of product b is lower than the relation of the private marginal utilities.

Trade is now opened up, and the production point is T_2 and the consumption point C_2. At point C_2, there is an indifference curve on the basis of which consumers react, and line 2 at point C_2 is tangent to this indifference curve.

Figure 4.2: Externalities in consumption

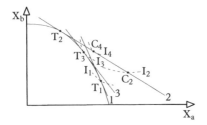

The socio-economic indifference curve is I_2. Since it is located above the socio-economic indifference curve at point T_1, which is autarky, free trade will result in a higher real welfare level.

However, there is another autarky situation which is better than the original one at T_1, and which is also better than the free trade situation at C_2. It is the situation in which the country imposes an expenditure tax on product a, producing the result T_3. In this autarky situation, the country is on indifference curve 3, which is further out in the plane than indifference curves 1 and 2.

Once an adjustment for the »distortion« in consumption choice has been made by means of an expenditure tax, trade may be opened up. If this is done, the production point will be T_2, and the consumption point C_4, which means that welfare increases as compared to T_3.

If trade is opened up without prior adjustment for the externality in consumption, welfare will be expressed by indifference curve I_2. If trade is opened up after adjustment by means of an expenditure tax, welfare will be expressed by indifference curve I_4.

The existence of an externality in consumption is not an argument against trade, but an argument for allowing trade, after an intervention adjusting for the externality in consumption. An expenditure tax is an optimal measure because it eliminates the market imperfection flowing from the externality in the consumption of product a.

4.4. Distortions in factor markets

If there is perfect competition in factor markets, the payment of labour and capital will be the same everywhere. It is now assumed that real wages in one sector are higher than those in another. Labour is paid on the basis of the value of the marginal product in each sector. In the first sector, the marginal productivity of labour is thus higher than in the second sector. The reason for the difference in the real wages of the two sectors could be that the trade unions in the first sector are more powerful than those in the other. The reason could also be that the first sector has a minimum wage level, and that this is not the case in the other sector.

The country manufactures two products, a and b. In the production of product a, wages are relatively high, and in the other sector,

Figure 4.3: Distortions in factor markets

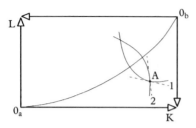

which manufactures product b, wages are relatively low. The consequence of this can be illustrated in figure 4.3, which displays a box diagram.

The relative factor prices are now different in the two sectors. It applies that:

$$\left(\frac{r}{w}\right)_a < \left(\frac{r}{w}\right)_b$$

This means that the country is no longer on the contract curve O_aO_b, characterized by the very fact that the relative factor payment is the same for the two productions.

The country is now outside the contract curve, for instance at point A, where the slope of tangent 1 is the factor price relation in the production of product a, and the slope of tangent 2 is the relative factor price for product b. Distortions in the factor prices will thus cause production to take place on a transformation curve, which does not correspond to the contract curve. In figure 4.4, the broken curve corresponds to the contract curve in the box diagram. The curve drawn with an unbroken line is the transformation curve under factor price distortion. If the country specializes wholly in production of either of the products, the volume of production would be the same with or without a factor price distortion.

At any point on the unbroken transformation curve, there is a marginal rate of transformation of dX_b/dX_a. If production factors are moved from sector b, in which wages are low, to sector a with its high wages, the cost reduction in sector b will be lower than the cost increase in sector a. Therefore it applies that $MC_a \cdot dX_a > MC_b \cdot dX_b$, where MC is the marginal cost. Consequently, at any point $dX_b/dX_a < MC_a/MC_b$. When there is perfect competition in the goods markets, the product price will equal the marginal costs.

Figure 4.4: Intervention other than tariffs

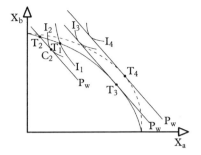

Therefore, the result is:

$$\frac{dX_b}{dX_a} < \frac{MC_a}{MC_b} = \frac{P_a}{P_b} \qquad (4.1)$$

In figure 4.4, the country is at point T_1, which is assumed to be autarky. P_a/P_b is larger than dX_b/dX_a at point T_1.

The indifference curve I_1 crosses point T_1. It is now assumed that at an international level, product b is relatively more expensive than in country A's autarky. When trade is opened up, the country will move its production point to T_2. The relative price will be P_{w}, and the consumption point C_2, which gives a lower level of welfare.

In the present situation, the level of welfare will drop when going from autarky to free trade. If the curvatures are different, or if the production point T_2 does not move so far to the left or if P_w becomes shallower, the welfare may rise under free trade.

However, the crucial factor is that free trade may result in a lower level of welfare. It can be deduced that a prohibitive tariff which takes the country from production point T_2 to production point T_1 will improve the country's welfare.

Though a tariff may improve welfare, other modes of intervention are even better. If production subsidies are granted for the production of product a, the country can take itself to production point T_3, where the slope of the tangent equals relative world market prices. By granting production subsidies, it is possible to move to indifference curve 3, resulting in a higher level of welfare than I_1, which reflects welfare under a prohibitive tariff. The problem with production subsidies is that the country is still on the »distorted« transformation curve.

If the country could move to the broken transformation curve, welfare would be further improved. This move may be effected by granting wage subsidies to sector a or imposing a wage tax on sector b. By means of such a measure, the same relative factor return may be obtained for the two productions. This means that in figure 4.3 a move is made from point A to a point on the contract curve O_aO_b. In figure 4.4 it would represent a move from the unbroken transformation curve to the broken transformation curve. Once the country is on the broken transformation curve and international trade is opened up, the production point will be T_4 and the indifference curve of the country will be I_4.

The example discussed here demonstrates that intervention may be carried out in different ways. There is a distortion in the factor market which means that (4.1) applies. The country is on the unbroken transformation curve. The best mode of intervention is a measure which eliminates the distortion in (4.1). This can be effected by granting wage subsidies to sector a, which will cause the marginal rate of transformation to equal relative prices. Factor subsidies are better than production subsidies, which are again better than tariffs. In our example, a tariff is better than free trade without intervention.

4.5 Distortions in international trade

The agricultural policy of the EU can be used as an example. This policy has resulted in world market prices for the subsidized products being lower than would otherwise have been the case. The schemes have also caused world market prices to fluctuate more than they would normally have done.

In figure 4.5, D indicates the demand for food and S the supply of food in the EU. Without intervention, the world market price would be P_{w1}, which in the figure implies that the EU would import food if there were free trade.

Because the EU wants the selling price for the agricultural sector to be P_1, and at the same time this is the price level for the consumers, consumption will be OX_1 and production OX_2. The surplus production X_1X_2 is exported, meaning that the world market price falls from P_{w1} to P_{w2}. The artificially high domestic price level P_1 is secured through an import protection which equals $P_1 - P_{w2}$, while

Figure 4.5: The EU high-price policy for agricultural products

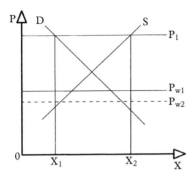

at the same time the export per unit is subsidized at a corresponding level.

If the agricultural producers in other countries do not receive support, their farm prices will fall from P_{w1} to P_{w2}. This can cause other
exporting countries to introduce export subsidies for their agricultural sectors or make importing countries introduce import duties.

Policy intervention within the EU will distort the world market
price. If this »distortion« is permanent in the sense that it can be
expected to continue in the foreseeable future, this intervention in
the market mechanism by the EU is not in itself an argument for
introducing either export subsidies or tariffs in other countries. If
other countries have alternative production possibilities, they
should opt for these possibilities and in return benefit from low
international food prices.

If these presumptions do not apply, it may prove rational to
intervene. It is very likely that the EU agricultural subsidies are not
sustainable in the long term. The world market price will go up if
this support is expected to be heavily reduced or to be phased out.
Therefore, it may be rational for other exporting countries to provide temporary export subsidies or for importing countries to introduce a temporary import protection. The philosophy behind this is
that if the agricultural sector is competitive in the long run, it
would be an improper allocation of resources to let the sector deteriorate, when in future, the distortion of the world market price
which causes problems will be eliminated.

If the EU does not take the initiative to abolish protection, other
countries may force the EU to negotiate, by implementing export

subsidies and import protection, with a view to the EU phasing out these support schemes.

In this case, export subsidies and import protection are not appropriate in themselves, but the measures can be used strategically to force the EU into a settlement phasing out its trade policy which causes distortions on the world market.

4.6 Ranking of instruments

The preceding sections give examples of distortions affecting production, consumption, factors of production and international trade.

When distortions are related to market imperfection or policy measures effected abroad, it raises the question of whether to engage in policy intervention. If intervention is chosen, how can it be carried out most appropriately? »Pure« trade policy instruments such as tariffs, import restrictions or export subsidies can be applied. Alternatively, »domestic« instruments with trade policy implications can be applied, such as duties or subsidies that may relate to production, consumption or factors of production.

The ill-considered use of instruments to eliminate market imperfection often entails a number of negative side effects which create new distortions. Let us use the example from section 4.4 to illustrate the problem and examine, for instance, a developing country with frozen real wages in the industrial sector. The real wages of the industrial sector exceed those of the agricultural sector. Furthermore, it is assumed that a number of externalities are connected with industrial production. Labour-training takes place, and by establishing a larger industrial production, the basis is laid for a better industrial environment, which may deliver cheaper inputs to industry.

The conditions are illustrated in figure 4.6, in which D is the demand for industrial products and S and S^1 are the private supply curve and the social supply curve for industrial production, respectively. P_w is the world market price. In the case of no intervention, domestic production will be OX_1, which means that the country imports the volume X_1X_4. This is not an optimal production. The most rational solution would be to produce the volume OX_2 and limit the imports to X_2X_4. The gain from this increase in production would be the area a.

Figure 4.6: Too high real wages in the industrial sector

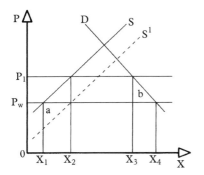

A domestic production of OX_2 can be achieved by imposing a tariff on the imports which equals $P_1 - P_w$. This would create a distortion on the consumption side. The consumer surplus is reduced by $(P_1 - P_w) \cdot OX_3 + b$. The increased producer surplus and the tariff revenue will be $(P_1 - P_w) \cdot OX_3$. In other words, the tariff causes a loss equal to the area b. This is contrasted by the gain a, which is assumed to flow from the elimination of excessive real wages in the industrial sector. However, distortions in the labour market will still exist even after a tariff has been introduced.

The tariff results in increased employment in the industrial sector, but this increase is not as large as it would be if wage subsidies were granted to the enterprises, causing an increase of labour intensity in production. In addition to not eliminating the original distortion, the tariff gives rise to a new distortion on the consumption side. Wage subsidies eliminating the original market imperfection are the best solution. The tariff is not even the second best solution, because the tariff entails two distorting side effects, viz. the continuing distortion in the labour market as well as the new distortion in consumption.

Production subsidies per production unit corresponding to $P_1 - P_w$ are a better solution than a tariff. Subsidies for production will increase production to OX_2, but these subsidies will only have the same effect on employment as a tariff, because distortion in the labour market is not eliminated in either case. However, the distortion on the consumption side caused by a tariff is avoided.

This example shows that when there is a given distortion, the various instruments can be ranked according to their suitability.

Table 4.2: Ranking of instruments in case of distortion because of too high real wages

Measure:	Distortions after the measure:	Number of distortions:	Ranking:
Factor subsidies	None	0	Best instrument
Production subsidies	Distortions in factor markets	1	Second best Instrument
Tariff	Distortions in factor markets Distortions in consumption	2	Third best Instrument

This ranking is made in table 4.2, and indicates that the number of distortions related to the instrument in question determines the suitability of the instrument.

The most important finding of the analysis is that it is absolute crucial to identify the problem. Which type of distortion is in play? Next it is important to choose an instrument which makes an adjustment as close as possible to the root of the problem.

This analysis has implicitly assumed that there are no financing problems related to the payment of subsidies. A tariff generates a public revenue, whereas subsidies require a tax revenue. If there are problems in obtaining a sufficient tax revenue, or if distortions arise from the increased taxation, the picture changes. If production duties or expenditure taxes are chosen as a source of finance, the duties must be of a general nature so that all production and consumption must be subject to the duties. If the market economy has not gained a foothold everywhere because of the existence of a parallel subsistence economy in certain commodity areas, increased taxation may result in differentiated taxation between different commodity markets. If income taxes are also relatively high, an increased level of taxation may influence the supply of labour. In addition, both general product taxes and income taxes require a well-developed administrative apparatus.

In particular, less wealthy developing countries often find it difficult to finance their public expenditure. The need for public expenditure is significant, but it is difficult to collect general product taxes and income taxes because the administrative apparatus is inadequate. Such a country will consequently find it difficult to finance subsidies, even though our analysis shows that in many cases subsidies are better instruments than tariffs.

Tariffs create distortions which can be avoided by granting subsidies, whereas subsidies entail financing problems. These problems do not occur in connection with tariffs, since tariffs generate a tax revenue, traditionally implying low administrative costs.

These considerations of financing may lead to the conclusion that it is often worthwhile to combine tariffs with subsidies to promote a given business activity. By granting part of the support through tariffs and part of it through subsidies, the distortion loss experienced with tariffs can be reduced. The desired support can be granted and it can also be self-financing if the tariff revenue covers the subsidy expenditure.

4.7 Multiple simultaneous distortions

There will often be more than one distortion present in a given market. In order to comply with the principle of choosing an instrument which intervenes as closely as possible to the problem, it is clear that several instruments may be required in such a case. Each instrument should be chosen with the intent to neutralize one distortion. It is a general phenomenon in economic policy that only in very rare cases can an instrument solve more than one problem. The task is to find combinations of economic measures which collectively provide the best solution.

If several distortions exist simultaneously, the theory of »the second best« applies. According to this theory, the best solution (the first best) is the one neutralizing all distortions simultaneously. All other solutions are »second best«, and these solutions cannot be ranked according to how many distortions are neutralized. At first glance, it may seem that a situation with two distortions is always worse than a situation with only one distortion. However, this is not the case as can be illustrated using the example below.

The market for air travel in Europe has been subject to a number of national regulations which have restrained competition. The market has been distorted because of restricted competition. There is further distortion, as the air carriers purchase fuel at the market price without duties. This private price is far below the social price of fuel. Air traffic produces significantly more pollution per transport kilometre than other forms of transport.

The set of agreements which has previously restrained competition in the air travel market is now being phased out. On the face of it, this would appear to be an advantage, because consumers gain access to cheaper air travel. Cheaper air travel will result in a shift in competition between the different forms of transport to the benefit of air traffic. The disadvantage of this is that air pollution increases.

The best solution would be to introduce a fuel duty so that the fuel price would equal the socio-economic price, which includes the environmental costs, while at the same time creating intensified competition by phasing out the rules which restrain competition. In other words, two instruments should be used to eliminate the two distortions in the market.

If, in a situation with two distortions, the only result of intervention is intensified competition, i.e. elimination of one distortion, while the other distortion, which is attributable to too low fuel prices, still exists, the outcome could be a situation which is worse than the initial one.

The central issue is that all other situations in which at least one distortion remains cannot easily be ranked in relation to each other. A situation with two distortions cannot generally be classified as being worse than a situation with only one distortion.

4.8 The infant-industry tariff argument

One of the oldest arguments in favour of tariff protection is the argument for infant-industry tariff protection advanced by the German economist Friedrich List in 1840. At the time, industrialization was going on in England, and Friedrich List believed that it would be impossible to establish a German industry unless it was protected, because England, being the first industrialized country, would enjoy a competitive edge. Time was a central factor, as German industry could not gain a foothold in the short term, but when this was eventually obtained through protection, German industry would be competitive in the long run. This means that tariff protection should be temporary. Once the industry has grown strong in the shelter of tariff protection, the protection should be scaled down and finally abolished.

It is natural to analyse infant-industry tariffs in conjunction with the theory of distortions. It would be rational to think that if all markets are perfect, and if there are entrepreneurs with knowledge and insight, these entrepreneurs would make investments which are profitable in the long run, without protection.

By presupposing the existence of perfect markets, the central argument for the infant-industry tariff is eliminated by definition. Imperfection prevails when an industry has not already been established, and tariff protection aims exactly at repairing this imperfection. However, the question is, what the market distortions consist of and whether a tariff would necessarily be the best instrument to neutralize them. Obviously, it may be difficult to set up businesses, particularly in developing countries with markets barely established, and even if markets have been established, they are often imperfect. Let us consider some examples.

There are *dynamic internal economic conditions* in individual enterprises, which are important. When an enterprise is established, its sales will often be limited to begin with, which implies that the production-related economies of scale enjoyed by established enterprises cannot be exploited by the new enterprise. This may hold back potential investors, because the venture is regarded as too risky. The function of the capital market may not be satisfactory either, which may make the acquisition of the necessary capital at reasonable interest rates difficult. There may be no suitably skilled labour immediately available to be employed in the enterprises. Unskilled labour must be brought in, and the costs of learning at the workplace and training must be borne by the enterprises themselves.

It is evident that the introduction of tariff protection will make investments easier and less risky. The question is, however, whether a tariff remains the best instrument against the distortions mentioned above. If the problem is that credit cannot be obtained at reasonable interest rates, it would possibly be a better idea to concentrate efforts on improving the capital market function for instance by granting interest rate subsidies. If potential entrepreneurs are averse to taking the risks connected with the project, one option could be for the state to extend enterprise allowances to new entrepreneurs. If the training of labour poses a problem, this activity could be subsidized. These alternative instruments are all more targeted than tariffs.

Also, a number of *dynamic external economic conditions* may render public intervention a natural choice. If the labour which is trained in an enterprise stays with the enterprise as assumed above, this is an internal matter for the enterprise, as it invests in human capital which will benefit the enterprise later.

However, one can imagine that the labour whose training the enterprise finances will leave the enterprise because other enterprises are willing to offer higher pay. This means that an investment in human capital has been made to the benefit of society, but not to that of the enterprise which paid for the investment. It is assumed here that trained labour does not finance its own training through lower pay in the training period. If the labour force is willing and if the unions allow a lower »introductory pay«, there is no problem. When the enterprise finances training without being able to benefit from it, because the labour leaves the enterprise after training, society gains an external advantage which the state should finance through subsidies to secure the establishment of the enterprise and to ensure that the enterprise does not incur losses when engaging in an activity which is beneficial from a socio-economic point of view.

Gradually, new enterprises acquire useful knowledge as production increases. This knowledge is disseminated to others, including competitors. New manufacturers of finished goods help establish an industrial environment in which there is a gradual evolution of potential for production of inputs for instance of machines for the manufacture of finished goods. Again, this constitutes an external economic advantage from which society benefits. These circumstances also speak in favour of securing the establishment of the new enterprises through tariffs. Again, the question is whether tariffs are better than the alternatives.

Whether the infant-industry tariff argument holds is very much a question of whether import substitution is a viable strategy to secure an industrialization which provides economic growth. We will return to this question in chapter 8.

In practice it is not always easy to identify the sources of the market distortions. Such an identification is of course necessary for a direct intervention. This may be an argument in favour of imposing tariffs to a certain extent. This is even more the case when the question of financing the measure is included in the discussion. As appears from the above analysis, the alternative to tariffs is usually a number of differentiated subsidy schemes which may be difficult to administer without entailing large expenses. In addition, subsidies are a burden to public finances, which are often quite strained in the first place. The imposition of a tariff does not cause such problems. However, a tariff is a source of distortion in itself. This may be acceptable if the tariff protection is only temporary, and will be phased out after the enterprises have gained a foothold in the market.

4.9 Considering non-economic goals

In the introductory section 4.1, it was mentioned that there are ample economic reasons for intervention when market imperfection exists in the form of different types of distortion. If, however, there is no market imperfection, but intervention is nevertheless made, the policy measures will create distortions. If policy intervention is based on a desire to attain non-economic goals, it must be carefully considered how large the economic distortions and ensuing losses the country is willing to accept in order to achieve these non-economic goals.

For the purposes of this discussion, non-economic goals are taken to mean goals with other priorities than economic efficiency. However, non-economic goals, legitimate as they may be, entail economic consequences, because the economic efficiency associated with a Walras equilibrium is not attained. A typical non-economic goal is the desire to maintain a certain degree of self-sufficiency in food production.

Non-economic goals can be attained in various ways by employing different instruments. As in the case of market imperfection, these instruments may be ranked according to the number of distortions they cause. Any given non-economic goal may thus be achieved in a more or less efficient manner. In order to rank the various instruments, a precise description of the non-economic goal is required. The ranking will vary depending on the specific non-economic goal. A country's agricultural policy may be used to illustrate this.

If the objective of a country's agricultural policy is to improve producers' incomes, the best policy for a small country would be to pursue a free trade policy. This would provide the largest aggregate consumption potential. If the country considers the incomes of the agricultural sector to be too low, direct income support may be granted to the sector, which does not affect the composition of production, but which causes the desired redistribution of income. Of course, there are transaction costs related to this measure. The costs in question are administrative costs flowing from the collection of taxes and distribution of public support, just as the calculation of the support for the individual recipient also requires resources. It may also be a problem if the increased taxation level adversely affects the supply of labour or gives rise to more clandestine (nontaxed) labour activities. If the costs in connection with direct income support are disregarded, it would be better to provide this kind of support than, for instance, production subsidies, as the latter increase production and thus have a distorting effect. However, production subsidies are better than tariffs, because tariffs cause distortions in production as well as in consumption.

If the purpose of the agricultural policy is to obtain a given volume of production in order to maintain a certain degree of self-sufficiency, direct income support will not help. This is because it is assumed that any influence of direct income support on the volume of production will only be very marginal. If the desired goal is related to production, the measure employed should be one which has a direct effect on production. This can be illustrated as in figure 4.7. Product a represents industrial products, and product b represents agricultural products.

Under free trade, the country produces at T_1 and consumes at C_1. Direct income support does not affect T_1. Consequently, direct income support is of no help if the aim is to produce $\overline{X}_b$ of product b. If production subsidies are introduced for agriculture, the production point will shift from T_1 to T_2, and the consumption point to C_2 However, the production point T_2 can also be reached through tariffs. In this situation, the production point will again be T_2, but the consumption point will be C_3. A tariff reduces welfare more than production subsidies. It is thus cheaper to attain the production goal through production subsidies than through tariffs.

If the purpose of the agricultural policy is to reduce imports to a certain quantity, import restrictions or tariffs would be better solutions than production subsidies.

The choice of the best instrument is thus very dependent on the

Figure 4.7: Securing a specific production goal

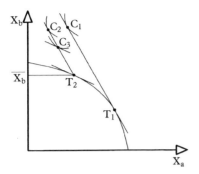

purpose of the agricultural policy. The present analysis has assumed various purposes which have been taken as given factors. They should not of course be regarded as given factors in the real world. In truth, the question should always be posed whether or not it is reasonable to pursue the specific non-economic goal in question. Here, the weighting of the socio-economic costs in relation to the goal enters the picture.

4.10 Summary

A number of marginal conditions must be met in order for a country to be in a Walras equilibrium, which implies that the country is in an optimal situation with regard to production, consumption and trade. It must thus apply that DRT = DRS = FRT.

When externalities exist, the social costs do not equal the private costs. The above-mentioned conditions of equilibrium should apply to socio-economic conditions. When individual citizens act on the basis of private-economic costs, the above equilibrium will not be reached when there are externalities.

Often, there are distortions in the economy which entail that the conditions of equilibrium are not met. There are different types of distortions, as analysed in sections 4.1-4.5. These distortions may be caused by market imperfection, including externalities. They may also be provoked by policy intervention. The policy intervention may be inherited from earlier times, and which cannot be said to be rationally motivated today. There may also be policy intervention which aims at realizing non-economic goals.

The chapter analyses whether distortions should be met with intervention. In the vast majority of cases, this would be appropriate. Intervention can be effected by means of several policy instruments. If the distortions are regarded individually, the different instruments may be ranked according to their appropriateness. It is a golden rule that the closer the intervention is to the causes of the distortion, the better the result.

One of the arguments often expressed in defence of import protection is the infant-industry tariff argument. All economies suffer from externalities and other imperfections in the market mechanism in the form of lesser-developed or defective markets. This applies in particular to developing countries. The theory provides ample arguments advocating other types of support than tariffs. Tariffs will rarely intervene directly to repair the existing distortions, and at the same time, tariffs create a distortion on the consumption side. Nevertheless, in practice countries are often forced to employ tariff protection to a certain extent. Among other things, this has to do with the public expenditure required by the preferred alternative instruments in the form of subsidies. The public fiscal problems experienced, not least by developing countries, are in themselves an argument for levying tariffs which increase public revenue and are easy to administer.

At the end of this chapter an example of the pursuit of a non-economic goal is given. If such a goal has been decided upon, it is important to find the instrument which will inflict the lowest costs on society.

Literature

Baldwin, R.E., »The Case against Infant-industry Tariff Protection«, *Journal of Political Economy,* 77, 1969.

Bhagwati, J.N., »The Generalized Theory of Distortions and Welfare«, in Bhagwati J.N., R.W. Jones, R.A. Mundell and J. Vanek (eds), *Trade, Balance of Payments and Growth,* Amsterdam, 1971.

Bhagwati, J.N. and T.N. Srinivasan, »Optimal Intervention to achieve Non-economic Objectives«, *Review of Economic Studies,* 36, 1969.

Corden, W.M., *Trade Policy and Economic Welfare,* Oxford, 1974.

Johnson, H.G., »A New View of the Infant Industry Argument« in McDougall, I.A. and R.H. Snape (eds), *Studies in international Economics,* Amsterdam, 1970.

Lloyd, P.J., »A More General Theory of Price Distortions in Open Economies«, *Journal of International Economics,* 4, 1974.

5. International trade co-operation

5.1 The background to GATT

Global co-operation in international trade first saw the light of day when the General Agreement on Tariffs and Trade (GATT) was set up in 1947. This co-operation was built upon an ideological foundation, a particular historical situation and a wish to ensure international co-operation through the establishment of international institutions.

The ideological foundations

Ever since the days of Adam Smith, the science of economics has been preoccupied with the advantages of free trade. It has been recognized that the theory advocating free trade presupposes the fulfilment of certain assumptions. If these assumptions are not fulfilled, then protectionism can become an option. The most marked example of this is provided by the argument that it is necessary to protect infant industries by means of import duties. Economic theory from the nineteenth century and the first half of the twentieth century provides examples of situations where protectionist measures were reasonable and justified. Nonetheless, the clearly dominant school of thought has been in favour of free trade which is supposed to provide increased welfare through the exploitation of comparative advantages.

The historical background

In the aftermath of the Second World War, there was widespread interest among nations to work for the establishment of international free trade. The background to this was the events of the 1930s, when the international division of labour completely collapsed. When the depression started in 1929, the United States resorted to protectionism in order to shield its industry in the hope of reducing unemployment. This had an effect on the outside world which, in turn, resorted to increased protectionism. This is an example of the »Beggar my Neighbour« policy, so-called because the trade policy followed by any individual country only aggravates the problems of all the others. When all countries decide to protect their industries, then protectionism is not an effective way to relieve unemployment. The result is that the international division of labour is disrupted. Countries also acted in an uncoordinated fashion on currency policy. In order to promote employment at home, country A would devalue its currency and would, for a time, improve its competitiveness at the expense of other nations. Country B, faced with rising unemployment, then decided to devalue in turn, leaving those countries which did not devalue to sink deeper and deeper into trouble and eventually resort to devaluation themselves. The end result was that, after the round of devaluations was completed, the relative currency parities were much the same as they were before the process began.

The experience of the 1930s, when there was no international co-operation in the spheres of trade and currency policies, demonstrated how badly wrong things could go if countries acted on their own in an uncoordinated fashion.

At the end of the Second World War, the United States was in a dominant position. During the nineteenth century, Great Britain, as the leading industrial nation, had argued the case for free trade. During the twentieth century, the American economy grew and by the end of the Second World War the United States held an undisputed position as the leading economic superpower. America proposed and promoted the idea of international economic co-operation based on free trade. As the tensions with the Soviet Union and the Eastern Bloc grew, America began to see a policy of trade co-operation with western European countries and others as part of an international political strategy for the containment of Communism. The Marshall Plan and American requirements for the internal liberalization of Western Europe were all part of this strategy.

Setting up international institutions

In order to ensure international co-operation it was agreed to establish a series of international organizations under the United Nations.

At the Bretton Woods Conference in 1944, the decision was taken to set up, as part of the United Nations framework, the International Monetary Fund (IMF) as well as the International Bank for Reconstruction and Development (IBRD) known as the World Bank. The IMF's role was to supervise and guide international monetary co-operation, the purpose of which was to ensure stable rates of exchange. The participating countries announced fixed rates of exchange to the IMF and these could only be changed in the event of fundamental imbalances in their balances of payments. The IBRD was originally intended to take care of post-war reconstruction, but instead it has become the institution which, by means of loans and assistance, has the purpose of promoting economic development in the developing countries.

With the IMF and the World Bank two cornerstones of international economic co-operation were established. It was the intention to establish a third cornerstone which should take care of international trade co-operation. In 1947/48, members of the United Nations negotiated the establishment of the International Trade Organization (ITO) but the treaty founding the organization was never ratified by the United States.

To prepare for the foundation of the ITO, a 23 nation committee was appointed and during its work in 1946/47, agreement was reached on a set of rules for tariffs and trade which was to form the basis of the ITO. Negotiations on tariff reductions also took place. In 1947, the General Agreement on Tariffs and Trade (GATT) became a reality. On the one hand, the 23 nations had agreed on a set of rules and, on the other, they had negotiated the first set of tariff reductions.

The GATT agreement was meant to remain in force until the ITO was founded, but as this did not happen the GATT agreement provided the framework for international trade policy co-operation. The number of countries, which participated in the co-operation increased from the original 23 to around 130 in 1995, when WTO was founded.

The aim of the GATT co-operation was to achieve two goals. Firstly, each country should follow the rules which lay down which trade policy measures were permissible. Furthermore the countries should adhere to the principle that an individual country should not act on its own, but through GATT. Secondly, GATT should organize international conferences, often referred to as »rounds«, with a view to dismantling national trade barriers and strengthening the regulations.

Eight rounds have been held, the Geneva Round in 1947, Annecy in 1949, Torquay in 1950/51, Geneva in 1955/56, the Dillon Round in 1960/61, the Kennedy Round 1964-1967, the Tokyo Round 1973-1979 and, finally, the Uruguay Round 1986-1994. The concluding agreement of the Uruguay Round brought about the setting up of the World Trade Organization (WTO) which since 1995 has continued the work of GATT.

5.2 The GATT principles

GATT co-operation was based on a set of basic principles. These were the principles of non-discrimination, reciprocity and that customs tariffs were the only acceptable form of protection. These principles have to be seen in the context of the various exceptions which existed within the GATT co-operation and which are described in section 5.3.

Non-discrimination

GATT co-operation was based on the notion of the Most Favoured Nation clause (MFN clause). When country A lowered the import tariff on a given commodity from country B, then any other signatory countries could demand the same tariff reduction. Any GATT country exporting to country A had the right to demand the same treatment as the most favoured nation. During the first five GATT rounds, agreements on tariff reductions for each product category were initially reached on a bilateral basis between the countries. The effect of the MFN clause was that all other exporters also benefited from the tariff reductions. In subsequent rounds, there was a shift towards negotiating general tariff reductions for a wider range of goods. During the Kennedy Round, for instance, the American delegation was authorized to negotiate national tariff reductions of up to fifty per cent.

The principle of non-discrimination applies to the specific commodity. A given commodity has to be treated in exactly the same manner, no matter from which country it is imported. The MFN clause does not prevent different exporting countries from being hit differently. Countries exporting to importers with high tariffs are worse off than exporters to countries with low import tariffs. The MFN principle goes back to the nineteenth century, where the principle was often used in trade treaties e.g. the Cobden Treaty between France and Britain in 1860. The American tariff policy of the 1930s also applied the principle. Since the Second World War it has been the United States, more than any other nation, which has striven to enforce the principle of non-discrimination.

Tariff rates reached as a result of negotiations at international trade conferences were bound tariff rates, which meant that they could not subsequently be raised. A member state might unilaterally decide to lower its rates, but the rates must be lowered for all GATT members.

According to the GATT rules, the principle of national treatment was also applied. This meant that once imported goods had passed the border, they were to be treated in exactly the same manner as goods of domestic origin. No country could thus levy taxes only on imported goods and not on domestically produced goods.

Reciprocity

GATT co-operation was founded on the principle of reciprocity. When a country lowers its tariff barriers, it is entitled to expect that other countries take corresponding measures to liberalize trade. The intention is to ensure that all countries benefit equally from the liberalisation of trade. There was a desire to avoid the so-called »free rider« problem. This arises when a country enjoys the advantages of other countries' tariff reductions, but wants a »free ride« at the expense of others and is unwilling to lower its own tariffs correspondingly. This gave rise to discussions as to whether the MFN clause should be made conditional. Only those countries that lived up to the reciprocity principle were to enjoy the benefits of the Most Favoured Nation clause. This would have eliminated the »free rider« problem. There was also a strong desire to eliminate the problems caused at negotiating rounds by the so-called »foot draggers«. The »foot dragging« countries are those which block agreements because they are unwilling to go far enough in what they offer at the negotiating table for final agreement to be possible. The problem with the conditional MFN principle was that it resulted in different tariff rates for different countries, which was in clear

Figure 5.1: Import demand and the tariff level

breach of the principle of non-discrimination. For that reason, the unconditional form of the MFN clause was adhered to.

Interpretation of the reciprocity principle gives rise to problems in practice. Does reciprocity mean that access to two given national markets should be the same or does it mean that the degree of alteration in market access should be the same? Country A has a protective tariff of 60 per cent while country B has one of 30 per cent. If foreign producers are to get equal access to both markets, then country A has to reduce its tariff by 30 percentage points. If the aim is to ensure that increase in market access is the same, it is by no means sure that this would be achieved by both countries cutting their tariff levels, for instance, by half. In the case of country B, a lowering of tariffs from 30 to 15 per cent could lead to a greater rise in imports than if country A lowered its duty levels from 60 to 30 per cent. So, perhaps, country A with its higher tariff should lower it by a greater percentage than country B with its lower tariff since the overall aim is to equalize access to both nations' markets. The level of import demand as a function of the tariff level might appear as it does in figure 5.1. for instance, where even a tariff of 30 per cent is almost as restrictive on imports as a level of 60 per cent.

If economic conditions in two countries are different, then a uniform lowering of tariffs would not be commensurate with true reciprocity. If two countries, one a developing country and the other an industrial country, each originally have a tariff rate of 30 per cent, which is reduced to 15 per cent then, in all probability, the developing country will be hit harder than the industrial country. This is because the developing country would be involved in building up its industrial sector and its ability to adapt to new trade conditions would be severely constrained by the fact that the chances of alternative employment are much more limited than in an industrial country.

Customs duties, subsidies and other trade policy instruments

GATT co-operation was based on the principle that the only way a country may protect its industry is through customs tariffs. The use of import restrictions was a widespread phenomenon when GATT co-operation started. According to Article XI of the GATT agreement, restrictions on imports were to be phased out and it was forbidden to introduce new import restrictions. Customs tariffs, however, were accepted although the intention was gradually to phase out this type of protection through agreements reached at international conferences held under the auspices of GATT.

That import restrictions were not allowed, whereas customs tariffs were, was due to the fact that restrictions are not as transparent. Conditions of export are far more clear cut for foreign exporters when they are faced by customs duties rather than import restrictions. Potential exporters do not know to what extent an import quota has been used up or not, and importers who hold import licences are in a strong position vis-à-vis the foreign exporters. It is not clear for the domestic consumers how much the import quotas protect domestic production. This would depend on world market prices as well as on the level of import demand. Any eventual consumer pressure, aimed at lowering national protection levels, would be greater in the case of tariffs than with import restrictions simply because it is easier to see the protective effect of tariffs.

Tariffs and import restrictions are direct obstacles to trade. Production subsidies granted to an area of production where a country is otherwise a net importer, would inhibit the import of these goods. Production subsidies for export industries and direct export subsidies promote exports. Subsidies for export industries are not in themselves obstacles to trade, but this type of support does raise exports above the level that unsubsidised exports would reach. It is clear that export enhancing measures have a distorting effect on patterns of international trade, so international trade co-operation has to take such subsidy policies into account.

According to GATT, production subsidies were not prohibited, but the member states were obliged to keep GATT informed about those subsidy schemes which indirectly affect both imports and exports. However, direct export subsidies were forbidden under Article XVI. Production subsidies incur greater costs to any national treasury than export subsidies. It is therefore assumed that countries are less inclined to subsidise production than exports. At the same time, production subsidies may serve the legitimate purpose of strengthening the domestic industries and businesses.

5.3 Exceptions to GATT principles

The GATT rules included some provisions which were at variance with the principles stated above. There are several independent reasons and arguments for these exceptions.

Exceptions to the Most Favoured Nation clause

The principle of the MFN clause is one of global non-discrimination. All countries which joined GATT were entitled to the same treatment in terms of tariffs. The significant exception to this in the GATT rules was Article XXIV which allowed countries to form regional arrangements in the form of customs unions and free trade areas. Such regional trade arrangements meant that a given country could discriminate in favour of other member countries and against non-member countries. This is in clear breach of the MFN clause.

The reason for the introduction of this exception to the GATT rules was a wish to ease European reconstruction through a gradual phasing out of protective trade barriers within Europe, but without obliging European countries to liberalize to the same extent vis-à-vis the United States. This was a goal which the Americans also agreed with, and was manifested in the Marshall Plan and its associated organization, the Organization for European Economic Cooperation (OEEC) which was to be the predecessor of the Organization for Economic Cooperation and Development (OECD). The OEEC was to ensure that the European countries mutually phased out their import restrictions, which was a condition for receiving Marshall Plan assistance.

Thus, under the shelter of the exception clause, the European Community (EC) began life as a customs union. The European

Free Trade Area (EFTA) was started between Great Britain, the Nordic countries, Switzerland, Austria and Portugal. Several subsequent regional trade associations have been established, such as the Association of South East Asian Nations (ASEAN) and the North American Free Trade Area (NAFTA).

Regional trade associations were accepted by GATT because it was recognized that closer co-operation between neighbours would be of value in its own right and that such co-operation would be hard to establish under the principle of a single-tiered, global MFN clause. At the same time, regional trade arrangements were seen as a step in the direction of increased global free trade.

A series of conditions have to be fulfilled before customs unions and free trade areas may be exempted from the requirements of the MFN clause. The co-operation has to comprise virtually all categories of goods and it is not allowed to raise the level of tariff protection towards the outside world. When a customs union is set up, its common tariff barrier must not exceed the average tariff level of the participating states before the customs union was set up.

Preferential trade agreements already in force before GATT co-operation began were also exempt from the MFN clause. This applied to those trade preference agreements between the former European colonial powers and their partners. These preference agreements subsequently developed into the Lomé Convention signed between the EU and the ACP countries (African, Caribbean and Pacific countries) which in formal terms was in breach of the MFN clause because the ACP countries were accorded preferential status when exporting to the EU.

The Generalised System of Preferences (GSP) was also established, which gave developing countries preferential status with the industrial countries. The developing countries' exports were either completely exempt from customs duties or could enter at a reduced rate.

Both the Lomé Convention and the various GSP agreements were recognized by GATT although they did give rise to much controversy as some countries, primarily the United States, expressed concern at the prospect of too many exemptions from the MFN clause.

Generally it can be said that GATT's interpretation of the rules and requirements concerning the establishment of customs unions, free trade areas and other types of preferential agreement was not overly restrictive.

Exceptions to the reciprocity principle

It has been mentioned already that it is not always clear how the reciprocity principle is to be understood. For a country to obtain increased access to other national markets, it has to open its own market to others. This is often the way matters appear in purely political terms, although sometimes a country may derive an economic advantage from liberalization without demanding reciprocal measures from others.

From the start of GATT, the question arose as to what the concept of reciprocity really means in connection with the relationship between the western European countries and the United States. The conditions were radically different in that Europe had to be rebuilt while the American productive apparatus was unscathed. In order to contribute to real parity it was natural that the United States should lower its tariff barriers at a faster rate than the western European countries lowered theirs, as was the case during the first years of GATT.

A similar problem arises in relation to the developing countries. A large section on trade and economic development, Part IV, was added to the GATT agreement in 1964. The rules allowed developing countries to avail themselves of otherwise prohibited trade policy instruments if this was done as part of a strategy to promote their economic development. In this particular connection, developing countries were granted an exemption from the reciprocity principle. The developing countries obtained trade advantages in the markets of the industrial nations without the latter demanding equivalent measures of economic liberalization in the developing countries in strict accordance with the reciprocity principle. During the first decades of GATT co-operation, this exemption was accepted from the pragmatic view that the developing countries did not participate much in the world trade. Besides, the industrial nations never liberalized their agricultural, textile or clothing markets, all areas where the developing countries have potential export opportunities, as will become apparent in the following.

Exceptions to the accepted use of trade policy instruments

Should a country find itself in a balance of payments crisis, it could then make use of import restrictions. This was in accordance with Article XII in the case of industrial countries and Article XVIII B in the case of developing countries. In practice, industrial countries have, in fact, made very little use of these escape clauses whereas developing countries have often resorted to them.

One of the underlying premises of the GATT system was that problems of macroeconomic imbalance which manifest themselves in the form of unemployment or balance of payments deficits have to be resolved through the use of macroeconomic policies including exchange rate policy. These imbalances were not to be dealt with by means of trade measures; they were to be dealt with in concert with the IMF and the World Bank which were the two other cornerstones of the international economic system. The industrial countries have lived up to these premises. However, this is not the case for the developing countries.

There were also exceptions to the rules in the area of duties where it was permitted to introduce anti-dumping duties as well as countervailing duties. The GATT rules define precisely what is meant by dumping and there are rules governing the introduction and use of anti-dumping customs duties, the purpose of which is to neutralise an unfair competitive advantage gained through the practice of dumping. Dumping occurs if goods are sold at a lower price level than the »normal« current level. A country may legitimately intervene with an anti-dumping duty when the dumping either causes substantial damage to a particular domestic sector or hampers its development. In the case of a country subsidizing export goods, the outside world may then introduce countervailing duties which correspond to the level of the original subsidy.

Sectors of industry exempt from GATT rules

GATT rules did not apply to certain key sectors: these were agriculture, textiles and services.

Several exceptions to GATT rules existed in relation to trade in agricultural produce. They comprise the ban on import restrictions along with the ban on export subsidies.

From the outset, there were a series of exceptions to the general ban on import restrictions in the GATT rules. Even this state of affairs was considered too restrictive by the Americans who, in 1955, obtained a temporary dispensation from GATT rules which soon proved to be permanent in practice. The United States wished to continue the agricultural policy it had implemented in the 1930s. The USA wanted the freedom to arrange its agricultural policy as it saw fit without any outside interference, which also meant the use of import restrictions. The result of this shortfall in international discipline was that the way was paved for the EC to build up its protectionist Common Agricultural Policy.

According to GATT rules, there was a general ban on export subsidies. This ban did not apply to so-called primary products, a category that includes agricultural products. These export subsidies were, however, to be used in such a way that the country in question did not get more than a »reasonable share of world trade« at an »earlier representative period«.

These exceptions to the rules, and the vaguely formulated requirements as to their application, has meant that in practice each of the industrial nations, in turn, was able to implement policies to protect and subsidize its agricultural sector. The Uruguay Round was the first time that an agreement was reached on agriculture with a view to creating better market access through the reduction of protection, limitation of subsidies for domestic producers and reduction in the use of export subsidies.

Textiles were also exempt from trade liberalization. There was excess capacity in the textile sector of many industrial countries throughout the 1950s while the supply of textiles from the developing world was increasing. This led to many of the industrial countries negotiating voluntary export restraint agreements with the new producers, principally Japan, Hong Kong and India.

In 1961, this series of bilateral agreements was replaced by a multilateral system upon which agreement was reached under the auspices of GATT. Eventual problems were expected to be short term and the agreement was supposed to ensure »regulated conditions of access« to the markets of the industrial nations in order to ensure against »market collapses« brought on by »sudden and significant rises in the importation of certain products from certain suppliers«. This agreement was short-lived, however, since the problems proved to be more permanent in nature than originally envisaged. A new long term agreement was reached and was replaced in 1974 by the Multi Fibre Agreement. This agreement, which covered 75 per cent of the trade in textile products made of natural or man-made fibres, has been renewed several times. These agreements run counter to the fundamental principles of GATT. They discriminate between imports from various countries and allow the use of import restrictions because at the heart of these agreements is the attempt to achieve a controlled trade through the use of restrictions. The Multi Fibre Agreement is based on bilateral quotas which are awarded to exporting countries which thus benefit from the so-called »quota rent«. These agreements give each country the possibility of making independent decisions and acting unilaterally instead of by multilateral decisions reached through GATT.

The Uruguay Round contained an agreement on textiles which was intended to phase out the system of regulated trade in textiles over a ten-year period.

Originally, GATT was a general agreement on trade in goods only. There were no rules about trade in services, such as transport, communications, financial services or those of the liberal professions. The explanation for this is that the trade in services did not play a significant part in overall world trade when the GATT agreement was set up. This has changed considerably since, which is why trade in services along with the protection of intellectual property rights were, for the first time, taken up by GATT in connection with the Uruguay Round. The trade in services is an area of particular interest to the industrial countries which is why they have pressed for the liberalization of this type of trade. Larger developing nations such as Brazil, India, Indonesia, etc., have been reluctant about this because they fear that the industrial countries, with well developed service sectors, will hinder them from building up their own equivalent service industries. In spite of this, however, it was possible, in connection with the Uruguay Round to reach an agreement about trade in services and intellectual property rights.

5.4 The results of GATT co-operation 1947-1970

When evaluating GATT co-operation, it is natural to break it up into two periods; the first starting with the establishment of GATT

until 1970 and the second from 1970 onwards up to the end of the
Uruguay Round.

Significant liberalization

The first period comprises the first five rounds of negotiations on
tariff reductions as well as the Kennedy Round of 1964-67. This
period was characterized by a massive lowering of trade barriers
between the industrial nations. On the one hand, there was a phasing out of import restrictions, except in the agricultural, textile,
coal and steel sectors, while on the other there was a considerable
overall reduction in protective tariffs. After the Second World War
the industrialised nations' estimated average level of protection for
manufactured goods was around 40 per cent. At the conclusion of
the Kennedy Round, the average level had been brought down to
about 10 per cent.

It was the first GATT rounds which brought about the particularly large tariff reductions, though the 1950s did not produce such
marked results. There were many reasons for this. To start with, it is
always easier to carry out the first reductions in tariff. The countries initially chose the categories of goods where the reduction of
tariff levels made the least impact. However, as the process of tariff
reduction was continued and extended, the whole issue became
more sensitive. Eventually, a level was reached where any further
reduction had a more serious impact on domestic industry. Then
new categories of goods, more dependent on tariff protection, were
included in the negotiating process. The other factor was that the
tariff reduction negotiations were bilateral and dealt with individual
commodities. Country A would produce a list offering tariff reductions on goods which would particularly interest country B, and
country B did the same vis-à-vis country A. When the number of
participating countries increased, it became more difficult to negotiate on a bilateral basis. Finally, European interest in GATT
waned as western Europe began to establish its own regional trade
co-operation. To this could be added the fact that the American
delegation was only given a limited mandate by Congress.

GATT co-operation got under way again with the Kennedy
Round. The United States pushed matters along as it was keenly
interested in lowering the European tariff barriers so as to reduce

the discrimination engendered by the construction of the European Community.

Congress voted for a trade bill which authorized the American administration to reduce the general tariff protection levels by up to 50 per cent. For those categories of goods where the United States and the EC had more than 80 per cent of the world trade, the administration was allowed to abolish tariff protection completely.

The United States not only feared the economic consequences of high western European tariff walls, it also feared the political consequences of looser transatlantic co-operation if tariff protection levels were not reduced.

The Kennedy Round also saw the introduction of a new system of negotiation. Instead of negotiating each category of product in turn on a bilateral basis, general tariff reductions for all categories of goods became the subject of negotiation. Disagreement arose between the United States and the EC as to whether tariff reduction should be linear, i.e., the same reduction in percentage terms for all goods, or whether the aim should be a harmonization of tariff rates so that the highest rates would undergo the greatest proportional reduction. The United States had tariffs with a far wider spread of levels whereas the EC had a far more uniform level for the various categories of goods as a result of the customs union then being constructed. The common tariff level of the EC was the mean average of the earlier tariff levels of the individual member states, as this was a necessary condition if the new customs union was to conform to the GATT rules. The result of the Kennedy Round was an average tariff reduction of approximately one-third while tariff levels were harmonised so that the highest rates were reduced the most.

It can be thus concluded that, with the notable exception of textiles, manufactured goods experienced significant liberalization. Import restrictions were abolished and there was a considerable lowering of tariff protection levels.

Continued protection

Notwithstanding the significant liberalization in the case of most manufactured goods, far from all the problems were solved. Firstly, agricultural products were exempt from liberalization. Secondly, liberalization did not encompass all categories of manufactured goods because the sensitive area of textiles had been left out. Thirdly, the reduction in the protection of raw materials and semi-manufactured goods had been proportionately greater than the reduction in the protection of finished goods. This meant that the lowering of nominal tariff rates did not reflect the continued and considerable effective tariff protection of many manufactured goods.

The United States was worried by the EC's Common Agricultural Policy which was then being built up. Common Market agricultural schemes, which implied high protection levels, were only possible because agriculture was completely outside the purview of the GATT agreement. There was a general ban on export subsidies in GATT, though there was an exception made for primary products including agricultural products. There was also a general ban on qualitative restrictions in GATT, though there again an exception was made for agriculture. In 1955, the United States obtained a general exception from the GATT rules on behalf of its farmers. The United States sought to reserve the right to implement the agricultural policy it had embarked upon in the 1930s. The Common Market used variable import duties in connection with its agricultural policy because they provided more effective protection than bound tariff rates. Variable import duties were not mentioned in the GATT agreement, but it is obvious that they clashed with the GATT principle that negotiated tariff levels were fixed, which meant that they could not be raised subsequently.

As the agricultural sector was not subject to GATT discipline, this made it possible for the EC to set up its own extremely protectionist agricultural schemes. At the same time, the United States took the opportunity to continue their subsidy policy for farmers.

In the manufacturing sector, textiles were in practice entirely exempt from GATT regulations. Within the area of textiles, industrial countries managed to introduce a comprehensive system of import restrictions in order to protect their own textile and cloting production against imports from developing countries.

Several agreements have been reached at international level on trade in textiles. The first textiles agreement was reached in 1961 and was meant to be short term. In 1964, a replacement came in the form of a long term agreement, which in turn was replaced by the Multi Fibre Agreement of 1974 which in its turn has subsequently been renewed. These agreements were reached under the auspices of GATT, even though they were at variance with GATT's fundamental principles.

Firstly, the textile agreements violated the principle that import restrictions were to be used solely as a means of solving temporary problems. Secondly, they clashed with the rule that import restrictions, if used, should never be applied discriminatorily. The textiles agreements meant that an individual importing country entered a series of bilateral quota agreements on an extensive range of textile products with the exporting countries, while according to GATT import restrictions, if used, were to be global. So, what was the difference between global and bilateral quota systems?

A global quota system is characterized by an individual importing country introducing a total quota for how much of a given product may be imported from the outside world. The various exporting countries then compete in order to get as large a part of the quota as possible. The bilateral quota system means that the importing country distributes a quota to each exporting country.

A bilateral quota system distinguishes itself from its global equivalent in two ways. Firstly, the extra profit generated by a quota system is distributed differently. In a global system, the quotas are usually granted to national importers either free of charge or for payment. This means that the extra profit in relation to the world market price either accrues to the importers if they get the quotas free of charge or to the state if the quotas are sold. The extra profit, known as the quota rent, devolves to the importing nation. In the case of a bilateral quota system, as in the textile agreements, the quotas are given to the exporters to whom the quota rent consequently accrues. If an importing country combines quotas with customs duties, it can recoup the quota rent in part or entirely.

The second difference concerns the nature of the market. Competition between exporters would be more intensive with a global quota system since there are more exporters. Where each exporting country receives a quota, there are fewer exporters and the possibility of forming an export cartel is greater. This is illustrated in Figure 5.2. where DD represents the importing country's demand for a product from a given exporting country. P_w indicates the price on the world market and, at the same time, the marginal costs of the firms producing for the world market. If there are no import restrictions, the country will import the quantity indicated by OW.

Figure 5.2: Prices when bilateral quotas are used.

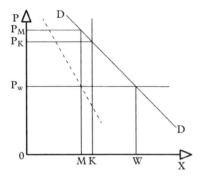

If a bilateral quota equal to OK is introduced and if the producers of the exporting country compete with each other, the domestic price will be equal to P_K and the quota rate $P_K - P_w$ would accrue to the exporting country. In the case of a bilateral quota being introduced where there is only one producer in the exporting country or the exporting producers form a cartel, the producer/producers can then obtain the monopoly price indicated by P_M as long as the producer/producers export OM which is a smaller quantity than the quota. The monopoly price, P_M, occurs at the point where the dotted line representing marginal revenues intersects the P_w line representing marginal costs.

The above example shows the interest that an exporting country might have in a bilateral quota system. To start with, the country obtains the quota rent and then it has the opportunity to obtain an even higher price for its exports as long as it exploits its monopoly.

In the case of a bilateral quota system, the importing country has to pay a higher import price. The import expenses will increase if the price rise in percentage terms is greater than the import reduction in percentage terms. Since the industrial countries have used bilateral quota systems, the motivating force cannot have been concern for the balance of payments. The true reason is to ensure that the domestic producers retain a larger share of the home market.

The idle capacity which occurs in the exporting country may then be used to produce goods which may eventually be sold in unregulated markets, or it may be redirected into the production of products not covered by the quota. In the latter case, the industrial countries might ask for more categories of goods to be included in the arrangement. The above illustrates that when quantitative regulation is instituted for one category of goods, it then tends to spread to other categories as well.

5.5 Changing world economic conditions

The trade system that was to be built up in the aftermath of the Second World War was characterised by the desire to obtain global free trade. The United States was the leading world power and had a decisive influence on the way international economic co-operation was shaped.

In the period 1950-1970 there were changes in international economic factors that changed views on trade policy, chiefly in the United States, but also in western Europe. These changes manifested themselves in three areas. First, new economic rivals appeared. Second, macroeconomic problems arose. And third, regional trade arrangements were established.

The new economic competitors

As mentioned above, the United States was the uncontested leading economic power in the immediate post-Second World War period, though this changed as time went by. New rivals made their appearance on the world market. It was obvious that western Europe would become an economic rival to the United States after its post-war reconstruction. This trend received the firm backing of the United States, because the Americans wanted, for political and strategic reasons, a strong partner and ally against the Eastern Bloc.

Japan also underwent reconstruction and made its entry onto the world economic scene during the 1960s when Japanese exports consisted mostly of more traditional products such as textiles and steel. These goods were not subject to strong rises in global demand and the industrial countries had already encountered major problems in these areas. As a consequence of the pressure of competition the first export restraint agreements were reached.

By the 1970s, the newly industrial countries emerged as economic rivals. They were countries such as South Korea, Taiwan, Hong Kong, Singapore, Brazil and Mexico which increased their export of labour intensive products, especially textiles.

In the same period Japanese exports continued to increase but there was a change in the commodity composition of the exports. Now the export of more manufactured goods such as cars and electronic products began to grow rapidly.

The result was that the United States and the EC were subject to more competition from several new producers. This competition made its first appearance in the more traditional industries such as textiles and other types of light consumer products which are typically labour intensive. Later on, competition arose especially from Japan, in growth sectors of industry such as high technology products. Large areas of the electronics industry were characterised by strong competition.

The new economic rivals thus applied pressure on the United States and western Europe on two fronts; the one consisting of traditional stagnant industries and the other of new, growing, technologically advanced industries. The strong growth in the new competitors' exports of traditional products made the necessary adjustment of industries in recession all the more difficult as the need for a drastic reduction of production grew. At the same time, expansion in what were otherwise growth-sectors seemed to become problematic in the face of growing competition in high-tech areas as well. This two-pronged pressure prepared the ground for a more protectionist trade policy.

In addition to this, the United States in particular felt that their political and economic power in the world was shrinking as a result of its reduced share in world production and world trade. The fear of losing ground internationally led to an increase in the demand for trade regulation, which meant, that on the one hand, the new rivals should restrain their exports to the United States and on the other, these countries should open their markets specifically to American products. A parallel can be drawn between this situation and that of Great Britain at the end of the nineteenth century when British industrial supremacy came to an end as a result of the rise of competitors such as the United States and Germany. British attitudes towards trade policy changed. The British had, until then, held that a free trade policy should be adhered to no matter what other countries did. However, this attitude changed with Great

Britain making its free trade policies conditional on other countries observing similar policies.

Macroeconomic problems

Generally speaking, it is easier to liberalize trade when economic conditions are good. If, however, economic problems arise, then those forces which seek to solve them by protectionist measures will gain greater influence in the formulation of economic policy.

The period up to 1970 was marked by considerable growth in the industrial countries resulting in a high level of employment. The international co-operation on pegged foreign exchange rates introduced at Bretton Woods, broke down in 1971. In 1973, OPEC drastically raised the price of crude oil, effectively trebling the price. This led to a considerable disequilibrium in the balance of payments for most industrial countries. The result was reduced economic growth, rising unemployment and increasing inflation. In many parts of the world, Latin America for instance, attempts were made to keep employment levels high through expansionary economic policies. Balance of payments deficits were financed by foreign loans at first, but subsequently increasing foreign debt gave rise to a more restrictive economic policy. The lower demand and increased unemployment in industrial countries and the increased economic problems in developing countries importing oil led to further pressure for the introduction of protective measures for import-competing industries.

Then there was the new economic policy introduced by the Reagan administration at the start of the 1980s. The combination of an expansionary fiscal policy and a tight monetary policy led to a rise in the interest rate which, in turn, led to a strengthening of the US dollar. This caused great difficulties for American business as its competitiveness was seriously impaired. The high international interest rate also meant that many developing countries, especially in Latin America, with large foreign debts to service ended up with even greater balance of payments problems. The general tightening of economic policy, which was meant to reduce balance of payments deficits, put an end to high growth.

There were thus several factors which contributed to a new period of low growth rates, rising unemployment, rising inflation as well as considerable balance of payments problems in the 1970s and early 1980s. There were, in other words, significant problems of macroeconomic imbalance. Under such circumstances, the desire to solve these problems through trade policy measures grew stronger. However, the experiences of the crisis in the 1930s showed that it was not possible to solve these problems by such means. Problems of macroeconomic imbalances require macroeconomic policy solutions. This is where international trade policy co-operation has to pass the test of resisting the protectionist pressure which always appears in times of economic crisis.

Regional trading blocs

While the idea of a multilateral removal of trade barriers was promoted in the forum provided by GATT, some groups of countries decided to enter into regional trade co-operation.

The most significant regional trade arrangements were established and built up during two distinct periods, the first of which was at the end of the 1950s and in the 1960s, and the second in the 1980s.

Strictly speaking, regional trade co-operation is a breach of the GATT idea of the multilateral removal of trade barriers, and against the principle of non-discrimination. However, an exception to this was provided for the GATT agreement of 1947, where, under certain conditions, countries may establish customs unions or free trade areas.

The United States supported the enactment of this exception in 1947 because of the opportunity it afforded to build up western European regional cooperation, which America favoured. A condition of receiving Marshall Plan aid was that the western European countries should start the abolition of import restrictions between themselves.

The EC co-operation comprising West Germany, France, Italy and the Benelux countries started in 1958. The customs union and the Common Agricultural Policy were established in the course of the 1960s. Since then, the co-operation has been extended to include more countries. In 1973, Great Britain, Denmark and Ireland joined the EC. Greece joined in 1981 and Spain and Portugal in 1986. The membership was increased further in 1995 when Sweden, Finland and Austria signed up.

The European Free Trade Area (EFTA) was set up in 1960.

During the 1960s it was an important trade co-operation agreement which has since lost its significance as most of the original members have subsequently joined the EC/EU.

In 1987, the Treaty of Rome, which had been the basis of the EC, was replaced by the Single European Act, the purpose of which was to replace the customs union with a single market that was intended to remove internal technical and administrative trade barriers. This goal was to be achieved through the establishment of a set of community rules pertaining to product standards.

Trade co-operation within the EC became ever more comprehensive, and this applied to both the number of participating countries and the extent of the common set of rules. Added to this the EC concluded a series of trade agreements with the remaining Mediterranean countries as well as treaties of association with ten central and eastern European countries which were former members of COMECON. COMECON, the Council for Mutual Economic Assistance, was a collaboration between the countries of the Socialist Bloc, viz. the Soviet Union, Central and Eastern Europe, Cuba, Mongolia and Vietnam. The purpose of COMECON was not the promotion of free trade but the planning of production and trade on a common basis in order to ensure that advantages were obtained through trade and that there was a balance of the internal trade flows. This collaboration was dissolved with the collapse of the Communist regimes.

Although the common tariff barrier of the EC has been gradually lowered, the rest of the world has had problems with the discriminatory elements of the EC trade co-operation. The United States has particularly criticised the rising protectionism which has been the result of the Common Agricultural Policy.

From the middle of the 1980s there were rising fears that the EC would turn itself into »Fortress Europe«, which would then discriminate increasingly against the rest of the world by allowing a free internal market while, putting up barriers against products from the rest of the world.

This fear contributed to the resurgence of interest in regional trade co-operations during the latter half of the 1980s. In 1988, the United States and Canada established a free trade area which expanded to become the North American Free Trade Area (NAFTA) when Mexico joined in 1992.

During the 1980s, co-operation between several southeast Asian countries was extended and structured in the form of the Association of South East Asian Nations (ASEAN). As a counter to the European and North American trade blocs, an expanded south east Asian economic association has been planned comprising Japan, South Korea, Taiwan and the ASEAN states. There were also plans for an Asia Pacific Economic Co-operation (APEC) comprising the above mentioned nations as well as Australia, New Zealand, the United States and Canada.

Also in Africa and Latin America many attempts have been made to establish regional trade co-operation in the form of customs unions or free trade areas. These trade agreements between developing countries have not met with the same degree of success as those between industrial countries with market economies. In developing countries, the market of any given country is often too small for economies of scale to be realised. There is, therefore, a natural tendency to try to create larger markets by means of free trade areas. The problem has been, however, to establish a co-operation where all the countries involved have felt that they benefit equally from the co-operation. Each participating country wants enterprises to be set up within its borders and, as long as there is no equal distribution of the new enterprises between the countries, some of them will feel that they are unfairly treated.

Through the establishment of customs unions, free trade areas and trade agreements, there has been a tendency towards an increasing regionalisation of trade co-operation. Strictly speaking, this is at variance with the GATT principle of non-discrimination. GATT has accepted customs unions and free trade areas, because these developments are seen as steps towards increased global free trade. However, the problem is that the GATT principle of non-discrimination has meanwhile been seriously undermined by these regional trade arrangements. When a regional trade area is set up, it causes trade problems for the countries outside the area. The outsiders are therefore interested in forming their own regional trade co-operation. The tendency to regionalise is spreading and has contributed to a general protectionist attitude towards the rest of the world.

The idea that customs unions and free trade areas represent a step towards multilateral free trade is only correct if there is a general lowering of trade protection between the regional blocs.

5.6 GATT co-operation 1970-1990

As a result of the changed trade conditions mentioned above, attitudes to trade were changed in a more protectionist direction first and foremost in the United States but also in the EC. In fact, the period between 1970 and 1990 can be described as that of the neo-protectionist wave.

During the Tokyo Round 1973 to 1979, many of the problems characterising the period were subject to negotiation. The negotiations included protection in the agricultural and textiles sectors, as well as non-tariff trade barriers and the abuses of the GATT rules of exception which abounded in this period.

The Tokyo Round did bring about a reduction in the average tariff protection level for manufactured goods by about one-third. Industry protection levels for finished goods thus fell from a level of approximately 10 per cent to around 7 per cent. Although a tariff level reduction of about one-third seems impressive, it has to be noted that tariff protection levels had already been considerably reduced.

The Tokyo Round did not get anywhere with regard to agriculture and textiles which remained firmly outside the general rules of GATT. The bilateral quota system for textiles was extended by means of the Multi Fibre Agreement of 1974. All in all, the Tokyo Round failed in its attempt to contain the neo-protectionist tide through the clarification and strengthening of GATT regulations.

In the period from 1947 to 1970, the old protectionist instruments were used. These were primarily in the form of customs duties supplemented by traditional import restrictions. A characteristic of the old form of protection was its relatively high degree of transparency. They were also the outcome of international customs negotiations. Furthermore, this type of protection was non-discriminatory as it applied equally to all exporters of a given product.

New forms of protection which were increasingly used in the period from 1970 to 1990 comprised different kinds of quantitative regulations, the use of subsidies as well as a rise in the application of the GATT rules of exception on anti-dumping duties and countervailing duties.

The protective instruments were implemented by individual countries without involving GATT. This clashed with the GATT principle that trade disagreements should be resolved within the GATT system. The new protective instruments were the result of administrative decisions at national level and were consequently far less transparent than customs duties. Neo-protectionism manifested itself in forms that were specific both in terms of product categories and countries. These instruments were differentiated to affect specific countries, which contradicted the GATT non-discrimination principle.

The new instruments of neo-protectionism were in clear breach of GATT's fundamental principles. Throughout this period, the GATT system came under increasing pressure. What follows is a discussion of the various instruments used at the time.

Voluntary export restraints agreements (VER)

The old industrial countries felt themselves under pressure when the new economic competitors appeared on the world scene. South east Asian countries in particular experienced high economic growth and they offered an increased volume of goods on the world market. This was above all true of Japan, and then of the so-called Newly Industrial Countries (NIC's) such as South Korea, Taiwan, Singapore and Hong Kong. Poorer countries such as Thailand, Malaysia and the other members of ASEAN have subsequently increased their export levels. NIC's have also appeared outside South East Asia; Brazil and Mexico are examples from Latin America.

The way of thinking behind the textiles agreements, whereby systems of bilateral quotas are built up, has spread to other sectors of industry. The United States and the EC entered agreements with the newly industrial countries with a view to limiting the import of traditional labour intensive industrial commodities, as well as with Japan in order to limit the imports of more advanced technology intensive products such as cars and electronics.

These VER's were based on the bilateral quota system which is also used in the Multi Fibre Agreement. According to Article XIX of the GATT agreement, import restrictions are only permitted as temporary measures designed to prevent market disturbance. Since import restrictions must not discriminate, only global quotas are allowed, not bilateral ones. So, the industrial countries cannot limit imports through restriction without infringing GATT rules. This is why the so-called voluntary export restraint agreements are proposed by the importers. The importing and exporting country agree that the exporting country will limit its exports to a certain level. These agreements can hardly be considered to be entirely voluntary because the industrial countries can threaten to impose import restrictions unilaterally if the exporting country does not sign up to a voluntary export restraint agreement. When seen from the point of view of the exporting country, voluntary export restraint agreements are as appealing as, for instance, the textiles agreements. The limitation of imports is controlled by the exporting countries and its producers, which is why the exporting countries get the quota rent. If there is only one producer in the exporting nation, or the number of producers is so small that an export cartel may be formed, the producers are then able to obtain an even higher sales price for their goods, namely the monopoly price as outlined in the analysis of Figure 5.2.

Both the importing and the exporting country may have an interest in reaching an agreement for voluntary export restraint because the importing country's own producers obtain greater production opportunities and the exporting country's products get a higher price in a protected market. Third countries may also benefit from these agreements besides the two contracting countries directly involved.

The importing country M has, for example, entered a customs union with country N. Outside the customs union there are two countries X and R, and country M signs a VER agreement with country X, which is the original exporter of the commodity to country M. These relationships are illustrated in Figure 5.3. DD represents country M's demand for the product and S_M represents country M's production. The horizontal difference between S_{M+N} and S_M represents country N's export to country M.

P_T represents the price of the product on the world market plus the common tariff of the customs union. At that price, country M's production is Q_1 and the export from country X is Q_1Q_6. Country M wishes to increase domestic production to the level Q_2. For that reason, a VER agreement is signed with country X limiting the export to Q_3Q_4. This agreement is also in the interest of country N, as it enables it to export the quantity Q_2Q_3 to country M. The VER

Figure 5.3: The effects of voluntary export restraints on various countries.

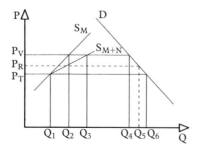

agreement creates a trade distortion. The price will be P_V but it will only be attained in the absence of exporters who, unfettered by agreements, may export at a lower price. If country R exports to country M at a price equal to P_R, which includes the common tariff, then both the production in country M and the export from country N will be reduced. Country R, however, would be able to export the amount represented by $Q_2Q_3 + Q_4Q_5$. Country X will export the same amount as before, although at a lower price equal to P_R. This example illustrates how more countries than the two directly involved may have an interest in the introduction of a VER agreement.

Voluntary import expansion agreements (VIE)

Voluntary export restraint agreements are measures which protect against imports. At the end of the 1980s, the United States entered into various bilateral agreements designed to increase American exports of specifically selected products. These VIE agreements may be seen as a form of export protection.

The point of departure was the American feeling of being put in a squeeze, especially in the 1980s, when it was difficult for US exports to compete. This was particularly true in relation to Japan and the newly industrialized countries of South East Asia. The United States contended that these countries had large enterprises working in both production and distribution that discriminated against the import of American goods. The United States thought that they themselves abided by the rules of GATT, but that this was not the case with some of their trading partners. The United States claimed that they were exposed to unfair trade conditions hurting their legitimate interests.

Already in the 1974 Trade Act, the Americans had inserted a »Section 301« which authorized the United States administration to negotiate with foreign governments concerning conditions in their countries that went against American business interests. Should such negotiations prove to be fruitless, the President had the authority to impose import restrictions on the countries in question. The usual American retaliatory measure was the imposition of high duties on certain of a given country's products. The use of Section 301 was in clear breach of GATT principles in several ways. To start with, tariff levels were raised, which was prohibited as tariff levels should be fixed. Then, the United States was acting unilaterally, i.e., on its own and not through GATT, on a contentious issue. Finally, Section 301 violated the principle of non-discrimination.

Section 301 was later renewed in the American Trade Act of 1988. This act enabled the US administration to indicate the countries which had introduced measures whose elimination would probably benefit American export interests, and which were regarded as unfair trade conditions. If these problems could not be solved through negotiation, then the US administration was entitled, according to the trade act, to introduce and enforce countermeasures. This revision is often referred to as »Super 301«.

Super 301 gave rise to several »voluntary« bilateral agreements where an importing country bound itself to import specified amounts of specified products from the United States. This is how the Americans secured a certain percentage of the Japanese market in semi-conductor chips for US manufacturers. The United States, also by means of a bilateral agreement, obtained a certain share of the Japanese beef market. The same applies to the American acquisition of a substantial part of South Korean agricultural imports.

These voluntary bilateral agreements for the expanded importation of selected American goods clearly contradicted GATT principles. They were discriminatory in relation to other exporters of similar goods from other countries. The result was that increased American exports replaced those of other, more competitive, countries. This was indeed an example of trade diversion as various importing countries had agreed to take in artificially large amounts of American export goods.

The United States objected to importing countries suggesting a general reduction in their tariff levels instead of entering bilateral agreements. Such tariff reductions would not ensure American exports because more competitive countries might benefit from the liberalization. In the United States itself, discussion of Section 301 gave rise to suggestions that where the US had a trade deficit with a given country, this should be sufficient reason to start bilateral negotiations with that country on voluntary import expansion.

The above was, of course, completely at odds with GATT which was based precisely on a multilateral trade principle where it is perfectly normal for a country to have a balance of payments deficit in its bilateral trade with another country. This is also in accordance with the theory of comparative advantages.

The fact that the United States had repeated problems with its balance of payments, with a massive overall deficit, was interpreted by the Americans as an indication of the extent to which other countries made use of unfair trade practices. Such a point of view does not take into account that the American balance of payments deficit was largely due to macroeconomic imbalances. These imbalances could only be solved through the correction of macroeconomic policies rather than by bilateral agreements which seriously jeopardize a non-discriminatory, multilateral trade system.

The American balance of payments deficit came about as a result of the economic policy of the Reagan administration, i.e., an expansionary fiscal policy together with a restrictive monetary policy. The result was high interest rates and a sharp rise in the value of the US dollar which severely impaired American competitiveness. During this period, Japan adhered to a policy of strict economic discipline which contributed to the large Japanese trade surplus.

These experiences demonstrate that macroeconomic imbalances, if not corrected through changes in economic policy, lead to a resurgence of interest in protectionist measures. These latter came in two guises, the first consisting of import protective measures such as voluntary export restraints agreements and the other of export protective measures such as voluntary import expansion agreements.

The use of subsidies

Trading conditions may be indirectly influenced through the use of subsidies. When there are restrictions on the possibility of using those instruments which directly affect trade, such as import restrictions or customs duties, there will be a tendency to use other instruments.

World economic conditions since the beginning of the 1970s have not been as good as before. For that reason, it is understandable that the use of production subsidies has increased. This is particularly true in sectors such as coal, steel and shipbuilding. Many developing countries have given up the strategy of import protection. Instead they have shifted to the use of various types of subsidy in order to build up export industries.

It is possible to use production subsidies without coming into conflict with GATT rules, as long as those subsidies are not of such a nature and size that they disturb trade patterns. The use of direct export subsidies is, however, prohibited, though there are border-line cases where it is hard to tell in practice whether the subsidy in question is of the export variety or not. It may be hard to ascertain whether the export credits are granted at a rate of interest below the free market rate. It may also be hard to decide whether subsidies for export promotion are an unacceptable form of export subsidy. When there is substantial intrasectoral trade, where the ability to compete depends on the exploitation of economies of scale, export promotion can be a significant tool.

Other measures affecting trade

There are several measures which can affect trade. Customs clearance at the border can take a long time. Rules on the valuation of imported goods may discriminate against imports. There are technical and health requirements, which a country may have in order to reassure the consumers of the quality of the goods. These requirements can assume the character of trade barriers because they discriminate against imported goods. If common product requirements are introduced, such as those of the Single Market, then each participating country wants the common requirements to be as close as possible to its own, as this would give its producers a competitive advantage. The public sector makes purchases and public authorities have an interest in seeing that national suppliers receive their orders, even though they might be more expensive than foreign suppliers. The intention, in this instance, is thus to give covert support for domestic producers. If, for instance, there is a firm desire to maintain a national armaments industry, then defence matériel is bought from domestic producers. Several countries also pursue regional policies which allow them, with the help of subsidies, to overcome the disadvantages of siting industries in regional development areas. If the subsidies received by those firms amount to more than the additional costs which the firms incur because they are situated in regional development areas, then these subsidies are too big and they may cause a trade distortion.

The above examples show that there are several ways of providing indirect support which is not particularly transparent. For this reason, efforts have been made to introduce common regulations for such measures. However, it is obvious that in practice it is extremely difficult to distinguish national initiatives with legitimate aims from those designed to protect national industries.

The use of exceptions to the rules

There are various exceptions to the rules in the GATT agreement. These exceptions allow the use of import restrictions in the case of balance of payments problems or if imports cause serious problems for a domestic industry. Many developing countries have cited balance of payments problems as the reason behind interventions in the economy whereas industrial nations have often cited market disturbance as the cause.

If foreign companies regularly practice dumping, thus causing persistent disturbance for domestic producers, inhibiting their competitiveness and jeopardizing their survival, it is entirely legitimate for the affected country to introduce anti-dumping duties. Such an anti-dumping duty has to be at such a level that it compensates exactly for the extent of the dumping and no more. Correspondingly, a country may take action against the effects of another country's subsidies schemes that disturb international trade. The countervailing duty that an importing country may introduce must not exceed the competitive advantage that the subsidies give rise to.

In practice, it is often difficult to determine whether the extent of the dumping taking place is indeed disruptive to the importing country. Equally, it is hard to establish how much of the rebate inherent in a low price is actually due to deliberate dumping. Similarly it is difficult to calculate the true price advantage gained from subsidies.

What can be stated is that throughout the period from 1970 to

1990, the number of cases of anti-dumping and cases concerning subsidies and the consequent countervailing duties has risen. This is a reflection of the economic problems that many countries in the world have been exposed to since 1970. In times of economic difficulties, there will always be a rise in the tendency to use whatever protective measures are allowed. The disturbing element in this trend has been that even minor price differences have been interpreted as being the result either of dumping or of unfair subsidies.

Evaluation of the significance of neo-protectionism

The extent to which the use of the new tools of trade policy has led to the constriction of trade is very much open to debate. What can safely be said is that the growth of world trade continued at a faster rate than that of GNPs. There are many ways of circumventing trade obstacles, for example in the form of voluntary export restraints. Firstly, a country may increase production of other categories of products not included in a VER agreement. Secondly, the exports may be forwarded via countries not included in the VER agreement. Thirdly, by means of foreign direct investment, production of the commodity may be placed in the importing country proper or in third countries not covered by the VER agreement.

There are various ways of looking at the period 1970-1990 when neo-protectionism was on the rise. It is possible to assert that the GATT rules were insufficiently developed to prevent the rise of new trade barriers. The trend towards liberalization which took place 1947-1970 was halted or neutralized to a certain extent by the neo-protectionist measures. Another point of view holds that when there are significant changes in the world economy, because there is recession in the industrial countries and in many developing countries and because there is a collapse of the international monetary system as there was in 1971, then, even with a strict set of GATT rules, it is difficult to avoid individual countries seeking some sort of protection. A fair evaluation of the period of increased protectionism could be that the damages was after all limited because the principle of multilateral free trade was preserved. It might even be claimed that the reason why the problems were not more serious, was the flexibility in the form of ambiguities and exceptions to the rules in the GATT regulations.

This latter, somewhat more positive view is easier to understand in the light of the happy outcome of the Uruguay Round of 1986-94. For a long time, it had been anyone's guess whether the Uruguay Round would reach a satisfactory conclusion which would strengthen the multilateral principle that GATT stood for.

Regionalisation of trade had developed and this increased regionalisation could have threatened multilateral international trade co-operation. The EC, which was a regional trade association, had grown from 6 members to 12. When it had become the EU, membership grew to 15 in 1995 and the EU now faces expansion eastwards with the inclusion of central and eastern European countries. There was a reasonable concern that the EC would concentrate more on its own internal development than on the multilateral elimination of trade barriers. At the same time the United States, with its Trade Act of 1988, began to widen the possibilities of unilateral intervention against other countries through the provisions of »Super 301«, and the United States and Canada, also in 1988, set up the North American Free Trade Area.

South East Asia had also been the scene of increased regional co-operation between, for instance, the ASEAN countries. There were plans for an expanded free trade area comprising Japan and the newly industrialized countries (NIC's), ASEAN members as well as Australia and New Zealand. Regional trade co-operation had also occurred in Africa and in Latin America.

It was clear that increased regionalisation of trade co-operation heightened the risk of trade clashes between the regional blocs as long as there was no revitalization of GATT co-operation.

5.7 The Outcome of the Uruguay Round

The Uruguay Round was the longest lasting GATT round. It started in 1986 and negotiations were concluded in 1994. It was the most comprehensive round of negotiations both in terms of participating countries, about 130, and in terms of the number of subject areas which were covered.

The Uruguay Round took place at a time when fears were growing that the neo-protectionism which had evolved during the 1970s and 1980s would continue unabated. The principles upon which GATT was built had been severely eroded and it was feared that these principles would be abandoned in the event of the Uruguay Round failing.

The Uruguay Round was often in a state of crisis, though in 1992 the last major hurdle concerning the rules governing agriculture was overcome by the Blair House accords between the EC and the United States.

The conclusion of the Uruguay Round presented the world with the most comprehensive set of rules relating to international trade that had ever been seen. This veritable complex of agreements builds upon the same principles as the original GATT agreement of 1947. The results are best illustrated by examining the main elements of this system of agreements.

The institutional framework around international trade co-operation was reinforced. GATT was originally an agreement that was to be supplemented by an international trade organization which, in the event, was never established. This meant that the co-operation gradually developed around the GATT secretariat in Geneva.

The end of the Uruguay round has meant that from 1995 onwards, there has been an international trade organization, the World Trade Organization (WTO). The institutional framework has thus been strengthened. Although the WTO Charter is not particularly comprehensive, it contains a description of the institutional and decision-making regulations and it specifically states that the WTO is a continuation of GATT in terms of fundamental ideas and practical work.

The most important decisions are to be found in the extensive set of agreements appended to the WTO Charter in the form of annexes as shown in table 5.1. There are four annexes in all. The first consists of three agreements about trade, services and intellectual property rights respectively. Originally, GATT co-operation only covered trade in goods as outlined in Annex 1A. Annex 1B is a new agreement which sets down the rules for trade in services. Annex 1C is also a new agreement which seeks to protect patents, copyright, registered trade marks and so on. The industrialized countries seek to prevent foreign companies copying new products which have been costly to research and develop.

Annex 2 is a set of agreements on how to resolve trade disputes. GATT was, at the beginning, a set of rules without an institutional framework, though in time procedures were developed under the auspices of GATT whereby panels of independent persons were

Table 5.1. Annexes to the WTO Charter

Annex 1	Annex 2	Annex 3	Annex 4
1A Multilateral Agreements on Trade in Goods	Rules and procedures for Dispute Settlement (DSB)	Trade Policy Review Mechanism (TPRM)	Country specific agreements on beef, dairy products, public purchases, civil aviation (Plurilateral Agreements)
1B Multilateral Agreements on Trade in Services (GATS)			
1C Multilateral agreements on Trade-Related aspects of Intellectual Property rights (TRIP)			

chosen to settle trade disputes. The resulting set of rules for dispute settlement has been reinforced in the Uruguay Round agreement.

Annex 3 is an agreement about the registration of each country's trade policy and subsequent regular analyses to ensure that the country in question is fulfilling its obligations. The idea is that greater transparency of the Trade Policy Review Mechanism can contribute to better discipline.

In the days of GATT, a series of agreements was reached, especially in connection with the Tokyo Round, that were only binding on those countries signing the specific agreements. Membership of the WTO means that all the agreements in Annexes 1 to 3 are binding. Annex 4 contains agreements between countries that only apply to those which have signed them. Annex 4 is open for new agreements in new areas where some member states may enter agreements which do not involve all WTO countries.

As mentioned earlier, the original GATT co-operation took place under Annex 1 A but, as table 5.2 shows, this annex contains several new agreements concluded in the Uruguay Round as well as those which were incorporated gradually into the GATT system and which were then altered in the course of new negotiating rounds.

The tariff reductions of the Uruguay Round are not immediately eye-catching; the other agreements are far more interesting. They

Tabe 5.2. Agreements under Annex 1A

1.	**Tariffs and general rules on trade**	2	**Agreements on specific sectors**
	General Agreement on Tariffs and Trade 1994 (GATT-94)		Agreements on agriculture Agreements on textiles and clothing
3.	**Exemptions**	4	**Agreements on indirect trade barriers**
	Anti-dumping measures Rules concerning subsidies and countervailing duties Protective measures concerning balance of payments problems and market disturbances		Technical trade barriers Sanitary and phytosanitary conditions (food products) Calculation of duties Inspection before shipment Rules of origin Rules concerning import licences
5.	**Miscellaneous**		
	Trade-Related Investment Measures (TRIM)		

concern agreements where new sectors were included in trade liberalization. They involve clarifying the exceptions allowed in the GATT rules. They are about agreements to prevent indirect trade barriers. Administrative, technical and health-related rules should relate to consumer protection policies, but such rules are often shaped so as to support a country's own domestic producers. Lastly there are rules relating to trade-related investment measures.

For the first time there is a GATT agreement on trade in agricultural products. The agreement contains a reduction of customs duties for agricultural products and it emphasizes that tariffs will be the only permitted form of protection. The agreement provides for a reduction of internal agricultural subsidies as well as a ceiling on the permitted level of export subsidies.

An agreement has also been reached on textiles and clothing which means that the bilateral quota system allowed under the Multi Fibre Agreement will be eliminated over a ten-year period.

Existing bilateral export restraint and import expansion agreements, which are in violation of GATT's article XIX, will be gradually done away with. In addition, the set of rules governing the use of subsidies has been clarified, and the same applies to rules concerning retaliation against dumping and subsidies. By strengthening the rules it is hoped to avoid their future abuse.

In order to prevent national technical and health-based regulations being used as trade barriers, the WTO has started to establish common product standards. This work is based on the agreement on technical barriers and the agreement about sanitary and phytosanitary conditions for food products. This is something which has already been done in the EU in connection with the Single Market. The idea is that if a commodity meets an approved standard, then no country can deny it access just because its own internal rules are stricter than the commonly agreed rules. It is clear that such a system restricts an individual country's ability to set its own standards of consumer protection. It also raises the issue of how far producer interests, including those of the multinationals, are especially favoured when it comes to shaping product standards.

The agreement on trade-related investment measures (TRIM) attempts to govern the special conditions which host countries may impose before they accept foreign investment. Host countries (especially those in the developing countries) often demand that a certain share of the semi-manufactures used in the production process should be purchased locally or that a certain proportion of production should be exported. TRIM draws attention to the fact that such demands conflict with the GATT principle relating to national treatment as well as the prohibition against quantative restrictions. Unless these demands on the foreign investor fall within GATT's exemptions then they must be removed.

From this it may be concluded that the Uruguay Round led to a strengthening of the GATT principles. Several new areas were brought under the GATT umbrella and its set of rules became more precise to avoid future abuse. The rules relating to dispute settlement are made more effective and there is now an open and transparent surveillance of the members' trade policies.

Even though the framework for stronger co-operation based on GATT's founding principles is in place, it is natural to ask how it will work in practice. Will there really be an elimination of the rise in protectionism seen since the 1970s? A strengthening of trade policy co-operation at a purely institutional level is an advantage because it is then possible to hope for a clearer division of responsibility between monetary and macroeconomic cooperation on the one side and trade policy on the other. One of the causes of the neo-protectionist wave has been that instead of using macroeconomic adjustments, including currency adjustments, attempts have been made to solve the problems of imbalances by increasing the use of trade policy instruments. Trade policy discipline is dependent on the implementation of the necessary macroeconomic adjustments to safeguard high levels of employment and the required structural changes in industries within a reasonable span of time.

It is important to look at trade policy in relation to other policies and this is among the challenges which the WTO now faces. The relationship between macroeconomic policy, including monetary policy, and trade policy has already been pointed out. Furthermore, environmental policy will become ever more important. How can trade rules be formulated so that countries either on their own initiative or through international environmental agreements ensure the promotion of environmental goals? Will violations of »reasonable« labour market rules, such as the right of workers to form trade unions, trigger trade sanctions in the future? Will observance of human rights be built in as a condition for enjoying the trade advantages that come with membership of the WTO?

Literature

Bhagwati, J.N., »The Threats to the World Trading System«, *The World Economy*, 15, 1992.

Curzon, G., *Multilateral Commercial Diplomacy*, London, 1965.

Dam, K.W., *The GATT: Law and International Organization*, Chicago, 1970.

Finger, J.M. and A. Olechowski (eds), *The Uruguay-Round: A Handbook on the Multilateral Trade Negotiations*, Washington, 1987.

GATT, *The Results of the Uruguay Round of Multilateral Trade Negotiations*, Geneva, November 1994.

Greenaway, D., *International Trade Policy: From Tariffs to the New Protectionism*, London, 1983.

Greenaway, D., R.C. Hine, A.P. Brien and R.J. Thornton (eds), *Global Protectionism*, London, 1991.

Meerhaeghe, M.A.G. van, *International Economic Institutions*, London, 1992.

Milner, C.R. (ed), *Export Promotion Strategies*, Hamel Hempstead, 1990.

Stern, R.M. (ed), *The Multilateral Trading System*, Ann Arbor, 1993.

Winters, L.A., »The Road to Uruguay«, *Economic Journal*, 100, 1990.

6. Customs unions

In the post war era, a large number of regional trade agreements have been entered into even though such agreements are actually in violation of the GATT principle of non-discrimination. Trade arrangements might take the form of customs unions, free trade areas and trade agreements.

A customs union is a co-operation in trade policy which entails that internal trade between the member countries takes place without tariffs and restrictions and that the member countries set up a common exterior customs barrier vis-à-vis other countries.

In a free trade area, internal trade among the member countries is free. No tariffs or import restrictions are imposed on goods originating in one of the member countries. Contrary to a customs union, each country keeps its own customs vis-à-vis countries outside the free trade area. This might create a problem, because exporters from non-member countries may try to export their goods to the member country that has the lowest tariff and then try to have the goods distributed to the other member countries from there. In order to prevent this, free trade areas must agree on rules of origin which stipulate how much of the value of the goods must have been processed within the free trade area for the goods to be sold from one country to another without tariffs and restrictions.

Customs unions and free trade areas extend either to all goods or to a majority of goods, and all internal tariffs on the relevant goods will be eliminated. Trade agreements are far more limited as they often extend to only a small number of goods and, at the same time, there may be quantitative restrictions associated with the concessions that are granted. Such concessions may be full tariff exemptions or tariff reductions.

Analyses of regional trade agreements are complicated by the fact that it is necessary to include at least three countries in the analysis. Initially, country A will treat imports from country B and country C in the same way. If country A enters into a trade agreement with country B, it means that exports from country B will be at an advantage compared to exports from country C.

In 1947, the GATT agreement allowed countries to set up customs unions and free trade areas under certain conditions even though such arrangements violated the principle of non-discrimination, because there was an interest in promoting regional cooperation in Europe. Both then and later, it has been stressed that regionalised free trade is a step towards increased free trade in general, and as such it is a step which also increases welfare.

However, this view calls for caution. Regional trade agreements are concerned with the theory of 'the second best'. This theory states that if there are two or more trade distortions in an economic system, it does not necessarily follow that eliminating one distortion will improve welfare. If country A has imposed tariffs on imports both from countries B and C, this counts as two distortions. If country A eliminates the distortion vis-à-vis country B in connection with a customs union between the two countries, welfare might be improved, but equally it might deteriorate, see section 4.7.

'The first best' solution is to eliminate all distortions. In the case referred to above, this means free trade with both countries B and C. All other solutions are 'second best' solutions which cannot be rated in terms of welfare. It does not necessarily follow that eliminating some distortions increases welfare.

6.1 Trade creation and trade diversion

When a customs union is created between countries A and B and country C is left outside the union, tariffs vis-à-vis country B will be removed. The situation changes from two distortions to one distortion. According to the theory of 'the second best', it cannot automatically be concluded that welfare will increase.

It is important to distinguish between two concepts, namely trade creation and trade diversion. J. Viner, the first person to distinguish between the two, assumed that demand for a product is completely inelastic and that production costs are constant despite the size of the production. This is illustrated in figure 6.1 where the vertical line D shows demand and C is the average costs in the

Figure 6.1: Trade creation and trade diversion.

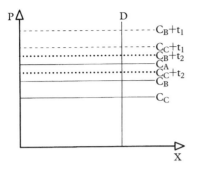

three countries A, B and C. The figure indicates $C_A > C_B > C_C$ which implies that country A has the highest production costs and country C has the lowest costs. If country A imposes tariffs of t_1, it follows that $C_A < C_C + t_1 < C_B + t_1$, which then implies that country A will produce the product itself as imports from both country B and country C will not be competitive after the tariffs have been added. Country A then enters into a customs union with country B which entails that $C_B < C_A < C_C + t_1$. This will result in country A no longer producing the goods as country B will take over the market after the tariffs, t_1, have been lifted on products from country B. This is an illustration of trade creation as a country's own more expensive production is replaced by less expensive foreign production. If all the production resources are exploited both before and after the creation of the customs union, welfare will be increased as the allocation of resources will have been improved.

On the other hand, if the tariff level in figure 6.1 is lower, for instance t_2, it follows that before the customs union is created, $C_C + t_2 < C_A < C_B + t_2$, which then again entails that country C will be exporting to country A. After the customs union is created, the situation will change to $C_B < C_C + t_2$, which means that country B will now take over country C's exports. A more expensive foreign supplier, that is country B, will take over the market from a less expensive foreign supplier, country C, because tariffs will not be imposed on country B's production. This is an illustration of a trade diversion as it leads to a misallocation when a cheaper foreign supplier, country C, is replaced by a more expensive foreign supplier, country B.

6.2 The effects of a customs union when demand is decreasing and supply is increasing

Based on the analysis in figure 6.1, it can be concluded that trade creation promotes welfare and that trade diversion harms welfare. However, the analysis is based on a number of assumptions. These assumptions are that product demand is completely inelastic and production costs are constant. If these assumptions are changed, the analysis becomes less simple. As it appears below, it can still be concluded that trade creation will always improve welfare in the importing country. A 'pure' trade diversion will always reduce welfare in the importing country. A 'pure' trade diversion exists when country A replaces a given quantity of of imported goods from a less expensive country, C, with the same quantity of imported goods from a more expensive country, B.

If product demand increases when prices fall, the trade diversion will coincide with an increase in consumption which will have a positive effect on welfare and thus reduce the loss of welfare generated by the pure trade diversion. If production costs increase when there is an increase in the production quantity, the customs union will not result in a pure trade diversion, but rather a combination of trade creation and pure trade diversion.

This is illustrated in the model shown in figure 6.2. The curves DD are falling demand curves and SS are increasing supply curves in the two countries A and B where country A is the domestic market that has created a customs union with country B. The rest of the world is represented by country C, which exports its products at a given world market price, P_V. Countries A and B are countries of the same size and they are both small compared to the rest of the world.

In the initial scenario, country A has imposed tariffs, t, on imports of a certain product so that the domestic price in country A is $P_V + t$. Before the customs union is created, country A imports a total quantity equivalent to $X_2 - X_4$. Country A imports a quantity, $X_2 - X_3$, which equals $X_2^\star - X_3^\star$, from country B. The rest, $X_3 - X_4$, is imported from country C.

Now country A and country B set up a customs union which means that country B will supply all country A's imports at a price of P_T as the external customs tariff in the customs union is assumed to be the same as country A's original customs tariff, t.

Figure 6.2: Simultaneous trade creation and trade diversion.

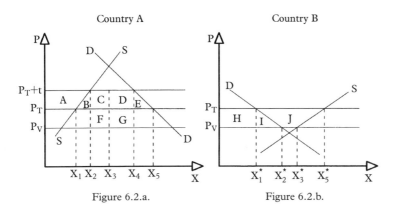

Figure 6.2.a.   Figure 6.2.b.

Imports in country A rise from $X_2 - X_4$ to $X_1 - X_5$. It follows that $X_1 - X_2$ represents a trade creation as a domestic production is replaced by imports from the partner country B. The fact that the quantity $X_3 - X_4$ is no longer supplied from country C but from country B represents a trade diversion. Finally, $X_4 - X_5$ shows an increase in imports as a result of the increased consumption following the lowering of the price in country A.

The overall change in welfare in country A consists of changes in consumer surplus, producer surplus and the revenue from the imposed customs in the following way:

Increased consumer surplus	: A + B + C + D + E
Reduced producer surplus	: A
Loss of revenue from customs	: C + D + F + G
Change in welfare in country A	: (B + E) – (F + G)

Each of the elements in the change of welfare has its own background. B represents the increase in welfare that is connected with the trade creation. $X_1 - X_2$ was previously produced domestically and this production is now replaced by less expensive imports. E represents the increase in welfare which is connected with the increased consumption which again is a result of the drop in the domestic consumer price. F is a loss of welfare which is caused by the deterioration of the terms of trade for the quantity of imported products that originally came from country B. G is the loss of welfare which can be ascribed to the pure trade diversion as $X_3 - X_4$ is the imported quantity that originally came from country C at world market prices.

In country B, the increase in welfare will be equivalent to the changes in the producer surplus H + I + J less the changes in the consumer surplus H + I. The increase in welfare will be J.

Whether or not the customs union will secure an overall improvement of welfare depends on the following:

Change in welfare in country A: (B + E) – (F + G)
Change in welfare in country B: J

Change in welfare in the
customs union: (B + E) – (F + G) + J

Based on the assumptions made in this analysis, for any given product which country A imports and country B exports, country B will always be at a gain in a customs union. Country A will realize gains if (B + E) > (F + G). Everything else being equal, the chances of this happening increase when:

- the smaller the imported quantity was to begin with,
- the more elastic supply and demand in terms of price,
- the closer the domestic price, P_T, is to the world market price.

If country A realises a net gain, the entire customs union will experience a gain as country B will always be at a gain in the outlined circumstances. If country A experiences a loss, country A's loss must be compared to country B's gain.

Even though country A experiences a loss in connection with the import of a given product, it does not automatically follow that country A will lose overall. In the above-mentioned example, only one product has been analysed. The picture might change for other imported goods, so that (B + E) is larger than (F + G) for these other goods. Additionally, country A also exports a number of goods. If figure 6.2.b. illustrates the conditions for one product that country A exports and figure 6.2.a. illustrates the import conditions in country B, it is obvious that country A will realize a gain.

Figure 6.3: Both countries were originally importers of a given product.

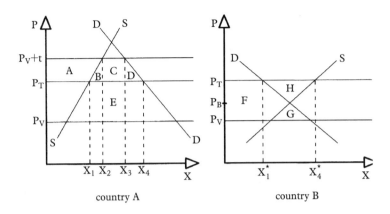

country A   country B

To measure the overall effect for country A of entering into a customs union, one must add up all the welfare gains and losses for all the products.

In figure 6.2, country B is always at an advantage in relation to the customs union, the assumption being that initially, country B was the exporting country. If country B started out as an importer of products from country C at world market prices, and if country B had not imposed tariffs on its imports, country B could suffer a loss. If both countries A and B started out importing the product, both countries could suffer a loss as a consequence of the customs union.

Figure 6.3 shows a case where country B, which was initially an importing country, becomes an exporter to country A.

The world market price is P_V. Country A has imposed tariffs, t, which means that the domestic price in country A is $P_V + t$ which again means that country A imports a quantity of $X_2 - X_3$ from country C. Country B imports at world market prices P_V.

If countries A and B enter into a customs union in which the common customs tariff is equivalent to A's original customs tariff, t, the price of goods in the customs union will be P_T, and country B will export the quantity $X_1^\star - X_4^\star$, which equals $X_1 - X_4$ in the figure for country A.

The following changes in welfare will occur:

Changes in welfare in country A:	B + D – E
Changes in welfare in country B:	H – G

This opens up for the possibility that both countries will suffer a loss by entering into a customs union. This example also illustrates the importance of the level of the common customs tariffs for the changes in welfare in countries A and B.

In the initial situation where the common customs tariff equalled the original customs tariff, t, in country A, it is assumed that both countries A and B would suffer a loss by entering into the customs union as (B + D) < E and H < G.

If the common customs tariff is higher than $P_T - P_V$, lowering the common customs tariff will have no effect in either of the countries. If the common customs tariff is lowered to less than $P_T - P_V$, country A will see a gain in welfare compared to a situation where the common tariff equals t. The lower the common tariff, the larger country A's gain will be.

Matters are slightly more complicated in country B. If the new customs tariff means that country B's domestic price lies between P_T and P_B, country B's loss will increase compared to the loss suffered under a common customs tariff equivalent to t. If the common customs tariff equals $P_B - P_V$, country B's loss will reach its maximum, G. If the external customs tariff is reduced to a level which is lower than $P_B - P_V$, the maximum loss suffered in relation to the price, P_B, will be reduced.

6.3 The effects of a customs union when economies of scale play a role

In the previous example, it was assumed that the supply curve increases when production increases. It is now assumed that there will be economies of scale connected with the production of a given product. The question is whether this means that there will be advantages associated with the customs union which are not taken into account when it is assumed that there is full competition with an increasing supply curve for the entire market. When the market expands, as a consequence of the customs union, it will be possible to produce goods at lower unit costs by rationalizing production, i.e. gathering production in fewer production units.

To illustrate this scenario, a number of assumptions have been set up which are illustrated in figure 6.4. Countries A and B are the

Figure 6.4: The effects of a customs union with economies of scale.

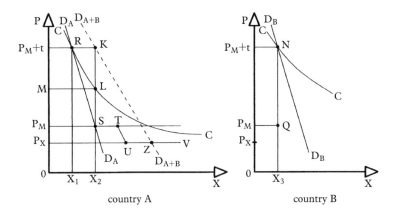

country A   country B

two member countries in the customs union. D_A and D_B show demand for the product in countries A and B, respectively.

The first assumption is that in each of the two countries there is actually or potentially a supplier on the market. The curves CC show the unit costs which must be covered in order for the company to be able to exist. The curves CC are identical in the two countries because production technology and factor return are the same in both countries.

The second assumption is that the world market price which countries A and B can get for the product is P_X. The import price that the two countries pay for imports from third countries equals P_M, which is higher than P_X, because transportation costs will be added to the price of imports from third countries.

The third assumption is that the curve CC always lies above P_X, which is the price that countries A and B can potentially get for their exports. From this assumption, it follows that neither country A nor country B exports their products to any third countries.

The fourth assumption is that countries A and B are not doing business with one another before they enter into the customs union.

In order to establish companies in countries A and B, the companies must be guaranteed a certain price $P \geq P_M + t$. Only in these cases will the turnover in the companies be equal to or higher than the total costs. Both countries have imposed tariffs, t, which gives a domestic price of P_M + t in the two countries and which again means that two companies can survive in the market, one in each country. The demand curve that the company in country A faces is P_M + t, R, S, T, U, V. At a price of more than P_M + t, country A will import the product from a third country. At a lower price t the demand will be RS. At a price of P_M, country A can take over the market in country B which means that ST equals OX_3. At the price, P_X, country A can sell its products on the world market.

When a customs union is established, tariffs, t, will be eliminated between countries A and B. This means that there will only be room for one company. If the company in country A takes over the market, the demand curve will be P_M + t, K, Z, V. Tariffs, t, still apply to imports from all third countries. If the company still sets the price at P_M + t, consumer surplus in the two countries A and B will remain unchanged. The company in country A will realize a gain which equals P_M + t, K, L, M. So country A will see a gain while consumers in country B will be in exactly the same situation as initially as the country's domestic production is replaced by imports from country A at the same price. Country B loses a company which means a loss of workplaces and it will also incur import costs.

The employment and the balance of payment problems that country B will experience in connection with the closure of its domestic company can be disregarded. It is reasonable to assume that in another sector where the conditions are similar to those in figure 6.2, a company in country B will take over the entire market and a company in country A will close. This can re-establish the same employment and balance of payment status as in the initial situation.

It was assumed that there was one company in each country in the initial situation. The result will be trade creation which is profitable to all the countries in the customs union. Other options exist though. For instance, there might initially only be one company in country A or there might be no companies in either of the countries.

In the situation where there is only one company in country A, country B will initially be importing goods from a third country. The price of imports will be, P_M, and country B will get a customs revenue equal to the area P_M + t, N, Q, P_M. When the two countries enter into a customs union, imports from the third country will be replaced by imports from country A. This means that country B will lose its customs revenue. Country B will instead import goods from country A at the price, $P_M + t$, which means that its terms of trade will deteriorate. Country A will still see a gain of $P_M + t$, K, L, M. Whether or not the customs union will do any good depends on whether country A's gains are bigger or smaller than country B's losses.

In the case where there is neither a company in country A nor in country B, the customs union will mean a loss in welfare. Countries A and B will lose revenue from customs equal to $(P_M + t - P_M)$ · OX_2, and their gains will only amount to $P_M + t$, K, L, M. In this case, the losses will always be bigger than the gains. If there is a trade diversion in both countries, the customs union will lose. If there is only a trade diversion in one country, the overall welfare of the customs union might go up or might go down.

It can therefore be concluded that if both countries initially produce the product in question, the customs union will experience an increase in welfare. If neither of the countries initially produce the product, the customs union will experience a loss. In the situation where there is one supplier in one country but no suppliers in the other country the overall welfare might go up or down.

In other words, introducing the assumption that there will be economies of scale does not have any impact on the conclusion that the more trade is created, the better, and the more trade is diverted the worse.

6.4 Non-discriminatory reductions of tariffs and customs unions

If country A enters into a customs union with country B, it will result in tariff discrimination between imports from country B and imports from countries that are not members of the customs union. This situation might obviously be compared to a situation where country A unilaterally reduces the tariffs imposed on both country B and other third countries.

It is assumed that the conditions are similar to those described in figure 6.2 with the accompanying text. The curves in figure 6.2 have been copied to figure 6.5.

In the first situation, country A, which has already imposed tar-

Figure 6.5: The effects of a unilateral reduction of tariffs by country A.

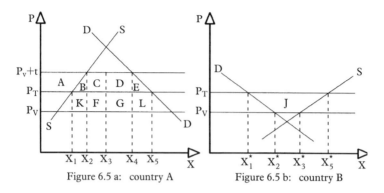

Figure 6.5 a: country A   Figure 6.5 b: country B

iffs, t, enters into a customs union with country B, so that the market price becomes P_T. In the second situation, country A decides unilaterally to lower its tariffs so that the market price in country A also becomes P_T. This means that the tariffs imposed by country A on all imports are lowered by $P_V + t - P_T$.

In the situation with the unilateral customs reduction, the total imports will, as in the case of the customs union, increase from $X_2 - X_4$ to $X_1 - X_5$, but the distribution of imports between country B and third countries will be different. In the customs union case, all imports will come from country B, whereas with a general tariff reduction imports from country B will remain unchanged $X_2 - X_3$. Imports from third countries will increase from $X_3 - X_4$ to a total of $X_1 - X_2$ and $X_3 - X_5$. So what are the effects on welfare in the two situations?

> Change in welfare in country A compared to the initial situation.
> Customs union case: $(B + E) - (F + G)$
> Tariff reduction case: $(B + E) + (K + L)$

If a customs union is established, it will result in a change in welfare in country A to the extent of $(B+E) - (F+G)$, see also the analysis in relation to figure 6.2. If country A implements a general reduction of tariffs, the new revenue from customs will be $K + F + G + L$. By reducing tariffs, country A will lose the customs revenue represented by areas C and D, however, this loss is set against an increase in consumer surplus. By reducing tariffs, country A will get income from tariffs which in addition to the original $F + G$ will also include K + L, which are the last elements of the change in welfare after tariffs are reduced, see above. It is thus clear that the welfare gains in country A in the tariff reduction case, compared to the customs union case, is K + L + F + G, which is the revenue from tariffs which country A will get when the country reduces its tariffs in general.

The analysis of country A's imports clearly shows that a non-discriminatory reduction of tariffs will always increase welfare compared to the establishment of a customs union. The establishment of a customs union can be seen to include two elements. In a customs union, the average tariff protection will be lower, because tariffs vis-à-vis country B will be zero and tariffs vis-à-vis third countries will remain unchanged, t. A customs union can therefore be thought of as consisting of two phases; a phase of general tariff reduction which is then followed by a phase of tariff discrimination. All the positive elements of a customs union are connected with the general reduction of tariffs and all the negative elements are connected with the tariff discrimination.

For country B as an exporting country, it is obvious that the customs union with country A will result in a gain of J, whereas if country A makes a unilateral reduction of tariffs, this will leave country B in an unchanged position compared to the initial situation. It is thus clear that country B will prefer a customs union to a unilateral reduction of tariffs when it comes to exports.

If we look at both countries together, it is obvious that a unilateral reduction of tariffs will increase welfare. It always follows that K + F + G + L is larger than J. It is therefore fair to ask if it is reasonable for two countries to enter into a customs union. The answer is not as simple as it appears from the analyses which have been carried out here. This is because the analyses do not take into account the adjustment problems.

If country A reduces tariffs unilaterally, the production in country A that competes with imports will drop. Imports will increase without a similar increase in exports to begin with. A balance of payment problem will arise. The gains associated with a reduction of tariffs will go to third countries which may have high levels of tariff protection on goods which country A has comparative advantages in producing. Third country tariffs may make it difficult or impossible for country A to export.

The analysis in figure 6.5 only deals with country A's imports. It is now possible to make a similar analysis of country A's exports and country B's imports. Figure 6.5b illustrates the conditions for exports from country A, and figure 6.5a the conditions for imports to country B. Also in this case, a unilateral reduction of tariffs by country B will result in an overall increase in welfare. Reducing tariffs in country B unilaterally will be better than creating a customs union. If both countries A and B introduced a non-discriminatory tariff reduction, it would be better than creating a customs union according to the analysis. However, the adjustment problems in country A are not alleviated by the fact that country B is also introducing a tariff reduction as country A's exports remain unchanged. What happens is that both countries' imports from third countries will increase without countries A or B seeing an increase in their own exports. Exports to third countries and the mutual exports between the two countries are constant. Again, it is the third countries that see increases in exports to both countries A or B. If the two countries A and B enter into a customs union, the increase in imports will result in an increase in exports to the partner country in the customs union. The adjustment in the production sector in the two countries will be easier and less far reaching.

Put in another way, a unilateral reduction of tariffs can be described as a »cold shower«. Firms that produce goods that are competing with imported goods will operate under harsher conditions, because they will experience keener competition without the benefit of new markets opening up to them. In a customs union, there are aspects of both a cold shower and the incentive of new export possibilities. The firms in country A are exposed to keener competition from firms in country B, but at the same time the protection of the markets in country B is removed in favour of the firms in country A.

In addition, imports from third countries will increase with the tariff reduction strategy but will decrease with the customs union strategy. If the third countries have imposed high tariff barriers which reduce exports from countries A and B or make them impossible, a unilateral reduction of tariffs will put these countries at an advantage, whereas with a customs union they will be penalized through a trade diversion. This might mean that it becomes easier for countries A and B to convince the third countries that they should lower their tariffs.

An overall assessment makes it difficult to claim that a unilateral reduction of tariffs will always be better for a country than to enter-ing into a customs union. How the customs union will work in the long run depends on how high the common customs tariff is.

6.5 The common tariff barrier and the effects of a customs union

In figure 6.5 and its associated analysis, it was assumed that the common customs tariff of the customs union was the same as country A's original customs tariff from before the customs union was established. As illustrated above, this can give rise to trade diversion. However, such diversion might be avoided if the common customs tariff is reduced compared to the original customs tariff.

The conditions which were described in figure 6.5 can also be described in a figure which shows country A's demand for imports, ID_A, and country B's supply of exports, ES_B, and a horizontal export supply curve for third countries equal to the world market price P_V. This scenario is illustrated in figure 6.6. The horizontal supply curve for the third countries indicates that the two countries A and B are small countries compared to the third countries. If countries A and B are large compared to the third countries, then the third countries' export supply curve will increase from left to right.

Initially, country A imposed import customs, t. This means that country B's export supply curve is $ES_B(t)$, which is the export sup-ply curve without customs ES_B plus the tariff, t. The vertical dis-tance between the two curves is constant as the customs duty is assumed to be at a fixed rate per traded unit. Tariffs will be added to the third country export supply curve which will give the export supply curve, $P_V + t$. Initially, the domestic price in country A equals $P_V + t$. This means that the quantity, X_1, is imported from country B and the quantity, X_1X_3, is imported from third coun-tries.

Now countries A and B enter into a customs union which means that country B's export supply curve will be ES_B, while the third countries' export supply curve continues to be $P_V + t$ if the com-mon customs tariff of the customs union equals country A's initial customs tariff of t. The result will be a lower price in the customs

Figure 6.6: The level of the common customs tariff.

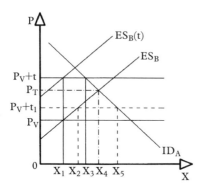

union, namely P_T. Country A will suffer a loss which is equal to the increased costs of the original imports from country B, the quantity X_1 which now costs P_T, and which was previously imported at world market prices, P_V.

At the same time, a trade diversion will occur as the import quantity X_1X_3 that previously originated from third countries at the price, P_V, is now replaced by imports from country B at the price P_T.

However, the loss which country A suffers as a result of the customs union might be reduced if the countries pick a common customs tariff that is less than $P_T - P_V$. If the common customs tariff is set at t_1, then $P_V + t_1$ will be the market price in the customs union. This means that the import volume from country B is reduced from X_4 to X_2, and that imports from third countries amount to X_2X_5. The lower external customs tariff of the customs union means that country A's deteriorated terms of trade stemming from imports from country B will be reduced while a trade diversion will be avoided. The lower customs tariff will open up for considerable imports from third countries at world market prices.

In the analysis, it was assumed that country A and country B were small countries in relation to third countries. If countries A and B, which have set up a customs union together, play a decisive role on the world market with respect to the product being analysed, it obviously follows that the export supply curve of the third countries will increase from left to right. This is illustrated in figure 6.7.

Third countries are referred to as country C and their export

Figure 6.7: A customs union might affect the world market price.

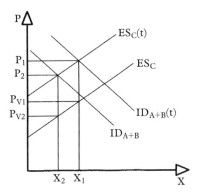

supply curve, ES_C, rises from left to right. When country C's exports to country A are subject to customs duties equal to t, $ES_C(t)$ will indicate the export supply curve for country C.

In this analysis country A is an importer and country B an exporter, like country C. The curve ID_{A+B} (t) is country A's demand for imports from country C, which is country A's total import demand minus imports from country B, when country B's exports are subject to customs duty t. The intersection between ID_{A+B} (t) and ES_C (t) indicates the price P_1, which is the internal price in country A, when country B and C's exports are subject to customs duty.

The quantity imported from country C will be X_1 and the world market will be price P_{V1}. When countries A and B enter into a customs union, country A will increase its imports from country B which means that country A's import demand for products from country C will drop to ID_{A+B}. It follows that the domestic price in the customs union will be P_2, imports from country C fall to X_2, and consequently, the world market price will fall to P_{V2}. The trade diversion which the customs union creates and which is reflected in a drop in import quantities from country C will reduce the import price in the customs union. In other words, we will see an improvement in the terms of trade vis-à-vis country C as a consequence of the trade diversion which, all things being equal, will reduce the negative consequences of the trade diversion. It is clear that country C will be the loser as it experiences both a trade diversion that reduces exports and deteriorated terms of trade.

6.6 What are best chances for a customs union to increase welfare?

The analyses in the previous sections show that in certain situations, a customs union can increase welfare while in other situations it can decrease welfare. The general rule is that there will always be some conditions that increase welfare and other conditions which reduce welfare. This is where the distinction between trade creation and trade diverison is decisive. As a rule trade creations increase welfare and trade diversions decrease welfare.

The chances that a customs union will increase welfare are therefore greatest the more trade it creates and the fewer trade diversions it causes. When are the chances for trade creation best and the risk of trade diversion least?

A number of different conditions come into play such as production conditions, the tariff level and the tariff structure before the customs union, the common customs tariff after the creation of the customs union and the number of member countries in the customs union.

The first conclusion which can be made is that the more uniform the structure of industrial sectors, the greater is the potential for creating trade. If the structure of the industrial sector, is less uniform, the risk of trade diversion is greater.

If the industrial structures in the two countries are alike, they will each have a food industry, a textile industry, a chemical industry and an engineering industry of the same size. If the comparative advantages of production are different, this will open up for specialization between the different industries. The greater the relative differences in production costs are for the different industries, the greater the inter-industry specialization will become in the two countries. The more uniform the production is with regard to product variants within a single industry, the less the companies in the different countries exploit the advantages of specialization, i.e. the advantages associated with producing a limited number of product variants. The customs union allows the firms to exploit these advantages through product specialization which leads to intra-industry trade. When the industrial structure is the same in the two countries, the likelihood that both countries import the same goods from third countries is much higher which means that the risk of trade diversion is lower.

The more dissimilar the structures of industrial sectors are in the two countries, the greater the likelihood that the two countries are already trading with each other before the customs union. Each of the two countries exports those products in which it is internationally competitive. Dissimilarity of industrial structures increases the likelihood that in areas where the partner country is not internationally competitive, the partner country imports goods from a third country before the establishment of the customs union. The risk that an inefficient member of the customs union will take over exports from efficient third countries is therefore greater. When the industrial structures are dissimilar in the two countries, the chances of trade creation are lower and the risks of trade diversion are higher.

This conclusion is supported by the fact that it is mainly industrial countries with the same economic level which harvest the advantages of entering into a customs union. In these countries the industrial structures are very similar, and there will be good opportunities for individual countries to obtain benefits if they enter into a customs union. This particularly applies to intra-industry trade creation where there are the advantages of specialization between firms with regard to product variants. The adjustment costs associated with intra-industry specialization are also considerably lower than in inter-industry specialization.

Customs unions between industrial and developing countries are more problematic. The industrial structures in industrial and developing countries are very different. The risks of trade diversion are much greater. At the same time, the trade creation that will take place will, to a much wider extent, be of an inter-industry nature which means that the adjustment to a new structure will be much more difficult.

Customs unions among developing countries have been put forward as a strategy to strengthen industries in developing countries. In most cases, the markets in individual developing countries are too small to take advantage of economies of scale which are necessary in order to reach efficient production levels. A customs union with a bigger 'home market' can solve this problem. A major problem for customs unions among developing countries is to ensure that all the individual member countries benefit equally from the formation of the customs union. If some of the countries are more developed than others it could easily mean that these more developed countries get all the gains. Even where the countries are at the same level, problems will arise if the market mechanisms which are supposed to guarantee the establishment of new companies do not work. If there are no private entrepreneurs who can take advantage of the new potentials, the public authorities must intervene to help set up new businesses. This calls for political agreement about where the companies should be located. As each country will look after its own interests and therefore would prefer to have as many production units as possible, experience shows that political disagreements can easily occur.

When customs unions are created among industrial countries, experience shows that it will lead to a considerable increase in intra-industry trade. Compared to poor countries, rich countries are characterized by a much more differentiated consumption pattern. The diversity between product variants that consumers prefer are much greater. The individual consumer also obtains a higher satisfaction by demanding a large number of different product variants. By creating a customs union between industrial countries, the product assortment will increase so the possibility of getting the best product variant and getting a larger product range increases. In developing countries, the consumption pattern is much less differentiated so developing countries will not experience the same advantages of increased product variation that industrial countries get.

Secondly, the tariff level and the tariff structure of the two countries prior to the customs union play a role. The tariff level and the tariff structure influence the industrial structure in the two countries. In general, if the two countries have a high degree of tariff protection there is reason to believe that both countries have their own production. The potential trade opportunities between the two countries after they enter into a customs union will therefore be considerable. How much trade will actually take place depends on the differences in costs in the two countries and the advantages of specialization for firms within the different industries. If the protection level is very high, chances of trade creation are good and the risks of trade diversion are small. If customs tariffs are low, the countries will have already specialized in the production areas where each of them has comparative advantages, so the chances of trade creation are small and risks of trade diversion are great. The example in figure 6.1 illustrates these conditions.

The customs structure also plays a role. There is a distinction between 'flat' customs tariffs, where the customs protection is the same for all products, and 'scaled' customs tariffs where the customs tariffs are very high on some products and very low on others. If it is assumed that each country has introduced high customs tariffs in areas where it is not competitive and low tariffs in areas where the country is competitive, there will be a considerable basis for trade creation if the two countries in the customs union start out with high and low customs tariffs in different product areas.

Thirdly, the level of the common customs tariffs is important for the result of the customs union. This has already been illustrated in section 6.5. If the common customs tariff is high, the risk of trade diversion that will lead to losses is high. This can be avoided by reducing the common customs tariff. If the customs union is large compared to the rest of the world and if the customs union continues to import from third countries, though to a lesser extent, the analysis in figure 6.7 shows that the customs union can force down the price of imported goods from third countries. Thus the customs union will get an improvement in its terms of trade. Third countries will lose in this situation since both export quantities and export prices will fall. The improved terms of trade in the customs union resulting from the trade diversion will in itself be an advantage to the customs union, but this gain must also be seen in the light of the losses which the trade diversion in itself will create.

If the common customs tariffs are lowered, the trade diversion and the losses associated with it will be reduced. On the other hand though, the improvement in the terms of trade will be small or non-existent. Total welfare will increase if the gain obtained from less trade diversion exceeds the loss of a less beneficial terms of trade.

This analysis has disregarded the fact that high common customs tariffs can inflict such losses on countries outside the customs union, which also have high levels of tariff protection, that they change their policy behaviour. The countries outside the union might see a benefit in cutting customs tariffs globally, so that a reduction of the protection level in the customs union will be met with a reduction of the protection level in third countries.

However, it does not follow that a customs union will lead to a global trade liberalization. The result might be that other customs unions are set up, leading to the creation of regional blocks each trying to increase discrimination against one another and against countries that are not members of customs unions. Unless there is a strong international set of regulations this can result in trade wars.

When countries are members of a customs union that has common customs tariffs, the countries in the union must agree on a common policy in relation to their participation in international tariff negotiations. It is obvious that a customs union has much stronger negotiating power than if each of the countries participates in international negotiations without coordinating their approach.

Fourthly, the more of a country's trading partners that are members of the customs union, the lower will be risk of trade diversion. The more countries that are members of the customs union, the greater the likelihood that the country that produces a product at the lowest cost is also a member of the customs union. The gains of a customs union for countries that already trade with one another depend on the potential for trade creation.

It is also an advantage of a customs union that the market structure for many products will change. If there are a number of small countries with customs protection there might be national monopolies or oligopolies in the individual countries. If these countries become members of a customs union, the national monopolies will be broken and the oligopolistic markets will see more suppliers. In other words the customs union will change the market structure so it becomes more competitive. It is also clear that competition will be keener if five small countries get together than if only two small countries set up a customs union.

6.7 Different kinds of regional integration

The EC/EU is the most developed regional co-operation. This co-operation started by setting up a customs union. Over time, co-operation has expanded into more and more fields. There are different kinds of integration as shown in figure 6.8 The most simple form of market integration is a free trade area where the countries decide to keep their own external customs tariffs or a customs union with common customs tariffs. A free trade area or a customs union usually only applies to industrial products and not to pri-

Figure 6.8: Different kinds of integration.

	Market integration			Economic – policy integration		Political integration
	Customs union	Common market	Single market	Monetary union	Economic union	
No customs and trade restrictions, common external customs.	X	X	X	X	X	X
Free movement of labour and capital.		X	X	X	X	X
Uniform product standards.			X	X	X	X
Fixed exchange rates and common monetary policy.				X	X	X
Common economic policy in general.					X	X
Common foreign and defence policy.						X
Common policy in general.						X

mary products like agricultural products. Agriculture was not part of EFTA nor of the customs union in the EC. For agriculture, the EC set up a number of market schemes to regulate the markets and allocate considerable subsidies to all farmers. Internal customs and import restrictions on agricultural products were eliminated and common regulations were set up for import protection vis-à-vis the rest of the world. It also meant that all member states had the same regulations on subsidies for exports to countries outside the EC. A common market goes one step further in that it not only opens the way for the free movement of goods but also of services, labour and capital. In a common market, production factors can move freely between countries. This applies to labour, financial movements of capital and direct investments.

The Treaty of Rome, which came into force on January 1, 1958, marked the start of the EC and it created the framework for the establishment of the common market. In 1987, the Single European Act came into effect. Its purpose was to set up a single market with common product standards with the elimination of all trade barriers and where individual member states could not give their domestic suppliers an advantage over suppliers from the other countries.

There are two problems which a customs union does not solve, but which it is the intention that the single market should solve. The first problem has to do with the countries' internal trade. The second has to do with the trade agreements which the individual countries enter into with countries outside the union.

The first problem which a customs union does not solve partly concerns hidden trade barriers and partly distortion of competition. A customs union will eliminate the more visible internal trade barriers, but it does not do anything about less visible trade barriers such as health and technical regulations for product standards. In order to protect consumers' health, a number of requirements may be laid down with regard to hygiene and product composition. In order to eliminate dangers from electrical apparatus and work-related injuries caused by machinery, certain technical specification must be observed. Such specifications are fully legitimate. However, if the product standards are not reasonably based on consideration for the consumer and society, but are based on consideration for domestic suppliers at the expense of foreign suppliers, such standards are hidden trade barriers. To solve this problem, when the Single European Act was signed, it was decided to introduce common product standards for all member states which individual countries cannot deviate from.

In order to get the single market to work without distorting competition, the member states must have a common set of regulations on government procurement and government subsidies to business. If a government can favour domestic suppliers without there being a commercial reason for it, this constitutes a distortion of competition. If a government can allocate money without limit, for instance, to shipyards, the competitiveness of the suppliers in each country will depend on how much money its government allocates. If the countries have different environmental standards, the environmental costs that the firms have to pay will differ from country to country which can again lead to a demand for common environmental standards (uniform regulations) or to an adjustment of the standards in the individual countries (harmonization). There will also be a pressure for more uniform regulation of competition. Monopolies and agreements that restrict competition cannot be treated differently in the member states.

Another problem that arises in connection with a customs union concerns the trade agreements that individual member states enter into with countries outside the union. In connection with the Multi Fibre Agreement, individual countries entered into bilateral agreements with textile producing countries outside the customs union which reduced the individual countries' imports. Individual countries have, on their own, signed agreements with the south-east Asian countries stipulating that the Asian countries will voluntarily limit their exports to the individual countries.

These agreements, which the countries enter into on their own, can result in prices varying in the different countries. An example of this is the banana market where each country had its own agreements which led to different prices on bananas. In order to avoid the movements of goods internally from one country, where the prices are low, to another country, where the prices are high, it is necessary to exercise customs controls at all borders to stop this trade which will otherwise reduce the value of the individual agreements. If the member countries want to eliminate border controls completely, the EU must act as a unified body when entering into agreements with individual exporting countries. In other words, the internal market means that individual member states can no longer enter into agreements on their own with countries outside the EU.

In 1993, the Treaty on European Union (Maastricht Treaty) entered into force. The important new thing about this treaty is that it reflects a wish to extend market integration by integrating economic policy through the creation of an economic and monetary union (EMU).

Aspects of the Maastricht Treaty also point towards increased political integration in the form of a common foreign policy, a common defence policy, a common police force, common external border control, etc. If the market integration is extended to include economic and monetary integration (EMU) and political integration, in general, then a political union is created.

6.8 Summary

In connection with regional trade agreements, it is important to distinguish between trade creation and trade diversion. When customs unions are set up, both trade creation and trade diversion will occur. The impact on welfare depends on the relationship between the two concepts. The more trade creation and the less diversion, the greater the advantages of the customs union will be. This applies both in cases of perfect competition and to economies of scale.

A customs union can be seen as a general reduction of customs tariffs by the members of the customs union, followed by discrimination between the countries within and outside the customs union. If all advantages are associated with the general reduction of customs and all disadvantages are associated with the discrimination, it must be concluded that a general reduction of customs is preferable. The difference is that by introducing a general tariff reduction, third countries will obtain greater advantages, whereas a customs union will secure mutual advantages for member states.

The common customs barrier which the customs union sets up has significant economic consequences. The lower it is, the smaller the risk of trade diversion. It is always possible to find a common protection level vis-à-vis the rest of the world which will put the rest of the world in the same position as prior to the setting up of the customs union.

A number of structural factors determine when the advantages of the customs union are greatest. The conclusion is that it is preferable if the countries that set up a customs union are alike. Based on the regional economic co-operation in the EC/EU, this section shows that regional co-operation can be more or less comprehensive.

Literature

Cooper, C.A. and B.F. Massell, »New Look at Customs Union Theory.« *Economic Journal*, 75, 1965.

Corden, W.M. »Economics of Scale and Customs Union Theory.« *Journal of Political Economy*, 80, 1972.

El-Agraa, A.M. »International Economic Integration« in Greenaway, D. (ed), *Current Issues in International Trade*, London, 1996.

Greenaway, D., T. Hylack and R. Thornton (eds). *Economic Aspects of Regional Trading Arrangements*, Brighton, 1989.

Hine, D.C. »International Economic Integration« in Greenaway, D. and L. A. Winters (eds), *Surveys in International Trade*, Oxford, 1993.

Kemp, M.C. and H. Wan, »An Elementary Proposition Concerning the Formation of Customs Unions«, *Journal of International Economics*, 6, 1976.

Pomfret, R., *Unequal Trade: The Economics of Discriminatory International Trade Policies*, Oxford, 1988.

Viner, J. , *The Custom Union Issues*, New York, 1950.

Wonnacott, G.P. and R.J. Wonnacott, »Is Unilateral Tariff Reduction Preferable to a Customs Union? The Curious Case of the Missing Foreign Tariff.« *American Economic Journal*, 71, 1981.

7. Trade and developing countries

After the Second World War, many of the countries in Africa, South Asia and South East Asia were still governed by European colonial powers. In the period up to the early 1960s, most countries in these areas gained their independence. Even though a number of the larger developing countries such as China, India, Pakistan and Brazil were co-signatories of the GATT treaty in 1947, it was the industrial countries that had decisive power when it came to shaping the international trade system.

One by one, a large number of the developing countries joined GATT and today almost all developing countries are members of the WTO. However, the developing countries have not played a very active role in the international trade and tariff conferences that have taken place under the auspices of GATT. The developing countries have mostly been interested in securing themselves exemptions from the GATT provisions. Not until the Uruguay Round did the developing countries play an active role.

Originally, the developing countries were mostly interested in exemptions from the GATT regulations. The developing countries particularly wanted to be exempted from the provision that they could not increase their tariff levels. The reason for this was that, in the beginning, the developing countries wanted to achieve industrialization through a policy of import substitution. They also wanted exemptions from the principle of reciprocity so that they were not committed to lowering their customs tariffs when the industrial countries lowered their protection level. Gradually, the developing countries found it important to increase their exports to the industrial countries. To obtain this goal they wanted preferential tariff treatment for their products when exported to industrial countries. Both the developing countries' own tariff protection and the preference schemes established with the industrial countries can be seen as the operation of the infant-industry argument. The developing countries were economically so far behind the industrial countries that both import protection through trade barriers and export promotion through tariff preferences were necessary tools. There is a distinction between 'conventional' reciprocity and 'real' reciprocity. Conventional reciprocity means that the developing countries are obliged to lower their import protection and they are not offered preference schemes. On the other hand, real reciprocity means that developing countries are allowed to keep or increase their tariff protection and, at the same time, they are offered preference schemes for their exports to industrial countries. According to the infant-industry argument, such schemes should only run for a limited period until the industries in the developing countries become competitive.

The original infant-industry argument was based on protection against imports, in other words a domestic redistribution from consumers to producers via higher domestic prices. Customs preference schemes differ from this because they lead to restribution from consumers in industrial countries to producers in developing countries.

Since the developing countries gained their independence, there has been considerable dissatisfaction with GATT. The developing countries have claimed that GATT does not adequately look after their interests. They have been very unhappy with the fact that both agricultural products and textiles have in reality been kept outside the realm of GATT.

Because of this dissatisfaction, in the early 1960s the developing countries suggested that a conference on trade and development should be held under the auspices of the UN. This brought about the first UNCTAD conference (United Nations Conference on Trade and Development) which took place in Geneva in 1964. This first conference has been followed by conferences in 1968 (New Delhi), 1972 (Santiago), 1976 (Nairobi), 1979 (Manila), 1983 (Belgrade), 1987 (Geneva) and in 1992 (Cartagena).

7.1 The effect of tariff preferences

How do tariff preference schemes affect developing countries? To answer this question, it is necessary to divide the countries into four categories. The first category consists of industrial countries which

Figure 7.1: The effects of a scheme with unlimited tariff preference.

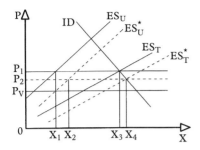

are net importers of a given product and which initially impose uniform tariff rates on all imports regardless of the country of origin. The second category consists of industrial countries which are net exporters of the product and which do not have any tariff protection. The third category consists of developing countries which are net exporters of the product and which have agreed with the net importing industrial countries on a scheme for easing the tariffs imposed on their exports. The fourth category consists of developing countries which are also net exporters but which have no agreements on preference schemes.

Under a tariff preference scheme, the participating developing countries either pay lower tariffs or no tariffs at all while exporting industrial countries and exporting developing countries that are not participating in the scheme pay full tariffs. It is assumed that the developing countries which participate in the preference scheme can export at the lower tariff rate without limit. The result is a diversion of trade as the developing countries that participate in the scheme will take over part of the export volume from industrial and developing countries that are not part of the scheme. Developing countries with higher production costs will now become competitive because of the tariff preference. This is illustrated in figure 7.1 where ID illustrates the import demand in the net importing industrial countries. ES_u is the export supply curve for the net exporting developing countries, which subsequently get tariff preferences, when their exports are subject to tariffs equal to $t = P_1 - P_V$. When the net exports from the other industrial and developing countries are added to the export supply curve the result is the total export supply curve, ES_T. This supply curve illustrates the supply when

everybody has to pay tariff, t. The domestic price in the net importing industrial countries will be P_1 and the world market price without a tariff is P_V.

Now all the developing countries with the prefix U are accepted
into a preference scheme which means that they do not have to pay
any tariffs. This means their export supply curve becomes $ES_U{}^\star$
which is lower than the original export supply curve to the extent of
tariff t. The total export supply curve will be $ES_T{}^\star$ as a result of the
tariff preference scheme.

Originally, exports from the developing countries which are later
accepted into the preference scheme amounted to OX_1, and
exports from the other exporting countries are X_1X_3. After the
preference scheme enters into force, exports from the first group of
countries increase to OX_2, and exports from the other group of
countries drop to X_2X_4. A trade diversion occurs.

At the same time, the market price will fall from P_1 to P_2 in the
industrial countries which have set up a tariff preference scheme.
This means that the world market price without a tariff will be P_2 –
t. The countries that do not participate in the preference scheme
will see a deterioration of their terms of trade and their export volume will be reduced. The developing countries that do participate
in the scheme will see an improvement of their terms of trade
equivalent to $OP_2 - OP_V$ and an increase in their exports.

An important assumption behind this analysis is that the developing countries getting the preference will get this preference no
matter how much they export to the industrial countries that grant
the preference. In most preference schemes, the preference only
applies to a certain quota. If the developing country's exports
exceed this quota, their surplus exports will be subject to tariffs
equivalent to those imposed on other exporters that do not participate in the preference scheme.

In figure 7.2, the import demand and the export supply curves
are the same as in figure 7.1. The new aspect is that the developing
countries that are granted a customs exemption only get this
exemption on a certain volume, OX_1, which, in figure 7.2, is equivalent to the volume that these countries were exporting before the
preference scheme was set up. The result is that there will be no
trade diversion. Exports from the countries that get preference and
the countries that are not part of a preference programme are still
OX_1 and X_1X_3, respectively. However, the preference countries will

Figure 7.2: The effects of a scheme with limited tariff preference.

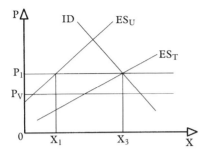

see an improvement in their terms of trade because they are exempted from tariffs. Their export price will be P_1, whereas before it was P_V. The importing countries will feel this improvement in the exporting countries' terms of trade as they will lose their revenue from customs duties equivalent to $OX_1 \cdot (P_1 - P_V)$. In other words, the preference scheme will transfer income from the industrial countries that offer the preference scheme to the developing countries that participate in it. The conditions for the exporting countries that are not part of the scheme will remain unchanged.

A preference scheme with a maximum quota requires a certain administrative system which will grant each country an export quota that must then be allocated to the exporting producers in the individual country. The exporting country can either allocate the quotas without charge or they can sell them. By selling the export quotas the government will get a revenue which can be used for subsidies to the industries considered to have comparative advantages in the country.

It is difficult to generalize about the effects of a preference scheme. The number of countries participating in a scheme is significant, as is the extent of the preference scheme with regard to the number of products affected. One possibility is for all industrial countries to offer a preference to all developing countries on all the products that the developing countries export. If there are no limiting of quotas, the developing countries will increase their exports, and the production in the industrial countries will be reduced. World market prices might fall, but the developing countries' terms of trade will improve because they will only have to pay a reduced customs tariff or no tariff at all. Such a preference scheme would lead to a general transfer of income from the industrial countries to the developing countries. In connection with such a programme, the industrial countries must implement certain structural changes. For goods that an industrial country does not produce itself, it will typically have no customs duty. If the industrial country produces a certain product itself, it will be competing with the developing country for market share and therefore, there will usually be some kind of protection. Frequently, industrial countries will have a high level of protection in areas where developing countries have clear competitive advantages. The protection that the industrial countries have is usually higher than indicated by the nominal customs tariffs. This is because tariff escalation. Raw materials from the developing countries are often not subject to tariffs, semi-manufactured products based on raw materials are subject to relatively low custom tariffs, and finished products are subject to high customs tariffs. This means that the effective protection on processing is much higher than indicated by the nominal customs tariffs, see section 1.7.

If the actual customs tariffs in the industrial countries reflect the lack of competitiveness of the industrial countries compared with products from developing countries, a general preference scheme might lead to new production units being created in the developing countries that have comparative advantages. This will, of course, give rise to certain adjustment problems for the weak industries in the industrial countries that might already be experiencing problems. Therefore, it can be difficult to secure political support for a general preference scheme that extends to all products from developing countries, without any limiting quotas.

Another approach is to create a preference scheme which only extends to some developing countries, to a limited number of products and with quota limitations. With such a system, trade diversion will not occur between the developing countries that participate in the scheme and the countries that are outside the scheme. Through the quota scheme, the adjustment of production in industrial countries will be minimal, while it will be possible to avoid trade diversion in relation to the countries that do not participate in the scheme. This means that the advantages to the developing countries that do participate do not necessarily harm the developing countries that do not participate. The extent of benefits to developing countries from being part of a scheme, depends not only on the size of the tariff preference, but also on whether the products covered by the preference scheme belong to product groups in which the developing countries have special comparative advantages. If the product groups included in the scheme do not cover products which are important in the development process, the preference scheme will have limited value. In addition it should be mentioned that it is difficult in practice to identify specific industries where the developing countries have comparative advantages. These will in any case change as the developing countries develop.

From the perspective of the developing countries, it is particularly unfortunate if the number of goods under the preference scheme is limited and does not extend to product groups where the developing countries have comparative advantage. It is also obvious that quotas will have a negative effect if the preference scheme includes products in which the developing countries have comparative advantages. They will not be able to expand their production capacity optimally because the volume that they can export on favourable terms will be limited. On the other hand, it cannot be denied that even a quota system might trigger investments which will give the companies export experience and allow them to improve production efficiency through 'learning by doing' which will enable them to compete on the world market even though the surplus export volume is subject to tariffs. This particularly applies to the more advanced developing countries.

It is a cardinal question whether the preference scheme is to include all developing countries or only some of them. The developing countries are a very heterogeneous group; some developing countries are so highly developed that it is reasonable to question whether they have not in fact become industrial countries. This applies, for instance, to the newly industrialized countries. Other developing countries have a much smaller production capacity and at the lower end of the income scale, there are the least developed countries. It could be argued that it would make sense to set up special preference schemes for the least developed countries which other developing countries would not profit from or which they would only profit from to a limited extent through small quotas.

It can therefore be concluded that the way preference schemes work depends, to a large extent, on how they have been set up. It is fair to ask if there are alternatives to preference schemes. Instead of preference schemes, tariffs could be reduced on all products from the developing countries. Rather than preference schemes that only extend to a limited number of products and which set up quotas, a general reduction of customs tariffs might be a better alternative. A general reduction of the customs tariffs will be of particular benefit to richer developing countries and will not really help the poorer developing countries. So it could be argued that there should be special preference schemes for the poorest countries. Alternatively, one could propose a general tax on all industrial countries to transfer wealth to the developing countries, or one could propose that a part of the present VAT should be transferred to the developing countries, scaled according to the level of development of the developing country in question. It is possible that the advantages that developing countries get under preference schemes are included in the calculation of the industrial countries' development aid programmes. If preference schemes were set up, this might result in a cut in the development aid otherwise granted to a developing country. So the question is whether direct development aid, including money transfers, is actually a better way of promoting economic development than preference schemes. Money transfers to developing countries can be used to subsidize industries which will offer comparative advantages in the long run.

It is not possible to draw any general conclusions as to whether preference schemes are better than money transfers. The result depends on the nature of the preference schemes and the efficiency of the development aid offered through the transfer payments. A solution might be to use both preference schemes and transfer payments.

Preference schemes might have the advantage that they offer potential markets for industries. If an export production is developed initially, it might become the basis of an export oriented development strategy instead of an inward looking import substitution strategy which is particularly problematic in small developing countries because of the limited market potentials..

7.2 The general preference system

One of the central questions that was discussed at the first UNCTAD conference was the establishment of a preference system for the developing countries (Generalised System of Preferences – GSP). The less developed countries, in particular, were interested in preference schemes instead of general multilateral reductions of tariffs based on the principle of the Most Favoured Nation clause. Tariff protection in the industrial countries vis-à-vis industrial products from the developing countries was generally higher than their protection against industrial products from other industrial countries. A general tariff reduction aimed at industrial products exported by the developing countries would be of particular benefit to the more advanced developing countries.

Negotiations to establish a GSP system were ongoing from 1964 until 1971. In 1971, the EC introduced a GSP system. Shortly after, Japan did the same, and in 1976 the US introduced its GSP system. These preference systems meant that most industrial products and semi- manufactured products from the developing countries were exempted from tariffs. On the face of it, this sounds like a major step in the direction of a comprehensive preference system for the developing countries. However, that was not the case because the programmes also had several limitations.

From the perspective of the developing countries, the product areas that the GSP programmes extend to are very limited. Both agricultural and fisheries products in raw and processed form are exempted. The same applies to textiles which are covered by the Multi Fibre Agreement. Basically, this means that the product areas in which the developing countries have comparative advantages are exempted from tariff preferences. Secondly, quotas have also been introduced so that the tariff exemption is limited to certain import quantities Thirdly, the programmes give no guarantees to the developing countries that they will continue in the future. The first GSP programmes ran for a period of 10 years and even though they were in fact extended several times, the time limitation creates uncertainty. Even more uncertainty is created by the different exemption provisions which the industrial countries have built into their programmes. The customs preferences may thus be repealed if so-called 'market disturbances' occur on the markets of the industrial countries.

The result of these programmes is that less than 20 percent of the exports from the less advanced developing countries is covered by the GSP programmes. It is the newly industrialized countries, a very limited number of countries, that have profited most from the programmes. 80 percent of the developed countries' imports under the programmes came from 7 newly industrialized countries, namely South Korea, Taiwan, Hong Kong, Singapore, Brazil, Mexico and Israel.

When assessing the programmes, it must also be taken into account that the tariff advantages that the developing countries originally got have been eroded as a result of the general reduction of tariffs between the industrial countries. The GSP programmes were introduced in the 1970s when tariff protection against typical consumer goods which the less advanced developing countries were interested in was usually 15 percent. If tariff escalation in the industrial countries is taken into account, the effective protection might have been between 20 and 30 percent. This preference margin was reduced when the industrial countries subsequently reduced their tariffs.

From the perspective of the less developed countries, the weakness of the programmes is that the product areas covered by the programmes do not include processed and non-processed agricultural products and textiles. It can be concluded that the programmes have had some limited value for the newly industrialized countries which have been able to make use of them, but that they have had no significant value for the less advanced developing countries.

7.3 Different kinds of price changes

Already at the first UNCTAD conferences, there were discussions on how to stabilize the international prices for raw materials. However, not until the UNCTAD conference in Nairobi in 1976 did the question of stabilizing raw material prices become a central question.

The background to the discussion was first of all that on many primary products there seems to be a long term tendency for their prices to fall compared to the prices of industrial products. Secondly, there is a tendency for the prices of primary products to fluctuate more than the prices of industrial goods.

Both of these aspects can create problems for the less developed countries whose income from exports stems mainly from primary goods. For many of the less developed countries 80 to 90 percent of their export revenue come from primary products. For developing countries that are highly dependent on the export of primary products, if the terms of trade deteriorate this is an obvious problem which will prompt these countries to try to reduce their dependence on revenues from exports of raw materials, either by adopting a strategy of import substitution or through an increase in the export of industrial products. Even if the terms of trade of the developing countries do not deteriorate, the constantly fluctuating prices of primary products can create problems because fluctuations in export revenue can disturb the development of developing countries.

When analysing price development and considering measures to prevent price fluctuation, it is important to distinguish between long term trends in prices and medium and short term price fluctuations.

Long term price development is determined by long term changes in demand and supply. For most food products and for products such as coffee, tea and cocoa, demand in industrial countries is only slightly on the increase because the income elasticity of demand for these products is very small, close to zero. For raw materials such as natural rubber, silk, cotton, wool and jute, a number of synthetic products have been developed which have partly taken over the market. Finally, technological advances have meant that today, less raw materials are needed for the production of industrial products. For instance, less steel is used in the production of machines and durable consumer goods, such as cars, etc. Also the supply side has seen major long term changes. Supply has increased when new oil resources have been found and when there have been technological advances in the production of agricultural products.

In the medium term, price fluctuations occur in connection with business cycles. In periods of growth, demand for raw materials increases and in times of recession, demand decreases. On the markets for raw materials, the price is fixed at the point where demand and supply meet and since supply is quite inelastic in terms of price, considerable price fluctuation can occur. For industrial products, there is monopolistic competition which means that when there are market fluctuations, firms keep their prices stable and adjust to the new market conditions through changes in their production volume. In the medium term, price fluctuations can also occur because production adjustments take time to work through, as shown by the 'cob web' theory. Price fluctuations of this kind have occurred in pork production and in the production of certain tropical raw materials such as coffee and cocoa.

There are also price fluctuations in the short term. Typically, they occur in the production of agricultural products where the weather and diseases can influence the size of the harvest from one year to the next. If the world market for agricultural products were free, the effects of good and bad weather in different parts of the world would eliminate each other and create more stability. Only if good or bad weather coincided in different parts of the world would there be major price fluctuations.

7.4 Measures against long term price changes

There seems to be a long term trend towards falling real prices for several primary products. It is necessary to be careful not to generalize too much since price development differs for different raw materials. It is thus clear that for tropical beverages such as coffee, tea and cacao and for natural fibres such as cotton and jute, the relative fall in prices has been steeper than for metals. Within the group of metals, the trend has also varied depending on the size of the supply compared to the demand for the different metals. When assessing a price trend, it is important to note which year is selected as the base year. In times of war prices of a number of raw materials will rise dramatically. If an analysis is based on a year with high prices, a fall in price will look more dramatic than if a year with more 'normal' price levels is taken as the base year.

Could or should governments intervene to prevent the terms of trade between raw materials and industrial products developing unfavourably for raw materials, thus harming many less developed countries? Measures could either be international commodity agreements which would in principle extend to both producing and consuming countries, or the establishment of international cartels consisting of the producing countries alone.

Setting up international commodity agreements is very complicated because countries have different interests. Developing countries do not necessarily constitute a bloc vis-à-vis industrial countries. Production of particular raw materials takes place in some developing countries but not necessarily in all developing countries, while many industrial countries have raw material production. Even though industrial countries are consumers of raw materials, so are developing countries. While it may be politically possible to set up commodity agreements, it is difficult to get them to work in practice because they require a number of agreements on production limitations by producing countries and agreements on 'forced purchases' by consuming countries. All parties must reach agreement on the price level, and the overall supply must be limited to the amount that consumers are willing to buy at that price. Such agreements put market forces out of play. New producing countries cannot enter the market unless the agreements are changed. If technological advances mean that supply is increased and demand is decreased, the agreements must be changed. Even if it is possible to maintain the agreements, it may be questioned how valuable they are for the producing countries. When the price level is unnaturally high, the producing countries must adjust their volumes and in the long run this adjustment could be considerable if there is decreasing demand and increasing supply. The EU's agricultural programmes excellently illustrate all the problems that arise when a system of bureaucratic pricing is set up which is totally divorced from the market conditions. International product agreements give both producing and consuming countries strong reasons for breaking the agreements.

Instead of international commodity agreements which, in principle, extend to all producing and all consuming countries, it is possible to set up a cartel of producing countries to oversee that production limitations are implemented, so that all the member states secure the monopoly price. Such cartels can only achieve their goals if consumers cannot use substitutes and if all the important producing countries are members of the cartel. An example of such a cartel is OPEC (Organization of Petrol Exporting Countries). Through specific agreements, a number of the major oil producing countries try to fix a certain world market price for oil. This happens through an agreement which grants the individual member country a certain production quota. The total effect is a limitation of supply which, with the existing demand, guarantees that the member countries are certain to get the intended price on the world market. The history of OPEC illustrates all the major problems which are associated with such an arrangement.

Even though oil is a product which cannot be substituted in a

number of situations, substitutes for oil do exist. For electricity and
heat generation there are alternative sources of energy, for example,
coal, natural gas, nuclear power and renewable sources of energy.
Also, high prices for oil have prompted a number of measures
which are aimed at reducing the demand for oil. Steps have been
taken in areas such as housing insulation, new energy-conserving
cars and machines. At the same time, the high prices for oil have
made it more profitable to exploit new oil sources, for instance, the
off-shore resources in the North Sea. The market power of the
OPEC countries is reduced partly through a fall in demand, and
partly through an increase in supply from new producers.

The history of OPEC also shows how difficult it is to sustain the
power of the cartel when the countries that constitute the cartel
have different interests. Iran, Nigeria and Venezuela are countries
with large populations that need as much revenue from oil as possible in order to develop their countries. Saudi Arabia and the other
producers of the Arabian Peninsula are countries with small populations which already have major foreign assets. Their need to
secure a revenue from oil exports is not as great. The ideal situation
for the first group of countries would be if they were granted large
production quotas while the major oil producing countries of the
Arabian Peninsula reduced their production considerably to make
sure that the total supply on the world market did not get so high
that the price of oil got too low. Saudi Arabia, in particular, has
been considered a 'buffer country' which would allow the other
countries to export large quantities while Saudi Arabia, by limiting
its own production, guaranteed a high price. Conflicts have arisen
because Saudi Arabia has only been willing to take on this role to a
certain extent. The result has been a lower price for oil than any of
the countries could ever have wanted. A cartel can, in some ways,
be compared to one single big country which has a major share of
the world production of a given product. Such a country might
experience improved terms of trade if export tariffs or production
limitations are introduced. The difference is that where the individual country can decide on such intervention unilaterally, a cartel
requires that everybody in the cartel agrees to a goal and on how to
achieve this goal.

It should of course be mentioned that oil is a non-renewable
resource and its maximum exploitation would create special problems. It could be desirable to ensure, through international co-

operation and through the pricing of oil, that the resource is not depleted too rapidly but that the existing resources are exploited over a period of time.

Moreover, oil consumption also involves a number of externalities in the form of environmental effects. International co-operation to introduce a tax on oil which takes these externalities into account could also be desirable.

From a global perspective, it can thus be reasonable to intervene in a number of situations to prevent falling prices. From the developing countries' perspective it would be desirable to try to improve the terms of trade for their products. The problem is, however, that it is difficult to get such a co-operation to work effectively. If initiatives could be taken, developing countries would immediately see an improvement of their terms of trade. Whether this would lead to an economic development which the developing countries could not otherwise have reached, by receiving the same financial support through different kinds of aid from the developed countries, can be discussed endlessly. If the raw material producing countries are to get higher prices for their products in general, market schemes must be introduced for a large number of raw materials. If the developing countries do not heed the market forces which will in the long run undermine the present market schemes with their advantages, the less developed countries may be trapped in a position as raw material producers instead of switching to alternative development strategies with a much better long term perspective.

7.5 Stabilization of prices in the medium term and in the short term

There is not much prospect in trying to neutralize the long term trend of falling prices for raw materials compared to industrial products. On the other hand, it makes much more economic sense to consider whether it is worth trying to eliminate price fluctuations in the medium and short term. Initially, it is always advantageous for both producers and consumers to have stable prices instead of widely fluctuating prices. For producers it is easier to plan, and for consumers it means that they will not have to face demand cuts when prices are increasing. If stable prices lead to more stable investments and a smoother development for the country as a whole, because the necessary foreign earnings are also more stable, a series of advantages will have been achieved.

In the following, two situations are compared. In one situation, prices are constant and in the other prices fluctuate around an average level which is equivalent to the price level in the first situation. If the two price situations also mean that income in the first situation is constant but fluctuates in the second, there is immediate reason to believe that price stability is to be preferred.

It is possible to distinguish between three approaches to risk, namely: risk neutrality, risk aversion and risk preference. If producers and consumers are indifferent to whether income is constant or fluctuating, they are risk neutral. If they prefer income stability instead of income fluctuation, they are risk averse. If they prefer fluctuating prices instead of stable prices, they have a risk preference. When it comes to financial risks of a certain size, most people will be risk averse. From a general welfare point of view, risk must therefore be reduced and income stability secured.

If a stable income also means that it is possible to make better long term decisions, for instance, in connection with investments, stable income will also mean efficiency gains.

Studies show that prices of raw materials fluctuate more than prices of industrial products. When it is considered that the majority of exports from the least developed countries consists of primary goods, that exports from each individual country are often concentrated on only a few raw materials, and that exports are often geographically concentrated in a few importing countries, the supposition must be that the least developed countries' revenue from exports must fluctuate more than other countries' revenue from exports. Studies seem to confirm this supposition. But at the same time, the studies seem to indicate that variations in export revenue can be ascribed to fluctuations in export volume rather than fluctuations in export prices.

The first question to arise is whether price stability on raw materials is to be preferred because it guarantees the less developed countries a more stable export revenue. The second question is whether a more stable revenue from exports promotes economic development in the developing countries. The results of the studies do not provide precise answers to this question. Some analyses do not show any connection between greater stability in revenue from exports and greater economic growth. This does not mean that

Figure 7.3: Price stabilization when changes in supply create price fluctuations

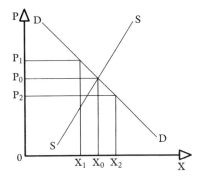

such a connection does not exist as there might be a number of other conditions which determine growth and which interfere so that a positive correlation cannot be read from the figures. Other analyses seem to point towards a positive correlation between stability in export revenue and the extent of investments in the developing countries.

In the above, it is assumed that price stability leads to stability in export revenue. The question is whether this assumption holds true. In such an analysis, it is necessary to distinguish between whether it is changes in supply or changes in demand that create price instability.

In figure 7.3, it is supply side changes that create the price fluctuation. It might, for instance, be changes in the weather conditions which result in the harvest being small one year and big the next. DD is world market demand for a given agricultural product. SS is world market supply during normal weather conditions and it is according to this supply curve that the producers make their plans. Producers expect to get a price of P_0, and they plan to deliver the amount X_0. If the crop fails, they will only be able to supply the amount X_1 to the market, and the world market price will be P_1. If the crop is exceptionally good, illustrated by X_2, world market price will be P_2. Because of the weather, supply will fluctuate around X_0.

If a system were set up by which it would be possible to increase supply by X_1X_0, in the case where the harvest is X_1, it will be possible to secure a world market price of P_0. In the case where the harvest is good, that is X_2, it will be possible to secure a world market price of P_0, as long as the supply is limited to X_0. If the system involved private stockholding so that supply will always be X_0 regardless of variations in the size of the harvest, it will be possible to ensure a constant price of P_0. It is possible to conceive of collectively financed stocks which would guarantee a constant supply.

So what would the consequence be of such a system which guarantees a constant supply and thus constant prices compared to a situation without intervention where the changes in supply will give rise to fluctuating prices?

The interesting aspect of this example is that, without intervention, prices and volumes will fluctuate in opposite directions which in itself helps stabilize revenue from exports even though volume and prices fluctuate. If the demand curve is isoelastic with elasticity numerically equal to one, revenue from exports will be constant. If the demand curve is isoelastic with elasticity either numerically less or greater than one, it might result in fluctuations in revenue from exports. If supply is small, revenue will be higher than the average when the demand elasticity is numerically less than one. Inversely, there will be a fall in revenue from exports if the supply is large. The opposite applies if the demand elasticity is greater than one.

If it is assumed that one country is selling a given product on the world market and that this country has introduced a national buffer-stock policy which will guarantee a price level of P_0, the country's revenue from exports will be constant. On the other hand, this does not apply to the producers' income if they get paid for their products as soon as they sell into stock. In good years, when the harvest is big, the producers will get an income of $OX_2 \cdot OP_0$, and in bad years, when the harvest is small, their income will be $OX_1 \cdot OP_0$.

What would the situation be, if an international buffer-stock system were set up to purchase stocks in years when the harvest is good and sell from the stock in bad years? Cash settlement to the producing countries would take place at the time of purchase of the stocks which would mean that in good years income would be $OX_2 \cdot OP_0$ and in bad years it would be $OX_1 \cdot OP_0$. In this case, the price stability system would result in fluctuations in foreign earnings. If the revenue from exports is paid directly to the producing farmers, they would also see fluctuating income as a result of the international system of buffer-stocks.

The conclusion is, therefore, that in situations where price fluc-

Figure 7.4: Price stabilization when demand changes create price fluctuations

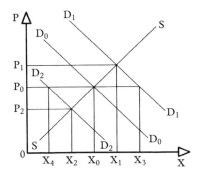

tuations are caused by changes in supply, price stabilization is not needed to stabilize a country's revenue from exports and the producers' income. However, it is clear that if price fluctuations on the world market causes price fluctuations in food prices on the home market, this can create problems for consumers, especially consumers with low income. If price stabilizing measures are introduced, they might contribute to larger fluctuations in the producers' income.

Price fluctuations might also be caused by changes in demand, for instance, in connection with cyclical fluctuations in economic activity. This situation is illustrated in figure 7.4 in which it is assumed that supply will immediately adjust to the new equilibrium prices which result from changes in the demand conditions. SS is the market supply and the DD curves are demand curves. D_0D_0 is demand under normal market conditions. P_0 is the equilibrium price and the supply will be X_0, which gives revenue from exports equivalent to $OX_0 \cdot OP_0$. During periods of growth, the demand curve will be D_1D_1, which results in a price of P_1 and a supply of X_1, which provides the exporting country with an income from exports to the tune of P_1X_1. During periods of recession, demand will fall to D_2D_2 which means a price of P_2 and a supply of X_2 and revenue from exports to the tune of P_2X_2.

In this case, fluctuating world market prices will also result in widely fluctuating revenues from exports because prices and volumes either both increase or both fall. If a system is set up to stabilize the price P_0, revenue from exports will also be stabilized.

An international buffer stock could also be a price stabilizing solution in this case. During periods of recession, the amount X_4X_o is purchased at a price of P_o, and during periods of growth, the amount X_oX_3 is sold also at a price of P_o.

It can thus be concluded that where changes in demand cause the price fluctuations, it is much better to intervene through a stock policy than where the price fluctuations are caused by changes in supply.

7.6 International commodity agreements

In the previous section, it was shown that price stabilization does not always lead to a stabilization in a country's income from exports or to a stabilization of the producers' income. If price fluctuations are due to changes in supply, it is more problematic, from the point of view of the producers, to intervene by using price stabilization, than in cases where the price fluctuations are due to changes in demand. In this connection, experience shows that price fluctuations are, to a much higher degree, contingent on changing supply rather than on changes in demand. It would therefore be a solution to set up a price stabilization system which would only be used to intervene when there are changes in demand, but not when there are changes in supply. Such a system would be difficult to set up. Consumers would feel uncomfortable with price fluctuations caused by changes in supply. Also, it will be difficult, in practice, to determine, at the time when intervention might be needed, whether the price fluctuations were caused by changes in demand or changes in supply.

Full price stabilization is not desirable because it puts the market mechanisms completely out of play. In practice, it would not be possible to enter into agreements which secure full stability. It is, therefore, quite natural that the aim of international agreements has been to take the top off increases in prices and the bottom off the decreases in prices.

International commodity agreements are built on the idea that there is a 'normal' price and that prices will fluctuate around this price from time to time. In figure 7.5, the price, P_o, lies at the point where 'normal' demand and 'normal' supply meet. Then, a ceiling is established indicating how high the price may rise and a floor indicating how low the market price may fall. In figure 7.5, these

Figure 7.5: Ceiling price and floor price formation

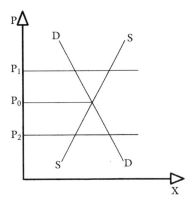

two prices are shown as P_1 and P_2, respectively. Within this price range, market forces are in place in the form of changing conditions for supply and demand which determine the price formation.

The content of the international commodity agreement determines the mechanisms which guarantee that prices will not be higher than P_1 or lower than P_2. It might, for instance, be a system with buffer-stocks or a system with international quotas.

If a system with international buffer-stocks has been set up, products will be sold from the stocks when the price is on the rise and likely to exceed P_1. Conversely, if the prices are getting close to or lower than P_2, products will be bought up on the market and the international stocks will grow.

Countries may also enter into agreements about international quotas. Producing countries will be allocated export quotas and importing countries import quotas which depend on the market price. If the price is high and close to P_1, producing countries are committed to increase their exports and importing countries are committed to reduce their imports. Conversely, when prices are low, producing countries are committed to reduce their exports and consuming countries committed to increase their imports.

Both kinds of agreement are intended to stabilize price formation. Setting up international product agreements often poses major problems and it has also proved to be difficult to get them to work. The difficulties associated with setting up quota agreements have already been illustrated in section 7.4. Similar problems apply to agreements on international buffer-stocks.

Firstly, all producing and consuming countries must be in agreement. It is important to avoid the 'free rider' problem which arises when some countries see an advantage in not being part of the agreement and saving costs by standing outside it, while profiting from the price stabilization which the system with buffer-stocks provides.

Secondly, it is necessary to procure adequate financial means to purchase products for the stock when there is surplus in supply. Conversely, it is necessary to have adequate stocks to be able to offer products on the market when there is a deficit in supply. There must be international agreement about sharing the costs that individual countries must pay to make sure that there are enough financial means to buy up products and to cover the expenses of holding the international stocks.

Thirdly, there must be agreement about the range within which prices can fluctuate without intervention. Price fluctuations which are caused by changes in supply, more than by changes in demand, do not necessarily create particular changes in the revenue of the producing countries. This might suggest adopting a wide price range. If only limited financial means are allocated to the programme, this also suggests opting for a wide price range. The less ambitious the countries are with regard to stabilizing the prices, the cheaper the programme will be.

Fourthly, if an international price stabilization system is to survive, there must be a realistic perception of how the price of a given product will change over the long term. If there is a long term tendency for prices to fall, problems will arise if the price level that is considered normal is not slowly reduced. Too high a price will result in purchases being made for stocks more frequently than products being sold from the stocks. The overall result will be growing international stocks which cannot be sold and which cost more and more to keep. If the intention of the stabilization programme is not only to eliminate price fluctuation in the short and medium term but also to guarantee a higher normal price, the programme will, from the beginning, face major problems. Even though it is the intention to adjust the normal price against the long term development, it might be difficult to do so in practice. This is because, in practice, it is hard to distinguish between medium term price fluctuations and price development in the long run.

Fifthly, an extensive international price stabilization system might make private stocks less attractive. If private stocks are reduced, the pressure on the international system to act as a buffer-stock will increase. Private inventory costs will be replaced by public inventory costs. To what extent private stocks are price stabilizing or price destabilizing depends on the nature of the price speculation. What makes private firms keep stocks is the prospect of making a profit. If prices increase over a period of time from t until t + 1, it is decisive for the private buyers whether they are expecting a further increase in prices in the period t + 2 or if they are expecting prices to fall.

If it applies that:

$$\frac{P_{t+1}}{P_t} > 1 \text{ causes } \frac{P^\star_{t+2}}{P_{t+1}} > 1$$

where P is the actual price and P* the expected price, the speculation will be destabilizing. The expected continued increase in prices will result in even more purchases being made for the stocks which will in itself contribute to prices going up in the period, t + 2.

If actual increases in prices give rise to expectations of a future fall in prices, it applies that:

$$\frac{P_{t+1}}{P_t} > 1 \text{ causes } \frac{P^\star_{t+2}}{P_{t+1}} < 1$$

which gives rise to price stabilizing speculations. People that have products in stock will sell from their stocks and that alone will contribute to prices being reduced in the period, t + 2.

The nature of the speculation can change from one period to the next. The more persistent the destabilizing speculation is on the private markets, the greater is the need to influence expectations through international stock policies. This influence will be exercised by selling more in times of price increases and purchasing more in times of price decreases. If the expectations actually stabilize the market, there is less need for international stock policies. Besides even though there is an international stock policy, producers and buyers may themselves take precautions against future price fluctuations by entering into futures contracts. Buyers and sellers enter into contracts which stipulate a fixed price of a product today for delivery at a given time in the future. If too much emphasis is put on the price stabilizing policies of buffer-stocks, this might make futures less attractive and thus eliminate the futures markets. If the futures markets work well, they are major contributors to price stabilization.

In the post-war era, there have been a number of international commodity agreements creating international buffer-stocks and quota programmes. Such agreements have extended to wheat, coffee, cacao, sugar, raw rubber, tin, copper, etc. However, the results have not been universally successful. Agreements have been broken; new agreements have been entered into and also broken. The general picture is that when the market is acting normally, agreements work, but typically they fall apart when the market experiences extraordinary price fluctuations. This is a major problem since it is precisely in situations of wide price fluctuations that such agreements are supposed to prove their worth.

In the mid-1970s, UNCTAD discussed an integrated programme for 18 different raw materials. The idea was to set up a common fund which was to be used to set up buffer-stocks for all 18 products. By creating a fund for a number of products but keeping it under one agreement instead of having individual agreements for all 18 products, the advantage should be a reduction of the financial investment in the programme. If the price developments for the 18 products were not the same, but varied from one product to another, the requirement for funding in an integrated programme would be less than the total of funds needed for individual product agreements.

The developing countries were the most active in trying to set up the integrated product programme. Their purpose was, partly, to eliminate price fluctuations through buffer-stocks and, partly, through production quotas, to raise the 'normal' price for the products included in the programme. Industrial countries especially criticized the integrated product programme. The industrial countries were of the opinion that the programme extended to products for which it was difficult to set up buffer-stocks and introduce production control. It was pointed out that the plan included products which were already covered by international commodity agreements. It was found that the programme did not take into account the history of unfortunate experiences that countries had with international commodity agreements. A major issue was how much money should be allocated to the programme, and the countries disagreed about how the costs of the programme should be covered and by whom. In 1979, an agreement was signed on the financing of a fund to set up a common system of buffer-stocks for a number of goods. The means allocated for this common fund were so insignificant that the programme has not had any importance whatsoever.

7.7 *Financial stabilization programmes*

As illustrated in section 7.5, it is not a given that price stabilization stabilizes the export revenue of the developing countries. If the price fluctuations are caused by changes in supply, which is most often the case, price stabilization can have a destabilizing effect on export revenue. This fact, combined with the bad experiences associated with price stabilization programmes, has given rise to the idea of trying to stabilize developing countries' revenue from exports directly.

The purpose of the price mechanism is to act as a signalling system which contributes to the rational allocation of the production and consumption of various products. If the price mechanism is put out of play, the allocation of production and consumption will be incorrect. To avoid this, there are many who argue against controlling prices, particularly when it comes to more long term price development. The problem is that the price mechanism determines the distribution of welfare between industrial and developing countries. When prices are fluctuating, especially when the fluctuations are caused by changes in demand, developing countries will experience fluctuations in revenues from exports and the industrial countries will see changes in the opposite direction in their import costs.

The problem could be solved by disconnecting income distribution from the price mechanism. A system could be set up which allowed prices to fluctuate freely if, at the same time, a system of international redistribution were created. The concept involves a system where countries agree to a normal price for a given raw material, and a normal export volume for each developing country. If the price and volume development in an individual country falls below the normal level, the importing industrial countries must transfer the difference between the normal and the actual incomes from exports to the developing countries. Conversely, the developing countries must transfer the difference to the industrial countries when their incomes from exports are higher than normal. Financing for these transfers must come from domestic taxes. In cases where the import prices in the industrial countries are lower than normal, this will be through a taxation of consumers in the industrial countries. The money that developing countries get through this kind of transfer can be used for transfer payments to the producers or to finance development programmes. In the converse case, when the income from exports is high in the developing countries, the producers in the developing countries will be subject to taxes.

By implementing such a system, the allocation function of the price mechanism will be disconnected from the impact of price mechanism on the distribution of income between industrial and developing countries. This idea is well-known within a single country where tax and social policies are used to try to establish a different distribution of income than that created by the price mechanism operating without any intervention.

To get this mechanism to work in practice is not easy. It is difficult to determine what the normal price is and what the normal export volumes are. Such a system would also be administratively demanding even though it might be questioned how much more demanding it would be compared to other programmes.

There are international programmes which follow the line of thought that lies behind the above suggestion to stabilize the export revenue of the developing countries. An example is the Stabex programme which is part of the Lomé agreement that the EC/EU had entered into with the ACP countries (countries in Africa, the Caribbean, and the Pacific). The ACP countries are former colonies of the European colonial powers. In connection with the establishment of the EC, the former colonial powers wanted these countries to be associated with the EC through preference programmes for their exports to the EC. In 1975, the Lomé Convention was extended to include the Stabex programme which is aimed at stabilizing the foreign exchange earnings from the EC/EU in the developing countries that participate in the programme. If the foreign exchange earnings drop below the 'normal' level, the EC/EU will offer them an interest-free loan which must be repaid later when their revenue from exports has increased.

The Stabex programme includes a number of agricultural products as well as iron ore, whether unprocessed or slightly processed.

However, all other products that have been processed are exempt from the programme. The Stabex programme has covered about 20 percent of exports from the member countries, but the limitations of the programme have meant that the programme has not had much importance.

The International Monetary Fund (IMF) has also implemented a Compensatory Financing Facility, the purpose of which is to grant loans to developing countries that are experiencing temporary problems on their balance of payments due to circumstances over which they have no control including falling international prices on their exports as well as small export volumes as a result of a poor harvest. Since the mid 1970s, when many developing countries suffered under the increase in oil prices, the programme has been used but again it must be said that the programme has been of limited importance. When assessing the loans offered to developing countries, the IMF would include an assessment of the countries' prospective future incomes from exports. Wrongful assessments of these prospects have often resulted in loans from the IMF having a destabilizing effect on the countries' foreign exchange earnings.

7.8 Summary

The first time that the developing countries played a central and more active role in the GATT co-operation was in the Uruguay Round. Until then the developing countries had mostly been interested in ensuring exemptions for themselves, for instance, in the form of tariff preferences for their own products and exemption from the principle of reciprocity, which requires developing countries also to liberalize their imports. Based on requests from the developing countries, a number of UNCTAD conferences have been held since the 1960s and they have dealt with issues of particular interest to the developing countries. In particular, tariff preference and programmes for stabilizing commodity prices of the developing countries have been popular topics.

The effects of tariff preferences depend on whether the preferences are unlimited or tied to a maximum quota. The GSP programmes that the industrial countries have implemented have had very limited value for the developing countries.

The developing countries have requested price stabilization programmes. A great difficulty in such programmes has to do with a realistic evaluation of the long term price development. Through export cartels among producing countries and stabilization programmes which extend to both producing and consuming countries, developing countries might temporarily get a higher price for their products but experience shows that the programmes are difficult to operate in the long term.

It seems to make more sense to try to eliminate price fluctuations in the short and medium term.

However, this is not without problems either, as price stabilization does not guarantee a stabilization of revenue. This has resulted in programmes which try to stabilize revenue from exports in the developing countries, but they have not been very successful either.

The unsatisfactory UNCTAD results have, without doubt, contributed to the fact that the developing counties have recently been more active in GATT co-operation.

Literature

Adams, F.G. and S.A. Klein, *Stabilizing World Commodity Markets*, Lexington, 1978.

Baldwin, R.E. and T. Murray, »MFN Tariff Reductions and LDC Benefits under the G.S.P.,« *Economic Journal*, 87, 1977.

Bhagwati, J.N.(ed), *New International Economic Order, The North-South Debate*, Cambridge Mass., 1977.

Bleaney, M.F. and D. Greenaway, »Long-run Trends in the Relative Price of Primary Commodities and in the Terms of Trade of Developing Countries,« *Oxford Economic Papers*, 45, 1993.

Finger, J.M. and D.A. de Rosa, »The Compensatory Finance Facility and Export Instability,« *Journal of World Trade Law*, 14, 1980.

Mac Bean, A.I. and D.T. Nguyen, *Commodity Policies Problems and Prospects*, London, 1987.

Newbery, M.G.D. and J.E. Stiglitz, *The Theory of Commodity Price Stabilization*, Oxford, 1981.

8. Trade and development

Economic growth which entails a growth in the total assets of society also influences international trade. The quantity of the different production factors may increase. The quality of the production factors may be improved through an increase in knowledge and technological enhancements. Economic growth which is exogenously determined affects the extent of trade, the composition of trade and the terms of trade.

Obviously, there is also a connection the other way around. Whether a country protects its industries or allows free trade, trade will have an effect on economic growth.

The trade policy that a country follows will have an influence on the economic conditions in the country including its economic growth. The question of which trade policy to implement is of particular relevance when it comes to economic development in the developing countries. Economic development can be defined as the process which takes place when a traditional society which uses a more simple technology that only gives a basis for a lower standard of living is restructured as a society with a more modern technology which allows for a higher standard of living.

It is obvious that a long list of conditions, both economic and non-economic, affect economic development. Trade is one of these factors. Since there is no widely accepted general theory of economic development today, it is no surprise that people hold different views of the importance of trade to economic development.

The purpose of this chapter is to describe the alternative trade policies than can be adopted as well as to describe their advantages and disadvantages.

8.1 Balanced or unbalanced growth

What does it take to create economic growth? Is it best to focus widely on all parts of industry or should the focus rather be on specifically selected industries? This discussion was at the top of the agenda in the 1950s.

Ragnar Nurkse was in favour of balanced growth, which means growth in all industries. If a shoe factory was built, it would result in a supply of shoes but the income generated by the shoe production would be directed towards a wider range of products. According to Nurkse, it would thus be necessary to invest more widely to increase the supply of goods to a point equivalent to the increased demand which the creation of income gave rise to. Nurkse held that the distribution of investments in different sectors must depend on the income elasticity for the individual goods from the various sectors.

The form of economic development that lies behind the idea of balanced growth is that a country's production structure must correspond exactly to its demand structure so that the country is self-sufficient. Nurkse thus disregarded the fact that sales from the shoe factory might not necessarily be exclusively to the home market. There might also be markets abroad. However, Nurkse did not think that developing countries as a whole could base their development on sales to industrial countries. Nurkse was of the opinion that the demand in the industrial countries for products from developing countries would be limited. There is little doubt that the development during the two world wars and in the period between the wars had a considerable influence on this view. The two world wars alone made exports to and imports from Europe and the US very difficult, while the period between the wars was characterized by extensive protectionism in Europe and USA.

The problem with the balanced growth strategy is that production is not completely divisible. An investment requires a minimum level. If investments are made in all sectors simultaneously, total savings will hardly be enough to finance the total investments. Expanding all sectors will take a number of years. If a balanced strategy is attempted, there is a risk that individual investments will be so small that there will be problems of competitiveness because the units will not be big enough to take advantage of economies of scale.

The opposite of balanced growth is unbalanced growth. One of the major advocates of this strategy was Albert Hirschman. A serious problem of balanced growth is the problem of capacity. It has already been mentioned that savings may not be enough to cover the need for investments. Hirschman points out another serious capacity problem, namely the lack of entrepreneurs. In developing countries, the number of entrepreneurs is very small and part of any development programme must aim to get more of them. Unbalanced growth creates bottlenecks in the economy, for instance, with regard to inputs and distribution opportunities. While such bottlenecks are not something to strive for in themselves, they can be used constructively to plan the next investments. Bottlenecks show precisely the areas which must be targeted.

Balanced and unbalanced growth have been presented as opposites here. In practice, a strategy is not either or but rather more or less balanced or unbalanced.

A completely balanced strategy where the country must be self-sufficient in consumer goods, semi-manufactured products, and investment goods is not ideal. Similarly it is not ideal to focus on only one industrial sector like, for instance, the textile industry.

In practice, it will make sense to strive for an in-between solution where specialization is built around industrial complexes where individual industries support one another. An example is an agro-industrial complex where the country produces agricultural products that can be used in the food industry or as industrial inputs, for instance cotton. Another example is a textile-industrial complex where cotton fabrics are manufactured and used for clothes. A third option is to focus on a machine-industrial complex where the country produces machines and tools using the technology which fits the country.

The question of how many industrial complexes a country should focus on depends on the level of development and the size of the country. The more developed the country is, the less problematic it is to focus on more industrial complexes. The larger the country is, the more sense it makes to focus on different complexes which again opens up for the possibility of taking advantage of regional differences in the composition of production factors. It is obvious that it would be more appropriate to adopt a more balanced strategy in a country like India than, for instance, Sri Lanka.

When developing countries select the areas to focus on, they can adopt different strategies.

Originally, developing countries were suppliers of primary products. One option is a strategy intended to expand these sectors. Alternatively, the focus could be on industrial production. Here, we are faced with two options. It is possible to select an import substitution strategy which calls for the establishment of national industries with a view to substituting previous imports. The other option, is to try to promote exports of industrial products.

In the following, the three different options will be presented. First, there is growth based on the primary sectors which means that foreign earnings are generated from the export of raw materials. Second, growth can be based on import substitution which means that the sectors that compete with imported goods are protected. This is often referred to as the inward looking strategy. Third, there is growth which leads to an increase in the export of industrial goods. This is usually referred to as the outward looking strategy.

8.2 Growth based on primary exports

The industrialization in Europe in the 19th century led to an extensive imports of raw materials. These included agricultural products such as grain, coffee, tea, cocoa, spices, etc. and raw materials for industry such as wool, cotton, jute, etc. The overseas markets also supplied various minerals.

These supplies of raw materials were a core element for the economic development of USA, Canada, Australia and New Zealand. Foreign earnings generated by trade combined with foreign loans paved the way for investments in these countries which in turn led to considerable economic development. Immigration of labour from Europe as well as tight cultural links were also important factors in the development.

Even within Europe, processed foods have played a decisive role in the development of certain countries. For a long time, both Denmark and the Netherlands profited from their major food exports to Great Britain.

Many overseas areas have exported raw materials but this has not made them developed countries. Most of the exporting countries were colonies, and it was European businessmen who were responsible for the production and who took the profits back with them to Europe. This hampered the economic development of the colonies in Africa and Asia which did not gain independence until after the Second World War. South America, on the other hand, gained independence in the early 1800s.

It is natural to ask whether developing countries can secure economic growth by focusing on expanding their traditional exports of raw materials. After the Second World War, most people would have answered »No« to this question. There were several reasons for that.

Firstly, world trade was not expected to grow strongly. In the 19th century and up until the First World War, world trade had grown rapidly not least the trade in raw materials. From the First World War and until the end of the Second World War, there was a fall in world trade. No one expected that this would change into a situation of rapidly increasing world trade.

Secondly, the Argentinean economist R. Prebisch and the British economist H. Singer came up with the Singer-Prebisch theory, which suggests that, in the long run, the terms of trade for primary products will deteriorate compared to industrial goods to the detriment of the raw material producing countries, i.e. the developing countries.

The central element of the theory is that demand for primary products has a tendency to increase slowly. For food and drink this is because income elasticity for these products is very small in the industrial countries. For natural fibres (cotton, silk, jute, etc.), the situation today is that synthetic fibres have taken over a substantial part of the market. For minerals, technological development has meant that the amount of raw material used per unit produced has been reduced.

Another element in the theory suggests that if there is perfect competition on the market for raw materials and no strong unions in the developing countries, production gains will lead to lower prices instead of a combination of higher prices and higher wages.

Several empirical studies have tried to prove or disapprove the Singer-Prebisch theory. Analyses show that raw materials cannot all be analysed under one category. For a number of minerals, price development has been better than the average for raw materials. The analyses also show that the results of the various studies are largely determined by the year selected as the base year for the study. If the base year is one with low prices on raw materials, all things being equal, this will be reflected in a more favourable development in the terms of trade of the raw materials than if the prices were high in the base year.

Different analyses have come up with different results as to whether the terms of trade for primary products are decreasing in the long term. One of the more recent studies, carried out by Bleany and Greenaway in 1993, shows that the terms of trade for raw materials, relative to industrial goods are falling by 0.5 percent per year.

Thirdly, it has been suggested that there is only weak linkage between raw material production and other production. »Linkage« refers to the fact that any given production of goods will create a basis for the production of other goods. It is possible to talk about backward linkage, forward linkage, and income linkage. If a country produces agricultural products, it must buy fertilizers, insecticides, fungicides, and machinery. Therefore, agricultural production opens up a market for the production of these goods (backward linkage). Forward linkage is the further processing of raw materials. If a country produces cotton, this will create a basis for establishing a textile industry. When a country produces agricultural products, income is generated which gives rise to consumer demand which can then be the basis for the production of consumer goods (income linkage).

If a country wants to help its own industries, it will be an advantage to focus on specific areas which will lead to production in other domestic industries.

It has been claimed that primary products do not have many linkages. One example that is often used is the extraction of oil and minerals. These production sectors are enclave economies which have few economic ties to the rest of society. These sectors are much more tied to the industrial countries in which the products are sold. Oil and mineral extraction requires expensive machinery and few workers. The surrounding community supplies only limited inputs, and only a small proportion of the production is used domestically. Backward and forward linkage hardly exists. The income linkage is also slight. The wages share is small because the production is capital intensive. The capital yield goes to the capital owners which can be foreign companies. It is possible for the government to get a share of the profits through taxation. This public income does not create development in itself, but it opens up the possibility for the government to launch new initiatives or to offer loans to private entrepreneurs.

The kind of economy described above is often referred to as dual economy; on one side, raw material production and on the other, the rest of society. There are few linkages between the two sectors so that the development of raw material production does not lead to development in the rest of society.

Oil and mineral extraction are examples of how a society will see few benefits in terms of development when the focus is on production of raw materials. The same applies to plantations, if they are owned by foreign companies. However, the lack of linkages does not apply to the production of agricultural products when the production takes place on a large number of privately owned farms where the owners' families make up the workforce. In this case, the income linkage is very important. If income increases in the agricultural sector, for instance, through productivity growth, it leads to a considerable rise in the demand for consumer goods. This might be the basis for industrialization.

There are a lot of forward linkages for many raw materials. One example is cotton which can be the basis for the development of a textile industry which can then produce and export textile products instead of merely selling non-processed cotton. Processing raw materials can be the basis for industrialization. However, the problem is that the industrial countries often have a high level of protection against processed goods. This is reflected in tariff escalation where raw materials can be imported without paying customs duties, but semi-manufactured goods are subject to certain tariffs, and processed goods are subject to even higher tariffs.

The arguments set out here have been crucial for the choice of development strategies in the developing countries in the 1950s and 1960s. The poorest of the developing countries have had no choice. They have had to focus on primary goods. Those developing countries which have had a choice have rejected a strategy based on increased exports of primary products. Instead they have focussed on the rapid development of the industrial sector. This can either be through an inward looking strategy of import substitution or through an outward looking strategy of industrial export.

8.3 Inward looking and outward looking development strategies

The import substitution strategy, or the inward looking development strategy, is characterized by the situation where a country tries to establish domestic markets for its own products by pushing imported goods out of the market. If a country imposes tariffs on imports or introduces import restrictions and if it gives subsidies to its own industries that compete with imported products, it discriminates to the advantage of the local industries which compete with imported goods. This is the substance of the import substitution policy.

Conversely, there is an export oriented policy when a government supports its exporting industries through subsidies. It is obvious that a policy which discriminates to the advantage of exporting industries is an export oriented policy. However, the conditions required for an economic policy in order for it to be referred to as export oriented are much less strict. A strategy which is neutral to international trade is also referred to as an export oriented or outward looking strategy.

The two strategies can be defined by using the effective exchange rate (EER) for the export sector and the import sector, respectively, as shown below.

For the importing sector, t_M is the tariff equivalence which shows how much different measures, such as, tariffs, import restrictions, production subsidies, etc. support the domestic industries competing with imports. If the nominal exchange rate is ER, the effective exchange rate for the importing sector is:

$$EER_M = ER\,(1 + t_M) \qquad (8.1)$$

For the exporting sector, t_X is the export tariff which must be deducted from the world market price before the exporting producers get their income, and s_X is the support in percent, which the exporting sector gets in the form of various subsidies. This means that the effective exchange rate for the exporting sector is:

$$EER_X = ER\,(1 - t_X + s_X) \qquad (8.2)$$

If $EER_M > EER_X$, it means that the country has opted for a policy which discriminates to the advantage of the import competing sector and against the exporting sector. This is the definition of the import substitution policy. Obviously, the larger EER_M is compared to EER_X, the more pronounced is the import substitution policy. If $EER_M = EER_X$, there is no discrimination, either against the import competing sector or against the exporting sector. This policy is referred to as the export oriented or the outward looking strategy. This will be the situation if a country decides to follow a non-interviontionist policy, i.e., it offers no support to either of the two sectors. Where there is an export oriented policy, this does not stop the country from protecting the import competing sector, as long as the exporting sector is supported to the same extent.

If $EER_M < EER_X$, the country discriminates to the advantage of the exporting sector. This situation, which hardly ever happens in practice, is referred to as ultra export oriented.

It is the relation between EER_M and EER_X, which is decisive when determining whether the country has chosen an inward looking or outward looking strategy. It means that the nominal exchange rate, ER, which is part of both (8.1) and (8.2) does not have any influence on whether or not the country discriminates against the import-competing or exporting sectors.

However, it cannot be concluded that the nominal exchange rate does not have any influence on the two sectors. As an example, we could look at the Euro area and the USA. The equilibrium exchange rate is, for instance, USD 1 = Euro 1, and by using (8.1) and (8.2) it is possible to calculate the effective exchange rates for the two sectors. If the Euro is overvalued, the exchange rate will be USD 1 = Euro 0,9. This means that the effective exchange rate for both sectors will be less than before. This again means that the competitiveness of both sectors vis-à-vis the home market will be reduced. The result will not be a change in the relative conditions for the two sectors which compete on the international markets, but for both sectors their competitiveness will be reduced in the domestic markets. When a currency is overvalued exports are reduced and import-competing domestic production can be replaced by imports. Both elements will lead to a deficit in the balance of payments.

If, on the other hand, a currency is undervalued, for instance, USD 1 = Euro 1,1, the sectors that compete on international markets will be in a position to raise wages compared to the home market sector.

The level of the actual exchange rate is not decisive for how the selected development strategy is designated when the developing strategies are defined by comparing (8.1) and (8.2). The actual exchange rate does not have any impact on the competitive situation between the import-competing and the exporting sectors. However, the exchange rate is important as it affects the competitive situation between industries exposed to international competition and home market industries.

8.4 *Import substitution – revaluing the currency*

The import substitution policy may result in a »stronger« currency. In figure 8.1, demand and supply of a foreign currency is shown as a function of the exchange rate on the y-axis. DD is demand for a currency which mainly stems from imports. The more expensive imports are, the lower the import expenses will be. SS is the supply of a currency which mainly stems from export revenue. Initially, the equilibrium exchange rate is ER_1. If the country follows an import substitution policy, demand for the foreign currency will move to the left. If exchange rates move freely, the new exchange rate will be lower.

When the nominal exchange rate falls, the effective protection of the import-competing sector will also fall, see (8.1), and, at the same time, the incentive to export will be reduced. In other words, there is a risk, that due to changes in the exchange rate, import substition will contribute to a reduction in import protection and even complicate the promotion of exports.

In (8.1) and (8.2), it is the nominal exchange rate that is used. Looking at development over time, inflation both at home and abroad does have an influence on the real exchange rate. The real exchange rate ER_R can be calculated as follows:

$$ER_R = ER \cdot \frac{P_F}{P_H}$$

P_F and P_H are price indices for the foreign countries and the domestic country, respectively. If the nominal exchange rate, ER, is constant, the real exchange rate will be revalued if the domestic price level increases more than the international price level.

If the import substitution strategy means that domestic inflation is higher than it would otherwise have been, the import substitution strategy will contribute to a real revaluation which undermines the intentions behind the strategy. It is obvious that when import protection is introduced, it will result in price increases which could otherwise have been avoided. Protection can also lead to higher inflation in the long run, especially if it is established through import restrictions. This is because competition is reduced when domestic industries are protected.

Figure 8.1: Import substitution may result in a stronger currency.

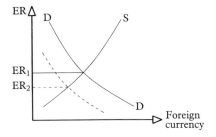

As has been illustrated here, a strategy based only on import sub-stitution can contribute to a real revaluation of a country's cur-rency. This means that the import-competing sector will be less protected than originally intended and it also becomes even less attractive to try to establish industrial exports.

8.5 Import substitution – a distortion of the price structure

It is evident that the infant-industry argument lies behind the import substitution strategy. Firstly, there is a wish to establish an industry which can sell its products on the home market. Sec-ondly, it is necessary to protect the industry against international competitors. This is because the domestic markets are often imperfect and externalities are related to the industries. Thirdly, the idea is that the protection has to be temporary. It must stop when the domestic industry has grown stronger and has overcome its initial difficulties.

When it comes to implementing the import substitution policy, a country has various choices. It is possible to impose a general cus-toms duty on all imported goods. By doing so, the country will have a uniform protection of all its domestic industries which actu-ally face or might face international competition. Such a general customs duty has the same effect on the importing sector as a devaluation. The difference is that a devaluation also helps the exporting sector whereas tariff protection in fact harms the export-ing sector because the tariff protection increases the domestic price

level. Unlike devaluation, tariff protection results in customs revenue to the government.

An alternative is to try to identify the industries which it would
be most profitable to protect. One way to do this would be to try to
calculate the competitiveness of different domestic industries compared to similar imported goods. To do this, the concept of domestic resource costs (DRC) is used and it is calculated as follows:

$$\text{DRC} = \frac{\text{Domestic production costs in domestic prices and domestic currency}}{\text{Currency saved due to domestic production in foreign currency (\$)}}$$

DRC thus shows the domestic costs in relation to the currency saved
in USD on a given production. All industries can now be ranked
according to the size of the DRC. It would make most sense to start
domestic production in areas where the DRCs are low. The first step
will therefore be to protect the industries that have low DRCs.

It could be asked whether it is reasonable to use import protection if the DRCs are low. If the DRCs have been calculated on the
basis of private domestic economic costs, and if the DRCs are
lower than the exchange rate (that is the number of domestic currency units being paid to for one foreign unit), it would be profitable for domestic entrepreneurs to invest even without protection.

The import substitution strategy is based on the assumption that
the private costs are higher than the social costs because of the
imperfections of the market and externalities. If the numbers for
the DRCs based on private costs are higher than the exchange rate,
it is not profitable to invest, seen from a private cost perspective. If,
on the other hand, DRCs are calculated on the basis of social costs
that are lower than the exchange rate, investments will be economically profitable from a social perspective, but will not be profitable
from a private economic perspective until the government provides
support for the industry. Calculations of DRCs based on social and
private costs can show which investments are profitable from a
social economic perspective and which need to be supported.

It is not easy to make these calculations. It requires an in-depth
knowledge of the functioning of the economy to make calculations
of the shadow prices of the production factors, that is the prices
which reflect the social costs. Such calculations also become ques-
tionable when there are changes in the economy.

An import substitution strategy will always discriminate in
favour of the sectors that are protected. The economy will be dis-

torted. The extent and nature of the distortions will depend on several factors. A uniform tariff level will have a less distorting effect than highly differentiated tariff levels. A high tariff level or import restrictions will be more distorting than a low tariff level.

The import substitution strategy can be limited to a certain number of goods or it can be gradually extended to more and more product groups. It is typical to start off protecting the production of certain consumer goods, for instance, textiles, shoes, leather products etc. The production technology is relatively simple and the work force mainly consists of unskilled workers. Later on, protection can be extended to durable consumer goods. Here production might be more complicated, more capital intensive and require more imports of semi-manufactured products. When the consumer goods sector has been developed, the country can choose to protect its production of semi-manufactured goods and maybe later the production of capital goods.

The idea behind import substitution is that the support must be temporary. It must allow the industry to gain a foothold. When this has happened, the support must be dismantled. When the more simple industries have been established with protection, this protection must be removed. It is then possible to move to the protection of new areas, but problems can arise in this connection. If, for instance, a country decides to protect its production of semi-manufactured steel products, the costs will increase for the companies that use steel. Protecting one sector will be like taxing another sector. Dismantling the support for the consumer goods sector while introducing protection for the semi-manufactured goods sector is difficult. The choice is often between either dismantling support for the consumer goods sector without introducing support for other sectors, or keeping the support for the consumer goods sector (maybe even increasing it) while extending the substitution strategy to new areas, for instance, semi-manufactured goods. To dismantle support for some sectors while starting support for other sectors is difficult.

South Korea, Taiwan and Singapore are examples of countries that introduced tariff protection of their consumer goods industries after the Second World War. Since the 1960s, this has either been reduced or compensated for by support for other sectors that have started to export their products. Another and very different example is from South America where many countries have extended the import substitution strategy to more and more areas. Low prices on raw materials in the period between the wars made these countries introduce the import substitution strategy and this has been continued in the post-war period. As protection was extended to more and more areas, the price structure became highly distorted and entirely failed to reflect the comparative advantages and disadvantages of the countries' different industries.

In this connection, it is worth remembering the concept of effective tariff protection. Moderate protection of a processed good can result in a highly effective tariff protection if raw materials and semi-manufactured products are not protected.

Implementing a far-reaching policy based on import substitution means that a country risks getting a highly distorted price structure which leads to inefficiency and bad investments.

8.6 Import substitution – distribution of income, savings, technology and employment

If the import substitution policy is applied excessively, a number of macroeconomic problems will arise.

First of all, it can lead to an unequal distribution of income. The industrial sectors that are protected will also see a rise in income. Workers in these sectors can use their unions to secure wage increases for themselves because their industry is protected. The general urban wage level will be artificially pushed up, making it difficult to set up export oriented industries. The losers will be that part of the urban population that cannot find work in the protected sector as well as the rural population.

Protection will also result in higher prices on industrial goods. Since the majority of the poor population live in rural areas, the industrial support will, in itself, make the distribution of income even more unequal. Agriculture is discriminated against on several levels. Firstly, agriculture will be taxed either through sales duties (export duties, etc.) or through artificially low prices on its products. The intention is to get revenue from taxes which can then be used to build up industries. Secondly, industrial protection means that the agricultural sector must buy its inputs and consumer goods at higher prices. Thirdly, import substitution means that the currency of the country might be revalued, see section 8.4, which is also detrimental to the agricultural sector. The overall result will be that the migration from rural to urban areas will increase. People move to the large cities in the hope of finding jobs and income.

Secondly, when a country tries to become industrialized by using import substitution, it follows that the necessary savings must come from the protected industries in addition to the savings that are secured through taxation of agricultural products.

In theory, a high degree of protection allows the protected industries to get high earnings which can then be used for investments. In practice though, the high protection will often be accompanied by less efficient production because the protected firms do not have to compete. At the same time, the wage level may be artificially pushed upwards. Moreover, the utilization of capacity is often low since the high prices on finished goods make it difficult to sell the goods. All in all, there are a number of negative elements associated with protection which make it difficult to secure the necessary savings level.

The savings that are accrued must then be spread over a number of investments. In this connection, there is a risk that the investments will be made in the same sectors where the savings are accrued. An alternative is to channel the savings into the credit market if such a market exists and is working adequately.

The alternative to expanding investments through taxation of agriculture and business savings is to stimulate private savings. This requires a credit market. Also the majority of the population must have an income level which allows them to save and, finally, it requires an incentive to save. This is where the real interest rate becomes decisive. The nominal interest rate must be adjusted to inflation so that the real interest rate is positive, otherwise, there is no incentive to save.

Thirdly, in the development strategy it is important to focus on areas in which the country has certain advantages. Usually, developing countries will have a large labour force of unskilled workers who must be trained further through employment. It is important that they become familiar with the new technology but it must be technology which is suited to the production conditions in the country in question.

Import substitution which replaces imports with capital intensive production is problematic. If the import substitution strategy leads to inflation, this will result in a negative real rate of interest and an overvalued currency which would also be a problem. If the currency is overvalued, it means that it will be cheaper to buy machinery from abroad, and a negative real rate of interest will also make it more attractive to replace workers with machines. This is even more true if the wage level is pushed up because of the import protection. It is clear that if the import protection helps capital intensive industries and if it changes the relative factor prices so that industries will use capital instead of labour, it will not result in the desired rise in employment.

Migration to the large cities will increase when industries are protected. However, the increased demand for labour is lower than the increased supply in the cities with migration. Migration to the cities also requires investment in the infrastructure for roads, sewers, schools etc. These investments are much higher than they would have been if the migrating work force had stayed in the rural areas. Migration to the cities ties up scarce investment resources.

When capital goods are imported from industrial countries, the technology applied will be related to the factor prices in the industrial countries where wages are high compared to the price of capital. The technology is not related to the factor prices in the developing countries where capital is relatively expensive and the price of labour is low from a social economic perspective.

What often characterizes the protected importing sector is overcapitalization, meaning that production is more capital intensive than it would have been, if the relative factor proportions of the country were taken into consideration. At the same time, the capacity of the industry is not fully utilized because of the high prices of the goods produced.

Developing countries' export oriented industries are labour intensive and, therefore, an outward looking development strategy which does not discriminate between industries might be a better strategy to secure increased employment and guarantee the adoption of technology which is adapted to the conditions in the country.

8.7 The export oriented strategy

In section 8.3, an export oriented strategy was defined as a strategy where EER_M/EER_X is about one or below one. An export oriented strategy is characterized by the fact that, to a large extent, it tries to take advantage of the market mechanism through integration into the world economy. The market mechanism reflects relative prices which constitute the incentives guiding economic development.

An export oriented strategy is not the same as a non-interventionist approach. The strategy recognizes that there might be market imperfections and externalities which make it appropriate to intervene. When a country decides to intervene, it is done in a way that the exporting sector is not disfavoured compared to the import-competing sector. Secondly, a completely different set of tools is used for the intervention. The country will not intervene directly in the market mechanism through restrictions as is the case, for instance, when a country imposes import restrictions. Instead, the country will try to modify the way in which the market mechanism works. One solution could be to grant subsidies to production and exports. It is crucial for the export oriented strategy to avoid the market distortions which can arise with import substitution. In section 8.4, it has been shown that import substitution can lead to a revaluation of a country's real rate of exchange which will harm the country's export opportunities. This happens directly when imports are reduced due to tariffs and import restrictions thus also reducing the demand for foreign currency. It may also happen indirectly if the import protection distorts price relations in the country. The more extensive the import substitution strategy is, the larger the price distortions will be and the more severe the misallocation of production and investments will be.

The export strategy also wants to avoid macroeconomic problems that might be associated with excessive import substitution. The export strategy does not discriminate against agriculture or the rural areas where the majority of the poor population live. The export strategy favours development of labour intensive industries so that the labour force will also be allowed to improve their standard of living.

The strategy which is based on import substitution will secure the necessary savings through firm savings in the protected import competing sector. The result will be that the country is forced to accept a more unequal distribution of income in order to secure the necessary savings. Besides this, it is far from given that import substitution will result in the necessary amount of savings. The surplus might not be big enough because of poor capacity utilization, high wages and inefficiencies in production. The export oriented strategy must secure the necessary savings through household savings. This requires that the real rate of interest, that is the nominal interest rate less the expected inflation, is positive. There must be an incentive to save. Experience shows that if there is an incentive to save, even low income households will set aside savings.

The export strategy does not distort the relative factor prices between labour and capital to the detriment of employment. Thus the risks, that production becomes too capital intensive and that the production technology used becomes too advanced, are avoided.

In short, the advantages associated with an export strategy almost match the disadvantages associated with import substitution.

8.8 *The view of development strategies has changed*

As already mentioned in section 8.2, in the 1950s developing countries were against economic development based on exports of primary goods. One of the persuasive reasons for this was that Singer and Prebisch put forward their theory that there was a long term trend for the terms of trade for primary products (raw materials and agricultural products) and industrial products to change, to the detriment of the primary products.

Developing countries, therefore, chose to focus on developing their industries. To do so they could choose between either an import substitution strategy where domestic industries would replace previous imports or they could try to build up industrial exports. They decided to go for the strategy based on import substitution.

The reason was that, like Nurkse, they did not think that the industrial countries could absorb the imports from the developing countries which would be necessary for the developing countries to reach the growth level they wanted. In the 1930s, world trade had collapsed completely and there were no expectations that world trade would grow strongly after the Second World War. If the developing countries thus focussed on exporting industrial goods, they feared that the industrial countries would continue with their import protection or maybe even intensify it.

From 1950 and until the mid 1960s, import substitution was the most popular approach. From the mid 1960s until the 1980s, there were two different development trends. Many countries continued with their import substitution policy, for instance in Latin America. Other countries gave up their import substitution strategy for more neutral export oriented strategies. From the early 1980s, the World Bank introduced a structural adjustment programme. The purpose was to remove the distortions which were seen in many of the developing countries. The World Bank granted medium term loans requiring developing countries to implement certain changes and adjustments. Import restrictions had to be lifted in whole or in part. The tariff level could be increased temporarily as a compensation for lifting the import restrictions, but in the long run, tariff protection had to be reduced. There was also a goal to arrive at a situation where there would be more uniform customs tariffs in order to avoid major differences in the effective tariff protection. The aim was for countries to replace import substitution with a more neutral strategy that also allowed for exports of industrial products.

The reduction of import protection had to be accompanied by an economic policy which did not promote imports or hamper exports. The overvalued currency, which often came with the import substitution, had to be devalued. It was equally important to avoid inflation. High inflation can in itself distort the price structure. If inflation is high and the nominal exchange rate is not devalued, the real exchange rate will be revalued to the detriment of the industries that compete on foreign markets.

8.9 What conclusions can be drawn?

Development of primary production

After the Second World War, nobody wanted to base their economic development on the production of primary goods. A decisive factor was the Singer-Prebisch theory which claimed that the terms of trade for primary products compared with industrial goods would deteriorate in the long run.

The question then is if there has been a long term tendency for the terms of trade for primary products to deteriorate. The answer to this question very much depends on which base period is used. The results also depend on whether oil is included in the analysis or not. One of the more recent analysis made by Bleany and Greenaway in 1993 shows that the relation between prices on primary products and industrial products is falling by approximately 0.5 percent per year.

When speaking about the deterioration of the terms of trade for primary products, it is important not to see these terms of trade as being identical to the terms of trade of the developing countries. The developing countries are a broad group of countries and a fair share of them actually export quite a lot of industrial products (especially the NIC's). Bleaney and Greenaway found that a fall of 1 percent in the terms of trade for primary goods will give developing countries a fall in their terms of trade of 0.3 percent.

A conclusion drawn from this must be that there is a trend for prices of primary products to fall compared to prices of industrial products. Of course, such a development will be particularly unfortunate for the countries that mainly export raw materials. If it is possible to obtain productivity gains in the production of primary goods, this will help to neutralize the negative consequences of a relative fall in the prices of primary goods. When a country can increase the exported volumes quantities more than the deterioration in the terms of trade, and this is normally the case, the import capacity of the country is increased.

A country should not down-prioritize the primary sector just because prices on primary products are falling. Most countries need the income from raw materials to get the necessary currency earnings. Besides, many countries have no alternative. If a country decides to implement an import substitution strategy, it risks neglecting the agricultural sector, as has been seen in several cases. An import substitution strategy means that resources are drawn away from the agricultural sector. If this happens in a situation where there are no increases of productivity in the agricultural sector, food production will be inadequate. This has forced many less developed countries to import foods.

The great risk associated with import substitution is that agriculture and the rural districts are neglected. Today, it has been recognized that first it is necessary to pump resources into agriculture to increase productivity to a level which enables resources to be drawn from the sector at a later stage.

Import substzitution

In sections 8.4 to 8.6, a number of disadvantages associated with the import substitution strategy have been outlined. The extent of these problems very much depends on how far-reaching the import substitution policy is.

Import substitution can be a very successful policy if the level of protection is moderate, and if it is focused on consumer goods where the country should have possibilities of building competitive industries. Import substitution stands a much better chance if it is combined with an economic policy which tries to eliminate the problems that the protection can give rise to (see sections 8.4 to 8.6). Import substitution is much more likely to be successful if it is made clear from the beginning that the support is temporary.

When a number of industries are being protected in order to replace imports with domestic production, first the price of imports will go up and the production mix may change if all resources are already being utilized. However, in developing countries the resources are not all fully utilized. The effect of the protection will therefore usually give rise to increased activity. Because of market imperfections, it will not be profitable to set up or expand domestic industries which replace imports unless the industries are supported. When the protection has been established the domestic industry will be competitive.

If the import protection is to be successful, it is critical that the production opportunities in the country are significantly increased. It is thus decisive how much the country's transformation curve moves. In figures 8.2 a and b, two cases of import substitution are illustrated. In the first case, the import substitution policy has failed and in the second case it has been successful. The difference between the two cases is how much the transformation curve moves over the period when the import substitution policy is being implemented. Initially, production lies at the point Q_1, and consumption at the point of C_1. Then tariffs are imposed on product b which is an industrial product that is imported. In the first case, production capacity will increase and the situation will be as in figure 8.2.a. The transformation curve moves only slightly to the right. Production will be at Q_2 and consumption at C_2, which lies below the consumption point C_1 under free trade. This is an example of failed import substitution. In the second case in figure 8.2.b, the transformation curve moves far to the right. This means that the consump-

Figure 8.2: Import substitution.

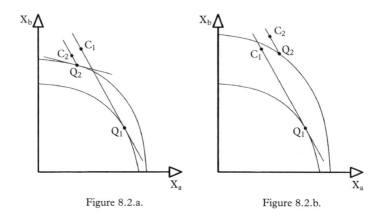

Figure 8.2.a.   Figure 8.2.b.

tion point will be at C_2, which is better than C_1, which is the consumption point under free trade. This is an example of how import substitution can be successful.

There are several historical examples of import substitution policies which have been successful. Germany and the USA were successful in their policies in the 19th century, as was Canada in the 19th and 20th centuries. In the post-war era, there are several examples of failed polices of import substitution. This applies to most of the Latin American countries. The problem has been that the disadvantages were so great because the countries chose a very high protection level and, they also decided successively to extend the protection from consumer goods industries to include semi-manufactured products and capital goods.

Empirical evidence from the post-war era

The decisive criterion in determining whether a strategy has been successful or not is the extent to which the strategy has allowed for economic growth and development.

Analyses seem to indicate that the countries that have had a policy of import substitution have had lower growth than countries that have either not used import substitution so extensively or which have used a more export oriented strategy. Such analyses have been carried out by Greenaway and Nam (1988).

Before making any conclusions, it is important to note the major problems that are associated with such studies. First of all, it is difficult to measure the degree and extent of import substitution and the degree and extent of an export oriented strategy. In section 8.3, the difference between import substitution and export orientation was described as the relation between EER_M and EER_X, which is the effective exchange rate for imports and exports respectively. This is a useful indicator in theory, but in practice, it can be hard to use. For instance, it is not always clear which sectors should be considered import and export sectors, respectively. There are many different instruments of support, each of which works differently, but which are still measured by a single indicator. This means that one has to be careful not to use that indicator too rigidly.

Secondly, it is clear that economic development can be ascribed to a long list of different conditions and a country's trade policy is only one of many factors. It is fair to ask how much of the growth in countries that have opted for the export oriented strategy can actually be ascribed to that strategy and how much is due to other factors. It is difficult to assess the importance of the selected trade strategy when the countries are so very different to begin with. Some countries that have already reached a relatively high income level may find it easier to grow than other countries at a lower level. However, it is a characteristic that it is precisely the richer countries that have chosen an export oriented strategy in most cases. The fact that the countries that have chosen an export oriented strategy have experienced more growth than the countries that have chosen an import substitution strategy is not necessarily related to the trade policy that they have adopted. It cannot be excluded that where many of the macroeconomic distortions are avoided, moderate import substitution can have a positive effect on development. If the intention that the support should only be temporary is adhered to, it is possible to avoid many of the negative consequences.

Thirdly, it does not necessarily follow that because certain countries are successful with an export oriented strategy that the same would apply to all other countries. The fact that certain countries have been successful with an export oriented strategy might be explained by the fact that other countries have chosen a strategy based on import substitution.

8.10 Summary

This chapter has been used to analyse different development strategies. There are advantages and disadvantages associated with focussing on primary production, on import substitution and on export oriented industrial production.

Empirical evidence does not allow us to conclude that one strategy is better than another. Whether to choose one strategy or another depends on the actual conditions in the country. In poor countries, it is important not to neglect primary production. Exports of raw materials are important for the country's foreign earnings and development of the agricultural sector is necessary so that the country is not forced to use its scarce foreign revenue on food imports in the future. In some of the more wealthy countries, it might make sense to use a moderate import substitution policy to build up industrial production in areas where the country will have comparative advantages in the long term. If a country is so rich to begin with that it already has some industrial production it will be natural to choose an export oriented strategy.

Nor is it reasonable for a country to have to follow the same strategy at all times. Conditions change in individual countries which means that it will be better to use different strategies at different times. When, for a period, a country has followed a strategy of import substitution it may be time for the country to dismantle its protection, which should only be temporary. It is therefore, quite natural for many countries first to adopt a strategy based on import substitution and later to move on to a more export oriented strategy. Many of the South Asian countries, the so-called NIC's, have used this approach.

Literature

Bleaney, M.F. and D. Greenaway, »Long-run Trends in the Relative Price of Primary Commodities and in the Terms of Trade of Developing Countries,« *Oxford Economic Papers,* 45, 1993.

Greenaway, D. (ed), *Economic Development and International Trade,* London, 1988.

Greenaway, R., and C.H. Nam, »Industrialization and Macroeconomic Performance in Developing Countries under Alternative Liberalization Scenarios«, *Kyklos,* 41, 1988.

Kirkpatrick, C., »Trade Policy and Industrialization in LDC's,« in Gemmell, N(ed), *Surveys in Development Economics,* Oxford, 1987.

Krueger, A.O., »Trade Policies in Developing Countries,« in Jones, R.W. and P.B. Kenen (eds), *Handbook of International Economics,* Volume 1, Amsterdam, 1984.

Milner, C.R.(ed), *Export Promotion Strategies: Theory and Evidence from Developing Countries,* Brighton, 1990.

Timmer, C.P., »The Agricultural Transformation,« in Chenery, H. and T.N. Srinivason (eds), *Handbook of Development Economics,* Volume 1, Amsterdam 1988.

9. Free trade or protection

Both the private and the public sectors produce goods and services. In the public sector, there are considerations, other than those purely related to the market, that influence supply and demand. In European societies, the private sector is based on the market where supply and demand determine prices.

There is a distinction between a laissez-faire policy, where the public sector minimizes its interference, and an interventionist policy, where the public sector intervenes. What are today called market economies could also be called »framework« economies, meaning that comprehensive regulation sets the framework within which the market mechanism operates. Examples of this could be rules about permitted products and production processes.

Obviously, certain health-related rules apply to food products, and certain technical rules apply to a number of industrial products in order to prevent accidents. Such rules take into account a number of consumer policy interests. For environmental reasons, production processes have to meet a number of requirements. These requirements act as restrictions, which put constraints on the types of goods produced and the production processes used.

The framework of the market mechanism reflects intervention. In addition to the framework it is also possible to intervene in how the market mechanisms operate, for instance through restrictions and prohibitions on imports and exports. This is known as administrative intervention. If a country imports a certain product, import restrictions may be introduced which constrain the import and thus increase the market price. An export prohibition on an item will result in the domestic price being lower than the price abroad. It is also possible to influence the way in which the market mechanism operates through economic intervention in the form of duties and subsidies. This kind of intervention may relate to production, for instance in the form of production subsidies. There can be intervention relating to the consumption, in the form of purchase taxes. Finally, intervention can be targeted against international trade, for instance in the form of import tariffs or export subsidies.

Discussions about free trade and protection are often associated with import protection and export support, i.e. intervention which is directly related to imports and exports. Measures which relate to domestic production or consumption in the form of subsidies and duties may be referred to as industrial policy intervention, and are thus not considered as trade policy intervention in a narrow sense. The reason why these types of intervention are nevertheless dealt with in relation to trade policy is that they have a significant impact on trade.

9.1 Free trade compared with autarky

Today, there are number of theories which seek to explain international trade. First of all, these theories should be considered as descriptive theories to explain trade patterns. What circumstances can explain why one country exports one type of goods and another country another type of goods? An analysis of the theories concerning international trade, leads to the conclusion that there is a natural distinction between traditional theory and recent theory.

Traditional theory, i.e. the neo-classical theory, is based on a number of assumptions. Traditional theory assumes a situation of perfect competition in markets for finished goods and factor markets. Furthermore, it is assumed that there are no externalities. Therefore, de facto prices always reflect the socioeconomic costs of production, as well as the socioeconomic utility of consumption.

Recent theories assume that products are differentiated. They no longer assume constant returns to scale. There may be economies of scale and benefits in connection with product specialization at the firm level. Finally, there may be external economies.

Traditional theory gives an exact account of the trade pattern. In neo-classical factor proportion theory, the countries' factor endowment explains the trade pattern. According to Ricardo's theory, differences in production conditions, reflected in differences in productivity, determine the pattern of trade.

The recent theories which take into account differentiated products, as well as economies of scale and enterprise specialization, succeed in explaining the substantial trade volume, but not the trade pattern.

The descriptive theories explain trade by using a comparative statics analysis, in which autarky is compared with free trade. These descriptive theories may also be used normatively by comparing welfare in autarky with welfare under free trade.

Such statics analysis leads to the conclusion that free trade is better than autarky. According to factor proportion theory this can be explained by the utilization of the relative differences in a country's factor endowment. According to Ricardo's theory this is due to the utilization of differences in production technology.

In recent theories, the benefit of free trade is related to economies of scale and enterprise specialization being utilized to a greater extent under free trade because the market is larger. Free trade also means that the competitive situation is different than in autarky. Increased competition gives advantages in the form of lower prices. Finally, free trade opens up for a wider range of goods. It becomes easier for the individual consumer to get the preferred type of product, and consumers are offered a larger diversity of product varieties.

The descriptive theories explaining trade may be used normatively to demonstrate that in a static context, free trade is preferred over autarky. This conclusion is not insignificant, but it is not very relevant either since, in practice, the question is whether free trade is to be preferred to a certain level of protection without eliminating all trade.

9.2 Free trade and the optimal tariff

In the following there is consideration of protection not in the sense of autarky, but rather in the sense that it reduces the extent of trade compared to a state of completely free trade. This is related to the question of how various trade policy measures influence welfare.

In chapters 1 to 4, the effects of trade policy measures were analysed. In chapters 1 and 3, the conditions of the neo-classical theories were assumed to apply. There is perfect competition on all markets, and no externalities. Under these circumstances, it would be best for a small country to opt for free trade. The higher the customs tariffs a small country imposes, the more will welfare be reduced compared to under free trade.

On the other hand, for a big country, which is able to influence its terms of trade through its economic size, the situation is different. If a large country imposes a customs tariff, the country's terms of trade will be improved. With low tariff rates, the improved terms of trade will outweigh the losses incurred due to the products being produced and consumed at home at higher prices than the world market price. With high tariff rates, the losses resulting from the price distortion will exceed the gains in terms of trade. This means that it is possible to identify a tariff rate at which a big country achieves the largest possible level of welfare. This is referred to as the optimal tariff.

From a national point of view, a big country will benefit from a certain level of tariff protection, which ensures better welfare for the country than free trade. This conclusion is based on the assumption that other countries will not respond with similar tariff protection. If the countries act uncoordinatedly, a country may, by trying to influence its terms of trade, end up in a situation where it is worse off than under the free trade.

The reason why the implementation of retaliatory tariffs is an obvious possibility is that when a big country imposes tariffs and thereby achieves a national benefit, it is to the detriment of foreign countries. Foreign countries will incur larger losses than the gains obtained by the big country through its protection. Therefore, the level of welfare will decrease globally if a big country imposes the optimal tariff. Globally, free trade remains the best situation. The losing countries can easily be tempted to recoup some of their losses by protecting their own industries.

With a neo-classical model of the Walras type, also known as the perfect competition model, a situation with no intervention will lead to a Walras equilibrium for the two countries, where the marginal rate of transformation (DRT) and the marginal rate of substitution in consumption (DRS) are equal in each country. Similarly, DRT is equal in both countries, since DRT is equal to the relative prices of finished goods. The situation arrived at is, at the same time, a Pareto optimum. If the big country imposes optimal tariffs, globally this will not lead to a Walras equilibrium, as the marginal rate of transformation (DRT) is different in the two countries. Therefore, globally this will not lead to a Pareto-optimal situation either.

In figure 9.1, the transformation curves of country A and coun-

Figure 9.1: Deducing the global transformation curve.

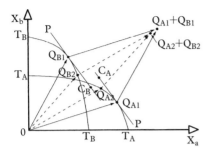

try B are shown as T_AT_A and T_BT_B. With the relative world market prices P_a/P_b, which are equal to the numeric value of the slope of the tangents P, we get the production points Q_{A1} and Q_{B1}.

The total worldwide production is found by adding the two vectors OQ_{A1} and OQ_{B1}, and we get the points $Q_{A1} + Q_{B1}$.

The consumption points are C_A and C_B, respectively, which means that country A imports item b from country B. If country A now imposes the optimal tariff, P_a/P_b for the manufacturers in country A will fall, which means that country A's production point will be for instance Q_{A2}. On the world market, P_a/P_b will rise, which means that country B's production point will be Q_{B2}. By adding these two vectors, we get a global production which is $Q_{A2} + Q_{B2}$. The total production of each of the two items falls when country A introduces the optimal tariff compared with the free trade situation.

In figure 9.1, the two global production points are found on the basis of world market prices in a free trade situation, which equal the slope of the tangent P. If the world market prices now assume alternative values, it is possible to deduce two global transformation curves, as illustrated in figure 9.2. T_I is the global transformation curve under free trade, whereas T_{II} is the transformation curve when country A introduces the optimal tariff. The two global transformation curves reflect the existing consumption opportunities.

Two countries, A and B, are to share the total production. For the sake of simplicity, we will assume that there is only one household in each of the two societies. Figure 9.3 shows the utility possibility curves illustrating the maximum utility value that the two persons in country A and country B, respectively, can achieve with

Figure 9.2: Global transformation curves with free trade and the optimal tariff.

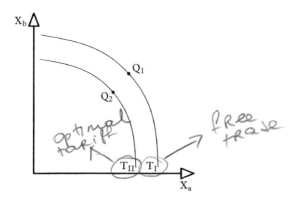

alternative distributions of income between the two countries. Curve U_I shows the maximum utility combinations with free trade. Curve U_{II} describes the maximum utility combinations when country A imposes the optimal tariff on the imported goods. The pivotal factor is that the utility possibility curve with the optimal tariff always lies within the utility possibility curve with free trade. Therefore, it is clear that free trade is potentially better than a situation in which country A imposes the optimal tariff. Initially point U_1 describes the utility combination under free trade. When country A imposes the optimal tariff, there will be the utility combination U_2, which means that country A achieves a higher level of welfare and

Figure 9.3: Utility possibility curves with free trade and with the optimal tariff.

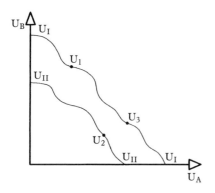

the welfare of country B decreases. Free trade is to be considered as the potentially better situation, because free trade, together with a redistribution of income between the countries can lead to point U_3, at which both countries are better off than if country A imposes the optimal tariff.

Whether free trade can in fact be considered the best situation without a redistribution of income is open to discussion. If some groups in a country are losing from free trade, it could be argued that, since free trade is potentially better for the country as a whole, there is a prospect of redistribution of income in the country in the long term, so that everybody will be better off. It is doubtful whether the same applies when international transfers from one country to another are required, as they are much more difficult to make in practice.

9.3 The effects of free trade and protection change over time

The analyses in sections 9.1 and 9.2 are snapshots. They show static situations where factor endowment and technology are given. Two situations are then compared. Trade is not seen from a dynamic perspective. However, economies experience growth which influences trade and terms of trade, just as it is evident that the trade regime chosen may influence the country's own growth, cf. chapter 8.

Growth in industrial countries may lead to only a modest increase in the demand of raw materials. This modest increase can make it difficult for developing countries which export raw materials to achieve sufficient export earnings. This applies particularly if there is a simultaneous deterioration in the terms of trade for raw materials. This situation is referred to as immiserizing growth, which means that increased production in a country may coincide with a deterioration of the terms of trade to such an extent that the country is worse off after the production increase than before.

The infant-industry tariff argument also considers the change in conditions over time. There are some market imperfections, and there are some positive externalities related to different industries. Therefore, it may be an advantage for a country to use temporary protection in order to compensate for some of the market imperfec-

tions and to benefit from the externalities. If there were no intervention, the differences in income levels between countries may
increase.

If both trade and factor movements are liberalized at the same
time, the likelihood of unequal growth in different countries may
be even greater. Some countries may develop into growth areas,
and other countries may become regional development areas.
According to the neo-classical theory, the reason for trade and factor movements is different factor endowment. Therefore, according
to the traditional theory, trade or factor movements will lead to an
equalization to the benefit of all parties. According to recent theories, technological differences, economies of scale and enterprise
specialization as well as benefits related to the establishment of an
industrial environment (external economies) determine trade and
factor movements. In such cases, trade and factor movements in
combination may lead to greater economic inequalities between
countries. To avoid major disparities it may be sensible to offer protection and support to the weaker regions.

There is little doubt that the establishment of an industrial environment is, in itself, an important part of the growth process. If it is
possible to establish an industrial environment, either through protection or through some other form of support, this is an argument
for public sector intervention in the economy.

In the neo-classical world, the markets are perfect and there are
no externalities. According to this model, the theoretical basis for
recommending free trade is also the basis for arguing that the public sector should not intervene in the markets at all.

However, if the recent theories are seen from a dynamic perspective, inequalities, which can be cumulative, may arise, and can
make intervention desirable.

9.4 Free trade and market distortions

In chapter 4, it was demonstrated that if the domestic marginal rate
of transformation (DRT) is not equal to the domestic marginal rate
of substitution in consumption (DRS), there is a distortion of the
market. This is also the case if either DRT or DRS is not equal to
the international marginal rate of transformation (FRT).

Such market distortions can arise in different ways. There may be imperfection in the economic system, i.e. the markets operate imperfectly because of institutional deficiencies. An example of this could be an imperfect credit market due to an insufficiently developed banking system. There may be imperfect competition on the markets because there are only few suppliers. Finally, externalities may lead to socioeconomic costs and benefits not corresponding with private costs and benefits.

Market distortions may also arise, even if the economic system is perfect in the sense that all markets operate perfectly, while there is perfect competition and no externalities. If this is the situation in a small country, which cannot influence its terms of trade, but which nevertheless implements import restrictions or grants subsidies to the export sector, distortions will arise. Such distortions are caused by the policy pursued.

The theory of market distortions developed in the 1960s and 1970s dealt with the methods of intervention in different types of distortion.

According to the theory of market distortions, attempts should be made to correct existing distortions. Where there are imperfections in the economic system, these distortions should be eliminated through intervention. If the market works imperfectly, intervention should be used to make it operate perfectly. If there are externalities, it is necessary to intervene to ensure that it is the socioeconomic costs and benefits that form the basis on which the private sector makes its decisions.

This may be done through various types of intervention. They are not all equally efficient, and the theory of distortions includes a ranking of the types of intervention according to their efficiency. According to the theory it is best to intervene as closely as possible to the source of the problem. Therefore, intervention in the form of trade barriers will often be a less than optimal approach. Even though trade intervention may eliminate one market distortion, it will often cause another.

The theory of market distortions proves that it may be highly reasonable to intervene. The theory also shows that in most cases, it is preferable to use other types of intervention than direct trade policy intervention. Therefore, the theory is an argument for avoiding direct trade intervention, and for pursuing an industrial policy with trade implications. Market distortions are usually domestic, so intervention should be carried out through instruments influencing the domestic market conditions.

Even though the distortion theory often comes to the conclusion that trade policy instruments should not be used, because they are often not the best way of intervening, the theory cannot be considered a strong argument in favour of free trade, in the sense of a situation in which there is no intervention to influence trade. The argument is that intervention and protection should be carried out otherwise than through trade policy.

If the economic system operates perfectly, i.e. the markets and the competition are perfect and there are no externalities, trade policy and industrial policy intervention will have a distorting effect. In this case, the political intervention causing the distortion should be phased out, unless the measures have non-economic goals.

In general, it may thus be concluded that if, without intervention, the market is characterized by distortions, it may be appropriate to intervene by means of industrial policy as well as trade policy instruments.

In the following, cases of imperfect competition and cases of externalitics will be looked at in more detail.

9.5 Free trade and imperfect competition

Recent trade theories focus particularly on the trade in markets in which there is not perfect competition. Originally, the purpose of the theory was to describe how the extent of trade and the trade pattern are influenced by imperfect competition. All literature on intra-sectoral trade is based on the assumption that products are differentiated, and that it is possible to obtain specialization advantages at firm level related to a reduction in the product range.

Since the 1980s, the theories have been used normatively by asking the question whether imperfect competition means that it is optimal to intervene by trade policy and industrial policy. The concepts of rent snatching and strategic trade policy were considered.

Rent snatching refers to the fact that through trade intervention, a country may gain a larger surplus than with no intervention. Strategic trade policy refers to the situation where, through its trade policy, country A influences the behaviour of manufacturers in country B so that country A's situation is improved.

As appears from chapter 2, the conditions vary a great deal in situations with imperfect competition. In some cases it is an advantage not to protect, whereas in other cases it may be worthwhile to protect by means of trade barriers or to support by granting subsidies. Again, in a third case it may be an advantage to impose tax on companies either through export tariffs or through production duties. It very much depends on whether the imperfection is found at home or abroad or both.

The number of companies on the domestic and foreign markets is also important, because the number influences the structure of the market. Moreover, the behaviour of market agents plays an important part. Do they behave conjecturally or autonomously? Price leadership may also exist. Finally, the shape of the demand curve is influential, as is the shape of the cost curve. Are there economies of scale, advantages of firm specialization, or constant returns to scale?

In a number of situations, free trade is an advantage. This applies in cases when there are few domestic import-competing companies. Here, free trade will ensure more competition. In other cases it will be worthwhile to impose import tariffs to snatch part of the monopoly gain which would otherwise fall into the hands of the foreign exporter. Tariffs may be imposed on high technology imports to ensure that domestic manufacturers get a larger share of the market which enables a particularly high production factor remuneration. If a country exports a product, which is sold by an oligopoly where the manufacturers behave autonomously, it may be optimal to introduce an export tariff. In other cases, seen from the country's perspective it may be sensible to grant export subsidies.

The essential point is that free trade is not necessarily the optimal solution in markets with imperfect competition. If all the necessary information on market conditions is available, it is possible to increase the country's level of welfare through pure trade policy intervention or through production duties and subsidies. Theoretically, there can be an argument for not following a free trade policy.

A more pragmatic, and thus also more policy oriented attitude leads to the conclusion that it is not wise generally to depart from the free trade principle because of imperfect competition.

First of all, the optimum policy requires complete information on the market conditions corresponding to the curves and assumptions on which the economists' analyses are based. As the optimum policy is highly sensitive to changes in the curves and to the assumptions in general, it is very easy to apply the wrong kind of intervention which will do more harm than good. In addition, it is not enough to analyse the conditions partially. Various types of intervention which from a partial view may seem sensible in isolation, may very well prove adverse in total.

Secondly, it should be remembered that if one country seeks to gain by intervening in international trade, other countries will be adversely affected, and may retaliate. The result may be widespread intervention which ultimately leaves all countries worse off.

Thirdly, it is necessary to question the size of the gains made by applying trade policy measures. Analyses seem to show that the advantages of optimal intervention are insignificant. When deciding how much importance to attach to such surveys, it is necessary to remember that most analyses of the effects of trade liberalization also reveal small gains. However, these analyses of liberalization only consider the static effects of a more efficient allocation of existing resources and a more efficient distribution of consumption between consumers. Empirical analyses find it difficult to capture the dynamic effects of trade liberalization. When free trade creates more competition, it may make companies more interested in technological progress. However, it is difficult, if not impossible, to quantify such an effect.

9.6 Free trade and externalities

According to traditional trade theory, external economies are of no importance. However, this is not the case with recent theory. A distinction is often made between technological and pecuniary external economies. The technological external advantages relate to the dissemination of knowledge possessed by one company to other companies. In an industrial country knowledge is generated under public as well as private management, and is disseminated between sectors and companies. This dissemination of knowledge often takes place outside the market.

The pecuniary external advantages are connected with the size of the market. The advantages are spread through a market. More inputs can be bought, often at a lower price. The larger the market for a finished product, the larger the market for inputs. When economies of scale apply to the production of inputs, the market must be of a certain size before companies producing semi-manufactured products and services are established. The advantages associated with a large concentrated market for a specific type of labour, also called labour pooling, should also be attributed to the external advantages of a pecuniary nature.

The traditional theory was based on the assumption of constant returns to scale and perfect competition. In itself, this eliminates the pecuniary external advantages. Thus, what remains are the technological external advantages associated with acquiring knowledge from outside. It has been said that these advantages are not limited to national environments, but rather that they are international. In the traditional theory and the assumptions on which it is based, there has been no room for external economies. Therefore, they have been disregarded.

The recent theory is characterized by the possibility of modelling the conditions of markets with economies of scale and externalities. This in itself has meant that the importance of external advantages has been accepted. There is little doubt that the existence of industrial environments plays an important role. They are built up over time. Once established they tend to grow stronger. However, it is difficult to explain how they come into existence. Chance can often be decisive.

Obviously, it is possible to affect the industrial structure through trade policy. Systematic attempts can be made to encourage industries which have external economies. In this way, general living standards can be enhanced.

As an example, we could imagine two identical countries. Each of the two countries is able to produce a large number of products by means of labour. With external economies, the productivity of the labour in the individual sector will depend on the size of the sector.

In the area where, perhaps by chance, the two countries first establish production of goods, each of them will achieve certain competitive advantages. Because of the external advantages, once achieved, the advantages will tend to be self-perpetuating. Only if there are significant changes to the relative production costs in favour of the country with the smaller production of the good concerned, can this country gain a larger share of the total production.

This is where the country's subsidy policy, including its trade policy, enters into the picture. By isolating its own market from competition from foreign manufacturers, a country can increase sales and thus benefit from the external advantages related to the sector. The external advantages are a key factor in the infant-industry argument, which was first advanced by F. List in 1840.

Only few attempts have been made to quantify the advantages that can be achieved through strategic trade policy, but existing analyses seem to show that the advantages are insignificant, cf. section 9.5. It is even harder to quantify the advantages of external economies. Nevertheless, it must be assumed that a realization of external economies gives advantages which are quantitatively far more significant.

The recent theory of trade policy demonstrates that, through trade policy, it is possible to obtain investments from which a number of external economies flow. A moderate general tariff protection may therefore be the decisive incentive to stimulate domestic investments, which can contribute to the beginning of economic development.

Up to now there has only been consideration of external economies. However, there are also external diseconomies in the form of pollution. In this connection, an obvious step is to implement restrictions on production processes. An alternative or a supplement to this would be to make use of economic incentives such as production levies.

The extent to which it should be possible to use trade policy instruments to promote sustainable development is one of the major questions, which will form part of future international WTO negotiations.

9.7 The free trade idea: science or ideology?

Almost all economists assume that the market mechanism should be used. However, they differ in their attitudes as to whether market forces should work freely or whether to intervene in markets.

Those in favour of intervention emphasize that the market mechanism is imperfect in many respects. There may be imperfect competition as well as externalities. Market adjustment may be slow because of large adjustment costs. This can also render market intervention an obvious choice.

Those who oppose intervention will often point out that the market imperfection is insignificant, and that market intervention entails great risks. This point of view is connected with the fact that the measures taken are often economically inappropriate and thus often likely to make things worse. Common expressions in this connection are »market failures« and »government failures«.

Pure trade policy measures such as tariffs, trade barriers and export subsidies are generally not popular with economists. It is not surprising that such measures are not favoured by the proponents of laissez-faire, i.e. a non-interventionist policy. But even those who endorse a certain level of intervention find pure trade policy measures problematic because other types of intervention may be better. However, this does not rule out trade policy measures from being the obvious choice in certain situations.

It is natural to ask whether this emphasis on the advantages of free trade is scientifically based. The answer must be that today, there is no clear scientific basis. On the contrary, there is a more policy oriented basis for free trade.

Scientific evidence for and against free trade

If all markets are perfect, as assumed in the neo-classical theory, a laissez-faire policy will result in a Walras equilibrium which will also be a Pareto optimum. In this theoretical world, there is perfect competition in the markets, and no externalities exist. The markets function perfectly, and the prices reflect socioeconomic costs. When there is no room for intervention of any kind, there is naturally no room for pure trade policy measures either.

This traditional theory provides scientific support of free trade. But the crucial problem is that the assumptions underlying this traditional theory are not in line with reality.

The theory of distortions does take this problem into account to a certain extent, cf. chapter 4. It is still assumed that the majority of markets exhibit perfect competition. A few markets may be characterized by distortions. The classic example is that of two labour markets with different wage levels. Furthermore, externalities may come into play. The prescription in this case would be to intervene to neutralize the cause of the market distortion. Since most distortions concern domestic markets and not international trade directly, industrial policy measures should be implemented rather than trade policy ones.

The theory of distortions states that while industrial policy measures are often reasonable, trade policy measures rarely prove the best form of intervention. The theory discounts the fact that industrial policy measures in the form of subsidies are a public expense, whereas a protective tariff is a public revenue. Many countries, not least developing countries, experience fiscal problems, which can lead to the implementation of trade policy measures as well.

The theory of distortions thus scientifically demonstrates that intervention is advantageous, while showing that some forms of intervention are to be preferred to others. The theory is thus an argument against certain forms of protection but it does advocate intervention in ways which affect the free market mechanism. Thus, the theory cannot be said to give scientific support for free trade without intervention.

Modern theoretical literature, which has developed since the late 1970s, is based on the assumption of imperfect competition. These theories have included assumptions of economies of scale and enterprise specialization, and of the existence of external economies. Normatively applied, these theories clearly demonstrate that there are advantages of intervening, either in the form of industrial or trade policy measures.

There is scientific support for the idea that, for an individual country, it may be an advantage not to have free trade. It is even possible that domestic protection can trigger such economic growth that foreign countries can benefit from it in the longer term. In much the same way as free trade is not a zero-sum game in which the advantage of one becomes the disadvantage of another, a temporary protective measure may yield advantages for both parties.

Recent theory provides clear support for intervention. It can be carried out with a view to utilizing the power over the market which comes through intervention. The measures can also be made in order to realize economies of scale or to achieve external economies.

The economic policy evidence for free trade

Even though scientific support for intervention exists, for reasons of economic policy the intervention must be applied with caution. First of all, the question is how much can be gained by intervening in the optimal manner dictated by the theory. Second, analyses show that the optimal measure is highly dependent on specific existing conditions. In one situation, a duty may be optimal. In another situation, in which the conditions are only subtly changed, the optimal choice would be to grant subsidies. The optimal intervention is highly sensitive to the actual conditions, which often are not known. When a situation exists in which the gain from applying the right intervention is modest, and the risk from applying a wrong measure is great, intervention should be subject to caution. Third, the use of trade policy instruments in one country may lead other countries to resort to similar measures. Thus, there is a risk of ending up in a situation in which everyone is worse off.

Selective intervention can create distortions. Measures of a more general nature are more acceptable. The economic policy dangers of intervention argue in favour of keeping to free trade. In exploiting external economies with special regard to development, there is an argument in favour of intervention, even in the form of trade policy intervention.

Going from theory to practice is not easy. On the one hand, there is clear scientific support for the argument that free trade without intervention is not always the best solution. On the other hand, empirical evidence shows that extensive intervention at the micro level, i.e. selective intervention in individual markets, may produce very negative results.

Different points of view

When considering intervention in the market mechanisms, various views are possible. There are gradations from those who advocate a laissez-faire policy to those who believe that extensive intervention through industrial and trade policy is preferable. To be more precise, the views can be divided into four groupings.

There is the first group, which is *strongly opposed to intervention*. The basis for this view is that many of the deficiencies that may exist in the market will eventually eliminate themselves. At the same time, this group is of the opinion that it is generally problematic to intervene in the market mechanism because this can easily lead to political abuse.

The second group is *moderately opposed to intervention.* There may be situations with such obvious market imperfection that moderate intervention is acceptable. This group also includes those who believe in responding to the actions of foreign countries if they put into effect measures that are harmful to the domestic market.

The third group can be described as *moderately in favour of intervention.* It is agreed that there are advantages in pursuing active industrial and trade policies, but at the same time it is recognized that there are dangers if the measures become too comprehensive. Therefore, the group wishes to limit the use of intervention to the obvious cases, and moderate intervention is to be preferred.

The fourth group is *strongly in favour of intervention.* In this group, it is believed that the markets are imperfect in many ways, so that intervention on a large scale is desirable in order for the markets to function better.

It is not possible to declare one viewpoint better than another on a purely scientific basis. Practical experience of intervention indicates that the right to intervene should in no way be waived when there are a series of goals to be achieved. On the other hand, experience also shows that extensive intervention aimed at improving conditions often ends up having the opposite effect. If the price structure is distorted, there will be an erroneous incentive system which can result in bad investments.

Often, the crucial question is not whether to intervene or not. The question is, how best to intervene.

Besides, it is not possible to set out general indications of the extent to which measures should be implemented. It entirely depends on the conditions in the country in question. Generally, it will be more appropriate to intervene in countries with imperfect market mechanisms than in the countries where the mechanism is fairly effective.

9.8 Macroeconomic disequilibrium

It has been shown above that it may be reasonable to apply trade and industrial policy measures, particularly in countries experiencing market distortions in the form of external economies.

There are a couple of circumstances which often prompt calls for protection. This applies when there are unemployment and balance of payment problems. Is it a good idea to correct a macroeconomic disequilibrium through trade policy?

Unemployment

There is no room for unemployment in the traditional neo-classical theory. The theory assumes that there is always full employment. In practice, however, this is far from always the case.

Therefore, the protectionist argument is often used in support of employment. Experience also shows that in times of high unemployment there is a tendency for countries to increase protection and to subsidize exports in order to secure employment.

Using trade policy instruments to ensure employment is not appropriate. The trade policy measures will change the competitive relation between domestic and foreign producers. If a country protects its own industrial sector, this may easily provoke foreign countries to do the same.

If a country has an employment problem, it should be solved through general economic policy, i.e. fiscal policy, monetary policy and exchange rate policy. Consideration may also be given to implementing labour market policy measures in situations where there are rigidities in the labour market.

Balance of payments deficit

In the general equilibrium model, the balance of payments is always in equilibrium. In reality, this is not the case. If there are temporary fluctuations which smooth each other out so that there is a long term equilibrium, this is not a problem, of course. A problem only arises if there is a long term deficit. In this case, a country may be tempted to introduce a form of import protection or to subsidize domestic production and exports.

A deficit in the balance of payments is indicative of a macroeconomic disequilibrium, and it should be resolved through an adjustment of the macroeconomic policy.

When there is a general problem of economic equilibrium, it is not appropriate to apply trade and industrial policy measures. There is also a question whether these measures will have the desired effect. If imports are reduced, the currency may be revalued. There is also of course, a risk of encountering retaliatory measures from other countries.

9.9 The lack of mobility of production factors

When world economic conditions change, individual countries must adjust to the new conditions. It may be difficult to make adjustments. For this reason, arguments are made, in particular by those affected, that protection should be introduced when an industry becomes subject to fierce competition. It may be reasonable to see the adjustment process from a trade policy angle.

Traditional theory assumes that the production factor remuneration is the same everywhere. This assumes that the factor markets are not rigid. Various rigidities will exist, however. First of all, the labour market will be influenced by trade unions that have agreed wage levels that are not adversely affected by an increased level of unemployment. Second, the production factors will not be fully mobile across business sectors even though there is a factor price differential. Labour with one professional skill cannot immediately be transferred to an industry which requires other skills. Labour, which becomes redundant in one geographical area, cannot immediately be put to use in companies in other geographical areas. The professional and geographical mobility of labour is thus restricted, particularly in the short term. The capital is tied up in specific sectors, which means that capital cannot in the short term be moved from one sector to the other. This can only happen in the longer term. This happens when one sector reduces its capital stock, i.e. it does not reinvest to maintain the size of the capital stock. Simultaneously, the other sector expands its capital stock through new investments. This means that capital is quite immobile even in the medium term.

The transformation curve of the country is consequently different in the short, medium and long term. This appears from figure 9.4, in which A is the production point in the situation where the relative prices of finished goods, P_a/P_b, equal the numeric value of the slope of the tangent P.

The production factors are immobile in the short term, meaning that the transformation curve is T_1T_1. In the medium term, it is

Figure 9.4: The transformation curve and time.

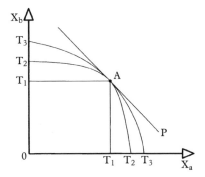

assumed that the labour market exhibits full mobility. The capital of the two sectors is still the same, because the capital is specific to the sector. The transformation curve is $T_2 T_2$ in the medium term. Only in the long term will the capital be mobile across the two sectors, meaning that the transformation curve is $T_3 T_3$.

Suppose that item a is electronic products and article b is textile products. In the initial situation, the country produces at point A. Now, the relative prices change, as the price of textile products declines while the price of electronic products remains the same. The production of item a is maintained. If the wages in the textile industry fall corresponding to the fall in the value of the marginal product of the labour, the production of textile products will remain unchanged.

The country will continue to produce at point A, but the price of labour will be lower in the textile sector. In the medium term, labour will move away from the textile industry and into the electronics business. In figure 9.5, which is a copy of figure 9.4, the point of production will move from A to A_1. At point A_1, the wage level will be the same in both sectors. However, this does not apply to the capital, where the capital earnings will be higher in sector a than in sector b. In the long term, capital will thus move away from the textile sector and into the electronic industry. This transfer is completed when the point of production is A_2. The points of consumption that correspond to the production points A, A_1 and A_2 are C, C_1 and C_2. From the location of these points it appears that there is a gradual increase in welfare during the adjustment process.

Figure 9.5: Adjustment with wage   *Figure 9.6: Adjustment without*
reduction.   *wage reduction.*

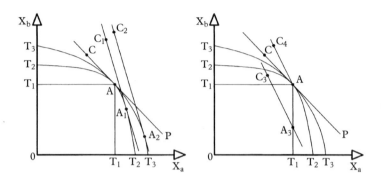

In the above course of events, it is assumed that the wage level in the textile sector is reduced as a consequence of the falling price of textile products. If the wage level is maintained by the trade unions, the textile sector will see job losses. The new production point could be A_3 as shown in figure 9.6. The corresponding consumption point is for instance point C_3, which gives a lower level of welfare than consumption C in the initial situation. Textile products are imported into the country. The fall in textile prices will improve the country's terms of trade, which is a positive effect, but at the same time, unemployment is created, which is an adverse effect. In figure 9.6, the negative effect of the unemployment is greater than the positive effect of the improved terms of trade, but this is not always the case.

As a consequence of the unemployment that will occur when the price of textile products falls without adjustment of the wage levels, the country may consider introducing a protective customs tariff. If a tariff is implemented which re-established domestic price relations corresponding to the initial situation, the production point will still be A. The consumption point will be C_4, which is always better than point C_3 and better than point C, which is the consumption point in the initial situation, before the fall of the price of textiles.

If a customs tariff is imposed which ensures employment, an immediate welfare gain will be obtained. If a permanent tariff is introduced, the production adjustment shown in figure 9.5 will not be achieved. Under free trade with wage flexibility the production point gradually moves from A to A$_1$ and later to A$_2$ resulting in an increase in welfare. The conclusion is thus that a tariff gives a temporary gain, but if the tariff is of a permanent nature, the adjustment in production, which will be even more beneficial in the longer term, cannot be achieved.

If a temporary tariff is introduced and at the same time its phasing out is scheduled, it is possible that the immediate positive effects of the tariff could be obtained and that an adjustment of the production structure could take place in the longer term.

9.10 Trade and distribution of income

Is the fact that the removal of an import protection changes the distribution of income an argument for continuing the protection?

In the traditional neo-classical model, an opening up of trade will mean that the distribution of income will be changed. According to the Stolper-Samuelson theorem, which forms part of the factor proportion theory, the earnings of one production factor will increase absolutely, while the earnings of the other factor will decrease absolutely. The production factor which is used intensively in the manufacturing for which demand rises will get higher absolute payment. The absolute payment of the other factor will fall.

If a good enjoys some import protection in the initial situation, a phasing out of this protection means that the domestic production of this good will fall. This results in an absolute fall in the earnings of the factor that is used intensively in the import-competing sector.

The question asked is thus whether free trade is better than a certain degree of protection. The Pareto criterion for a welfare increase in a given society is that no person suffers an impairment of his or her welfare. Going from a certain level of protection to free trade, the earnings of one of the production factors will be lower if the free trade is not combined with a redistribution of income.

Figure 9.7 shows the country's consumption possibility curve at given international terms of trade over which the country does not exercise any influence. In the case of free trade, the country can, as a maximum, have the combinations of goods indicated by the straight line F$_A$, the slope of which is determined by the relative prices of goods in international trade. In autarky, F$_C$, which is the

Figure 9.7: Consumption possibility curves for a country.

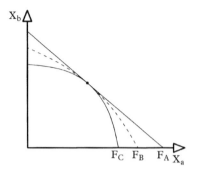

country's transformation curve, indicates the consumption potential. If a tariff is imposed which reduces trade without eliminating it, the consumption possibility curve F_B is achieved.

Utility possibility curves corresponding to each of the three situations can be drawn up for the two households in the country, cf. figure 9.8. The curves U_A, U_B and U_C each show the maximum utility combinations for the two households 1 and 2, corresponding to consumption possibility curves F_A, F_B and F_C, respectively. It applies to all the curves that when you move from the right to the left along the curvatures, it expresses a redistribution of income to the detriment of household 1 and the benefit of household 2.

The three utility possibility curves U_A, U_B and U_C, which reflect the maximum utility combinations obtainable under free trade, reduced trade as a result of protection, and autarky, respectively, are Pareto-optimal situations in connection with redistribution of income between the two households.

The interesting and crucial factor is that U_A is further to the right than U_B, which in turn is to the right of U_C. This does not signify that the situation under free trade is »better« than the situation with a certain degree of import protection.

Let us assume that the utility combinations are C in autarky, B in an import protection scenario which reduces trade, and A in a free trade situation. Going from autarky to reduced trade as a result of protection will increase the welfare of both households. Going from reduced trade as a result of protection to free trade will reduce the welfare of household 2.

The free trade situation, A, cannot directly be said to be better

Figure 9.8: Utility possibility curves for two households.

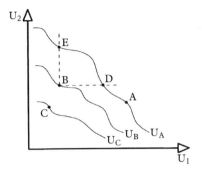

than situation B, where the country is protected to some extent. What can be deduced, however, is that free trade is potentially better than the situation with a certain level of tariff protection. The reason for this is that U_A is always to the right of U_B. This implies that in connection with free trade it is always possible to carry out a redistribution of income giving a point of utility on U_A between D and E. In this case, the utility of both households will increase.

If it is true, that free trade can always be combined with a redistribution of income improving the welfare of everybody, it can hardly be argued that import protection should be maintained for reasons of income distribution.

9.11 Different views on trade policy

If each country pursued a trade policy out of consideration for the interests of the whole, the fact that trade liberalization changes income distribution cannot be an argument for not bringing about liberalization. In practice, governments will often pursue their policies on the basis of the wishes of various lobby organizations.

Different lobby organizations have different power and influence. Consumers make up a large group, which is very heterogeneous apart from the fact that they would all like consumer interests to be considered. The advantages that consumer organizations obtain are of benefit to all consumers regardless of whether they contribute financially through membership. The advantages obtained by the individual consumer are small, because they have to be shared between all consumers. Costs, in the form of membership and active participation in the furtherance of consumer interests, are high in relation to the benefits, particularly since the benefits will also go to consumers who are not supporting the consumer case. Moreover, consumers have conflicting interests. Employee groups may be interested in protecting the business sector in which they are employed even though it may result in higher consumer prices.

Agricultural organizations have a smaller number of members, but they have far more cohesive interests with respect to securing increased protection. The costs imposed on society by this protection in the form of higher food costs are borne by the rest of society. As mentioned above, the loss experienced by the individual consumer is small, but the reward obtained by the agricultural sector is distributed among a smaller number of producers who each make a considerable gain. The interest in contributing actively, whether financially or through personal involvement in the work, is greater because the individual producer receives a considerable reward as payment for his or her contribution.

Trade unions in the food industry will often support protection of the agricultural sector, as the agriculture subsidies can be regarded as a precondition for securing employment in the processing sector.

Within the whole industrial sector, conflicting interests exist between the import-competing industries and the export industries. Export industries will often oppose protection, fearing that the country's own protection of its domestic market may provoke retaliatory measures by foreign countries to the detriment of the country's own exports. Even if this risk is non-existent, the export sector should oppose protection, as this will, other things being equal, cause the cost level, which determines the competitiveness of the export industry, to be higher. Semi-manufactured articles and investment goods may become more expensive. Higher food prices are transformed into a push for higher wages, which will impair competitiveness. The export sector's interests in free trade are harder for the general public to understand than the interests of the import-competing sector. The impact of the import sector will thus often be stronger than that of the export sector.

Although there is an asymmetry with regard to the power and influence of different lobby organizations, which can explain why the advocates of protection are still able to get their wishes granted, there are some general features in the present situation which weaken their position.

The reason for this is to be found in the rapidly increasing economic integration between countries. The economic integration or the globalization of the world economy has taken place through trade and foreign direct investments.

International trade has seen a far stronger growth than the economic growth of individual countries. This means that far more companies engage in exports. This in itself should increase the understanding of the fact that protection of the domestic business sector is a two-edged sword. In addition, the volume of foreign direct investment, including the extent of the activities of multinational companies, has intensified. The firms in a country invest abroad and itself becomes a host to foreign firms.

The purpose of a foreign investment can be limited to production for sale in the host country. Often, however, the purpose is also to export goods from the host country to other countries, including the country of the parent company. If there is a move to protect the trade and industry in a country, the companies in that country which have foreign direct investments can see an interest in opposing such protection. The result could easily be that other countries, to which subsidiaries abroad are exporters, will also introduce protective measures. The more foreign subsidiaries a country has, and the more these subsidiaries export from their host countries, the more problematic it becomes for that country if a new protectionist wave arises.

Generally, if in one country industries experience problems from foreign competition, the possibility of making investments abroad means that the alliance between companies and trade unions in demanding protection is weakened. An alternative to protection is that the domestic production relocates in whole or in part to another country with more favourable production potential. This will weaken the companies' interests in protection.

Naturally, the emigration of production will harm the employees. Trade unions can, however, use the potential of foreign direct investments to further their own interests in increased employment. They can, for instance, support the introduction of protection against foreign competition unless the foreign competitors set up business locally, which will increase domestic employment.

9.12 Summary

The purpose of this chapter is to summarise the guidance given by economic theory with respect to the question of free trade or protection.

The first conclusion that can be drawn is that international co-operation on trade policy is crucial. This is because trade policy measures implemented by an individual country affect the country's trading partners. If a certain international discipline is not exercised in respect of an acceptable scope for the trade policy of individual countries, the result may be a situation which is detrimental to all countries.

The next question is then whether the objective should be a pure free trade strategy or whether a number of trade policy and industrial policy measures should be accepted as measures available to the individual country.

Here, the economic theory is equivocal. Looked at from the view of the traditional theory in which information about technology is accessible to all, in which there is perfect competition and constant returns to scale, and in which there are no externalities, the answer is unambiguous. Free trade is the best solution on a global basis. A large country, which through the pursuit of a policy can influence its terms of trade, can obtain a welfare increase by using trade policy measures. This happens at the expense of other countries so that global welfare is reduced.

However, seen from the point of view of more recent theories, in which the same technology is not available everywhere, in which imperfect competition may exist as well economies of scale and enterprise specialization, and in which externalities occur in the form of industrial environments, the picture is somewhat different. If there is no intervention, cumulative processes may create greater inequalities between the countries. In a situation of imperfect competition, the individual country may benefit from intervention. Where market distortions are in play, it is reasonable to intervene in order to eliminate these distortions. Here, the question arises as to which measures to employ. Since many distortions occur at a domestic level, it will often be more appropriate to choose industrial policy measures rather than trade policy ones.

Nonetheless, a moderate use of trade policy measures could be considered appropriate in a number of situations with particularly

Index